Journal

of
Soviet and Post-Soviet
Politics and Society

Vol. 5, No. 1 (2019)

Special Section

Russia's Annexation of Crimea I

JSPPS 5:1 (2019)

GENERAL EDITOR AND ISSUE EDITOR-IN-CHIEF:

Julie Fedor, University of Melbourne

GUEST EDITORS:

Gergana Dimova, University of Winchester

Andreas Umland, Institute for Euro-Atlantic Cooperation, Kyiv

JSPPS Editorial Team

Julie Fedor, *University of Melbourne* (General Editor)
Andrey Makarychev, *University of Tartu* (Editor)
Gergana Dimova, *University of Winchester* (Reviews Editor)
Andreas Umland, *Institute for Euro-Atlantic Cooperation, Kyiv* (Consulting Editor)

JSPPS Advisory Board

Hannes Adomeit, College of Europe, Natolin
Timofey Agarin, Queen's University, Belfast
Mikhail Alexseev, San Diego State University, CA
Catherine Andreyev, University of Oxford
Anne Applebaum, The Legatum Institute, London
Anders Åslund, Peterson Inst. for International Economics
Margarita Balmaceda, Seton Hall University, NJ
Harley Balzer, Georgetown University, DC
John Barber, University of Cambridge
Timm Beichelt, European University Viadrina, Frankfurt (Oder)
Mark R. Beissinger, Princeton University, NJ
Thomas Bohn, Justus Liebig University, Giessen
Giovanna Brogi, University of Milan
Paul Chaisty, University of Oxford
Vitaly Chernetsky, University of Kansas, Lawrence
Ariel Cohen, Institute for the Analysis of Global Security, MD
Timothy J. Colton, Harvard University, MA
Peter J.S. Duncan, University College London
John B. Dunlop, Stanford University, CA
Gerald M. Easter, Boston College, MA
Alexander Etkind, European University Institute, Florence
M. Steven Fish, University of California at Berkeley
Gasan Gusejnov, Higher School of Economics, Moscow
Nikolas K. Gvosdev, U.S. Naval War College, RI
Michael Hagemeister, Ruhr University, Bochum
Stephen E. Hanson, College of William & Mary, VA
Olexiy Haran, Kyiv-Mohyla Academy
Nicolas Hayoz, University of Fribourg
Andreas Heinemann-Grüder, University of Bonn
Stephen Hutchings, University of Manchester, UK
Stefani Hoffman, The Hebrew University of Jerusalem
Mikhail Ilyin, Higher School of Economics, Moscow
Wilfried Jilge, University of Basel
Markku Kangaspuro, University of Helsinki
Adrian Karatnycky, Atlantic Council, New York
Andrei Kazantsev, MGIMO, Moscow

Jeffrey Kopstein, University of Toronto
Hrant Kostanyan, Centre for European Policy Studies
Paul Kubicek, Oakland University, MI
Walter Laqueur, Georgetown University, DC
Marlene Laruelle, George Washington University, DC
Carol Leonard, Higher School of Economics, Moscow
Leonid Luks, The Catholic University of Eichstaett-Ingolstadt
Luke March, University of Edinburgh
Mykhailo Minakov, Kyiv-Mohyla Academy
Olga Onuch, University of Manchester
Mitchell Orenstein, Northeastern University, MA
Nikolay Petrov, Higher School of Economics, Moscow
Andriy Portnov, Humboldt University, Berlin
Serhii Plokhii, Harvard University, MA
Alina Polyakova, Atlantic Council, DC
Maria Popova, McGill University, Montreal
Alex Pravda, University of Oxford
Mykola Riabchuk, Ukrainian Academy of Sciences, Kyiv
Per Anders Rudling, Lund University
Ellen Rutten, University of Amsterdam
Jutta Scherrer, École des Hautes Études en Sciences Sociales
Dieter Segert, University of Vienna
Anton Shekhovtsov, The Legatum Institute, London
Oxana Shevel, Tufts University, MA
Stephen Shulman, Southern Illinois University, Carbondale
Valerie Sperling, Clark University, MA
Susan Stewart, SWP, Berlin
Lisa M. Sundstrom, University of British Columbia
Mark Tauger, West Virginia University, Morgantown
Vera Tolz-Zilitinkevic, University of Manchester
Amir Weiner, Stanford University
Sarah Whitmore, Oxford Brookes University, UK
Andrew Wilson, University College London
Christian Wipperfürth, DGAP, Berlin
Andreas Wittkowsky, ZIF, Berlin
Jan Zielonka, University of Oxford

Bibliographic information published by the Deutsche Nationalbibliothek
The Deutsche Nationalbibliothek lists this publication in the Deutsche Nationalbibliografie; detailed bibliographic data are available on the Internet at http://dnb.dnb.de.

Bibliografische Information der Deutschen Nationalbibliothek
Die Deutsche Nationalbibliothek verzeichnet diese Publikation in der Deutschen Nationalbibliografie; detaillierte bibliografische Daten sind im Internet über http://dnb.d-nb.de abrufbar.

Cover picture: Polite People, a monument to the russian soldiers who participated in the annexation of Crimea in 2014. Simferopol.
132825237 © Leonid Andronov | Dreamstime.com

Journal of Soviet and Post-Soviet Politics and Society
Vol. 5, No. 1 (2019)

Stuttgart: *ibidem*-Verlag / *ibidem* Press

Erscheinungsweise: halbjährlich / Frequency: biannual

ISSN 2364-5334

Ordering Information:
PRINT: Subscription (two copies per year): € 58.00 / year (+ S&H: € 4.00 / year within Germany, € 7.00 / year international). The subscription can be canceled at any time.

Single copy or back issue: € 34.00 / copy (+ S&H: € 2.00 within Germany, € 3.50 international).

E-BOOK: Individual copy or back issue: € 19.99 / copy. Available via amazon.com or google.books.
For further information please visit www.jspps.eu

© *ibidem*-Verlag / *ibidem* Press
Stuttgart, Germany 2019

Alle Rechte vorbehalten
Das Werk einschließlich aller seiner Teile ist urheberrechtlich geschützt. Jede Verwertung außerhalb der engen Grenzen des Urheberrechtsgesetzes ist ohne Zustimmung des Verlages unzulässig und strafbar. Dies gilt insbesondere für Vervielfältigungen, Übersetzungen, Mikroverfilmungen und elektronische Speicherformen sowie die Einspeicherung und Verarbeitung in elektronischen Systemen.

All rights reserved

No part of this publication may be reproduced, stored in or introduced into a retrieval system, or transmitted, in any form, or by any means (electronical, mechanical, photocopying, recording or otherwise) without the prior written permission of the publisher.
Any person who performs any unauthorized act in relation to this publication may be liable to criminal prosecution and civil claims for damages.

CONTENTS

Special Section: Russia's Annexation of Crimea I

Legal Loopholes and Judicial Debates: Essays on Russia's 2014 Annexation of Crimea and Its Consequences for International Law
GERGANA DIMOVA 1

The Obligation of Non-Recognition:
The Case of the Annexation of Crimea
AGATA KLECZKOWSKA 7

Russia's Legal Position on the Annexation of Crimea
DASHA DUBINSKY and PETER RUTLAND 45

Business as Usual: Sanctions Circumvention by Western Firms in Crimea
MARIA SHAGINA 81

***

The Return to Patriotic Education in Post-Soviet Russia: How, When, and Why the Russian Military Engaged in Civilian Nation Building
HÅVARD BÆKKEN 123

Political Parties and the Institution of Membership in Ukraine
MELANIE G. MIERZEJEWSKI-VOZNYAK 159

REVIEWS

Ognian Shentov, Ruslan Stefanov and Martin Vladimirov, *The Russian Economic Grip on Central and Eastern Europe*
KIRIL KOLEV 213

Alexander Cooley and John Heathershaw, *Dictators without Borders: Power and Money in Central Asia*
Ana-Maria Anghelescu 216

Irene Kacandes and Yuliya Komska (eds.), *Eastern Europe Unmapped: Beyond Borders and Peripheries*
Aija Lulle 221

Chris Miller, *Putinomics: Power and Money in Resurgent Russia*
Vera Rogova 224

Marci Shore, *The Ukrainian Night: An Intimate History of Revolution*
Elliot Dolan-Evans 227

Lawrence Douglas, *The Right Wrong Man: John Demjanjuk and the Last Great Nazi War Crimes Trial*
Aleksandra Pomiecko 230

About the Contributors 235

Russia's Annexation of Crimea I

Guest edited by

Gergana Dimova and Andreas Umland

Legal Loopholes and Judicial Debates: Essays on Russia's 2014 Annexation of Crimea and Its Consequences for International Law*

Gergana Dimova

These three articles on the 2014 Russian capture of Crimea and its aftermath are the first instalment of a series of special sections in *JSPPS* which aim to provide critical and in-depth coverage on this momentous event in contemporary European history.[1] The annexation's repercussions are ongoing, and were especially palpable on 25 November 2018, when Russian war ships fired on three Ukrainian ships near the Kerch Strait between the Azov Sea and Black Sea. Our special sections, here and later, investigate the legality and impact of the annexation from judicial, political, international, and domestic angles. They bring together scholars with expert knowledge to weigh in on some of the thorniest issues when it comes to assessing the annexation and its various after-effects on international law and East European politics. They seek to complement and advance above all the existing scholarly legal literature on the issue.[2]

---

* The author wishes to thank Andreas Umland and Julie Fedor for their input and editorial suggestions.

[1] See also earlier, in this journal: Andrew Wilson, "The Crimean Tatar Question: A Prism for Changing and Rival Versions of Eurasianism," *Journal of Soviet and Post-Soviet Politics and Society* 3, no. 2 (2017): 1–46.

[2] For references on some of the relevant English- and German-language judicial literature on Crimea's annexation, see the following list from Andreas Umland, "Whom Does Crimea Belong to? Russia's Annexation of the Ukrainian Peninsula and the Question of Historical Justice," *VoxUkraine*, 29 August 2018, voxukraine.org/en/were-there-any-real-historical-grounds-for-the-annexation-of-crimea-by-russia-no/: Hans-Joachim Heintze, "Völkerrecht und Sezession: Ist die Annexion der Krim eine zulässige Wiedergutmachung sowjetischen Unrechts?" *Humanitäres Völkerrecht: Informationsschriften* 3 (2014): 129–38; Otto Luchterhandt, "Die Krim-Krise von 2014: Staats- und

The paper by Agata Kleczkowska, "The Obligation of Non-Recognition: The Case of the Annexation of Crimea" comprehensively assesses to what degree Russia breached international law by incorporating Crimea. It examines the issue through the lens of the doctrine of the obligation of non-recognition. Kleczkowska asserts that this obligation merits special scholarly attention as it has been commonly invoked in response to violations of international law. Despite its increasing usage, however, this obligation has no formal definition. To address this definitional deficiency, the article furnishes detailed historical and legal background for the doctrine and then discusses the statements issued by a number of international actors with regard to the doctrine's application to the Crimean annexation.

In particular, Kleczkowska asks: To what extent did international actors feel obliged to not recognize the Russian annexation of Crimea? According to the author, the United Nations

völkerrechtliche Aspekte," *Osteuropa* 5–6 (2014): 61–86; Anne Peters, "Das Völkerrecht der Gebietsreferenden. Das Beispiel der Ukraine 1991-2014," *Osteuropa* 5–6 (2014): 101–34; Christian Marxsen, "The Crimea Crisis—An International Law Perspective," *Zeitschrift für ausländisches öffentliches Recht und Völkerrecht* 74, no. 2 (2014): 367–91; Benedikt Behlert, "Die Unabhängigkeit der Krim: Annexion oder Sezession?" *IFHV Working Paper* 2 (2015) www.ifhv.de/documents/workingpapers/ wp5_2.pdf; Veronika Bílková, "The Use of Force by the Russian Federation in Crimea," *Zeitschrift für ausländisches öffentliches Recht und Völkerrecht* 75 (2015): 27–50; Tom Grant, *Aggression against Ukraine: Territory, Responsibility, and International Law* (London: Palgrave Macmillan, 2015); Otto Luchterhandt, "Der Anschluss der Krim an Russland aus völkerrechtlicher Sicht," *Archiv des Völkerrechts* 52, no. 2 (2014): 137–74; Christian Marxsen, "Territorial Integrity in International Law—Its Concept and Implications for Crimea," *Zeitschrift für ausländisches öffentliches Recht und Völkerrecht* 75 (2015): 7–26; Tassilo Singer, "Intervention auf Einladung," in *Ukraine. Krisen. Perspektiven: Interdisziplinäre Betrachtungen eines Landes im Umbruch*, eds. Evgeniya Bakalova, Tobias Endrich, Khrystyna Shlyakhtovska, Galyna Spodarets (Berlin: wvb, 2015), 235–60; Oleksandr Zadorozhnii, *Russian Doctrine of International Law after the Annexation of Crimea* (Kyiv: K.I.S., 2017); Majid Nikouei and Masoud Zamani, "The Secession of Crimea: Where Does International Law Stand?" *Nordic Journal of International Law* 85, no. 1 (2016): 37–64; and Władysław Czapliński, Sławomir Dębski, Rafal Tarnogórski, and Karolina Wierczyńska (eds.), *The Case of Crimea's Annexation under International Law* (Warsaw: Wydawnictwo Naukowe Scholar, 2017).

compared highly unfavorably to the United States when it came to formulating and declaring their respective obligations with regard to this doctrine in a resolute and precise manner. The UN Security Council failed to take a stand as Russia, being its permanent member, predictably vetoed the proposed resolution.

The UN General Assembly was more decisive in its adoption of a resolution titled "Territorial Integrity of Ukraine," which declared the referendum held in the Autonomous Republic of Crimea and the city of Sevastopol on 16 March 2014 to be invalid. The UN General Assembly also passed two resolutions in regard to human rights in Crimea. Nevertheless, Kleczkowska maintains that the UN's general position was ultimately weak because it failed to mention Russia by name. The UN's responses were less forceful than its reaction to Iraq's invasion of Kuwait in 1990, for example. Against the backdrop of the UN's overall ambiguous stance, the resolutions by the EU and OSCE indicate that the obligation of non-recognition was better formulated and enforced by regional organizations.

Dasha Dubinsky's and Peter Rutland's article "Russia's Legal Position on the Annexation of Crimea: A Critique" examines systematically both Russia's rationalization for forcefully incorporating Crimea and the Western take on it. While the article finds Russia's arguments wanting in legal foundation and factual basis, it recognizes that Russia made a certain effort to justify the Crimean annexation as allegedly in line with international law. Against this background, Dubinsky and Rutland suggest that it would be premature to dismiss Russia outright as a rogue state. The Kremlin, in their opinion, actually had a high stake in making the annexation appear legal. That is because Russia, being a major world power, benefited and still benefits from a whole number of pre- and post-annexation international treaties and institutions.

What, then, were Russia's arguments in justification of the annexation and how do they line up against the basic principles and concrete norms of international law? First, Dubinsky and Rutland consider Russia's contention that the Crimean people had a right to self-determination that was supposedly exercised through a "referendum" on Crimea's status on 16 March 2014.[3] While pointing out the inherent ambiguity of the legal definition of a "people," the article initially approaches this proposition as a plausible argument in view of the strong sense of regional identity on the peninsula and the specific historical fate of the Crimean Tatars. The authors also consider a second justification raised by Russia: that the Russians in Crimea had a legal right to secede from Ukraine, because they felt that Ukraine's territorial integrity was invalidated due to the flight of former Ukrainian President Viktor Yanukovych and what many Crimeans perceived as an unconstitutional transfer of power to the new acting President Oleksandr Turchinov. The authors argue that—whatever the empirical foundations for this narrative—this apology has no legal merit since a governmental transition or even a revolution does not invalidate a state's claim to the inviolability of a country's borders and territorial integrity.

The third argument made by Russia, and considered by Dubinsky and Rutland, is that the annexation was legal in so far as many ethnic Russians felt physically threatened and that, allegedly, they were no longer allowed to speak Russian in Crimea. The authors point out that there were 858,000 ethnic Russians compared to just 268,000 ethnic Ukrainians living on Crimea, at the time of the transfer. While Dubinsky and Rutland note that a UN report acknowledged that Russians in Crimean feared for their security, they also assert that most of these apprehensions were the result of purposeful fearmongering conducted by Russian government-controlled mass media. Their article suggests that it was mainly Russian state television, freely accessible and highly popular on the peninsula, that was responsible for such excessive agitation.

Fourth, the article contends, Kremlin used the secession of Kosovo from Serbia as a proto-typical case to provide yet another justification for Crimea's exit from Ukraine. Kosovo's declaration of independence in April 2008 was invoked by Putin, because its legal

---

[3] See also: Roy Allison, "Russian 'Deniable' Intervention in Ukraine: How and Why Russia Broke the Rules," *International Affairs* 90, no. 6 (2014): 1255–97; Olena Podolian, "The 2014 Referendum in Crimea," *East European Quarterly* 1 (2015): 111–28; and Umland, "Whom Does Crimea Belong to?"

framework casts general doubt as to whether international law prohibits one-sided declarations of independence. The Kremlin instrumentalized this ambiguity to argue that the Kosovo precedent allegedly allowed states like Russia to apply their own loose understanding of the principles of state sovereignty and of an ethnic minority's right to self-determination.

The last article of this section, Maria Shagina's "Business as Usual: Sanctions Circumvention by Western Firms in Crimea," inquires why, after four years of sanctions, Western companies' activities in Crimea have not only not ceased, but have, in some cases, even increased. The author's investigation addresses both the theoretical literature on sanctions and some practical implications for companies wishing to do business in Crimea and Russia. Using the case of Crimea, Shagina's article provides new empirical evidence with regard to the existing debate on why sanctions are not always an effective foreign policy tool for changing the target's behavior.

Shagina uncovers specific legal loopholes that Western firms exploit. She attributes some of the conditions enabling sanctions-avoidance to the nature of the sanctions themselves. Specifically, Shagina shows that EU sanctions are less flexible and comprehensive than US sanctions because the EU had to obtain the unanimous consent of all (then) 28 member states. The process of reaching a unanimous decision was both time-consuming and procedurally fragile.

In terms of implementation, EU sanctions are also lacking in that the principal decision is made at the European level but has to be practically enforced at the level of each individual member state. This discrepancy has opened up 28 political gaps whose width varies according to each state's ability and willingness to put officially adopted EU sanctions into real effect. Another loophole that Western firms exploit for sanctions circumvention arises from the differences in the sanctions imposed by various nations, such as, for example, those by Japan, which opted for only immaterial measures against Russia.

Shagina's article explores the central ways and conditions of sanctions-busting from the point of view of certain concrete firms involved. These conditions are categorized into three types: (1)

sanctions avoidance, i.e. cases where no rules are broken, but the activities are considered immoral; (2) sanctions evasion, i.e. cases where there is a deliberate intention to refrain from compliance and the evasive practices are liable to administrative and criminal penalties; (3) sanctions "avoision"—a term coined by Arthur Seldon (1979) by combining the words "avoidance" and "evasion."[4] This hybrid category covers cases where there are unclear boundaries, where doing wrong is not of itself an indication of purposeful evasion, and where firms provide evidence that they tried to behave properly.

The wealth of examples showcasing these categories constitutes the central contribution of Shagina's article. One instance of sanction "avoision" is the use of "flags of convenience," where ship owners register their vessels with a country which is not facing sanctions. This technique works in so far as current legislation posits that rules of the country of registration (and not of the country of ownership) apply. Another example of sanction "avoision" entails German and Dutch companies providing machines for the building of the Kerch Bridge with the justification that the machines were assembled in Russia and that these EU companies had tried, but failed, to ascertain that the machines would not be used on Crimea.

The three articles in this special section complement each other in their attempt to recast the Russian annexation of Crimea as a set of problematic issues, with far-reaching repercussions. The analyses should be of interest to a range of readers from diplomacy, academia, the policy-making community, and civil society. They may be useful to, among others, legal scholars and practitioners in search of new cases and arguments relevant to the issues of legal loopholes and judicial argumentation regarding the general status of annexed territories and its specific aspects such as, for instance, the conditions, hindrances, and penalties for conducting or not conducting business with them.

---

[4] Arthur Seldon, "Prologue to Avoision: The Moral Blurring of a Legal Distinction Without an Economic Difference," in *Tax Avoision: The Economic, Legal and Moral Inter-relationship between Avoidance and Evasion*, ed. Alfred Roman Ilersic (London: Institute of Economic Affairs, London, 1979), 51-70.

The Obligation of Non-Recognition: The Case of the Annexation of Crimea

Agata Kleczkowska

Abstract: *The aim of this article is to discuss the obligation of non-recognition arising out of the illegal use of force by Russia against Ukraine and the subsequent annexation of Crimea. The thesis underlying the article is that these events amounted to a gross violation of international law, and consequently, States are under an obligation not to recognize Crimea as part of the Russian Federation. The article starts with a section which briefly defines the obligation of non-recognition, tracing its evolution and examining the content of the obligation. The second and main part discusses the case of Crimea, highlighting the most important facts, discussing the statements on this case issued by the UN GA and the UN SC, and examining the stance adopted by other international organizations and States on this issue.*

Introduction

In November 2013, when the Ukrainian authorities announced that they had suspended the preparations for the conclusion of an Association Agreement with the European Union, it would have been hard to imagine that the crisis prompted by this decision would lead to one of the most flagrant violations of international law in recent decades: the annexation of the Crimean Peninsula by the Russian Federation. Even more unsettling is the fact that half a decade later, the international community has still not managed to address this situation effectively.

While the Russian use of force and annexation of Crimea has become a major topic of discussion in the international legal scholarship, the doctrine of law does not present a uniform position on the situation in Crimea, and nor have comprehensive studies on the consequences of this situation been carried out to date. There are some scholars, both outside and inside Russia, who reject the notion that by incorporating Crimea, Russia was in breach of international law.[1] Moreover, so far there has been little detailed scholarly discussion on the legal consequences of the annexation, including the most important of these, that is, the obligation of non-recognition.[2]

The obligation of non-recognition[3] of illegal situations is one of the gravest consequences of the violations of international law.

---

[1] See e.g. the statement by Karl Albrecht Schachtschneider, "Putin hat die Krim nicht annektiert," available at *YouTube*, 16 April 2015, https://www.youtube.com/watch?v=Y8OJo7D7gPI; Anatoly Y. Kapustin, "Circular Letter to the Executive Council of the International Law Association," *MGIMO University* website, 6 June 2014, https://mgimo.ru/about/news/departments/252984/; and "Statement of the Association of Lawyers of Russian Federation Concerning the Situation in Ukraine and Legitimacy of Conducting the All-Crimean Referendum on the Status of Crimea on 16.3.2014," quoted in Oleksandr Merezhko, "Crimea's Annexation by Russia—Contradictions of the New Russian Doctrine of International Law," *Zeitschrift für ausländisches öffentliches Recht und Völkerrecht* 75 (2015): 186. Maria Issaeva even claims that "Among Russian international legal scholars there were almost no critical voices (...)" raised against the annexation; Maria Issaeva, "Quarter of a Century on from the Soviet Era: Reflections on Russian Doctrinal Responses to the Annexation of Crimea," *Russian Law Journal* 5, no. 3 (2017): 87. For more opinions supporting the annexation see summary made by Oleksandr Zadorozhnii, "To Justify Against All Odds: The Annexation of Crimea in 2014 and the Russian Legal Scholarship," *Polish Yearbook of International Law* XXXV (2015): 139–69.

[2] For some rare examples of scholarship on this topic, see e.g. Enrico Milano, "The Non-recognition of Russia's Annexation of Crimea: Three Different Legal Approaches and One Unanswered Question," *Questions of International Law Zoom Out* I (2014): 39–51; idem, "Reactions to Russia's Annexation of Crimea and the Legal Consequences Deriving from Grave Breaches of Peremptory Norms," in *The Case of Crimea's Annexation Under International Law*, eds. Władysław Czapliński et al. (Warsaw: Scholar Publishing House, 2017), 203–06; and Władysław Czapliński, "The Crimean Crisis and the Polish Practice on Non-recognition," *Questions of International Law Zoom Out* I (2014): 73–84.

[3] Both legal instruments and doctrine of law use a variety of terms for this obligation: "obligation not to recognize as legal"—ILC, "Third Report on the Content, Forms and Degrees of International Responsibility (Part Two of the Draft Articles), by Mr. Willem Riphagen, Special Rapporteur," UN Doc. A/CN.4/354 and Corr.1 and Add.1 & 2, (12 and 30 March and 5 May 1982), 38; "obligation of non-recognition"—Separate Opinion of Judge Higgins, Legal

Despite the fact that there is no legal definition of this obligation, given the statements on this subject issued by various States and international organizations and present in the doctrine of law, one may assume that it arises as a result of violations of international law by a State such as the illegal use of force (and its consequences, such as illegal territorial acquisitions); breach of the right to self-determination; racial discrimination;[4] or breach of a peace treaty.[5] Thus, the illegal situation created by such violation of international law should prompt a reaction on the part of other States, one which first and foremost should refuse to recognize any such situation as being legal.

The aim of this paper is to fill the existing gap in the legal scholarship and discuss the obligation of non-recognition towards the use of force and subsequent annexation of Crimea. The novelty of this research lies in the broad perspective adopted here: the paper discusses the statements issued by a range of different actors, including the relevant United Nations General Assembly (UN GA) resolution and United Nations Security Council (UN SC) draft resolution; categorizes the attitudes adopted by States; and highlights the exceptions to the obligation of non-recognition

---

Consequences of the Construction of a Wall in the Occupied Palestinian Territory, Advisory Opinion, ICJ Reports 2004, par. 38; and Maurizio Arcari, "The Relocation of the US Embassy to Jerusalem and the Obligation of Non-recognition in International Law," *Questions of International Law: Zoom-in* 50 (2018)); "obligation not to recognize as lawful"—Yaël Ronen, "Status of Settler Implanted by Illegal Territorial Regimes," *British Year Book of International Law* 79, no. 1 (2008): 231-32; S. Talmon, "The Duty Not to 'Recognize as Lawful' a Situation Created by the Illegal Use of Force or Other Serious Breaches of a Jus Cogens Obligation: An Obligation without Real Substance?" in *The Fundamental Rules of the International Leqal Order*, eds. Christian Tomuschat and Jean-Marc Thouvenin (Leiden: Brill, 2006), 108; and "duty of non-recognition"—Alison Pert, "Duty of Non-Recognition in Contemporary International Law: Issues and Uncertainties," *The Chinese (Taiwan) Year Book of International Law & Affairs* 30 (2012); and Vera Gowlland-Debbas, *Collective Responses to Illegal Acts in International Law: United Nations Action in the Question of Southern Rhodesia* (Dordrecht: Martinus Nijhoff Publishers, 1990), 282.). Nevertheless, it seems that the meaning of these terms does not differ in substance. In this article, the term "obligation of non-recognition" will be used.

4 Pert, "Duty of Non-recognition," 69.
5 Gowlland-Debbas, *Collective Responses to Illegal Acts*, 281.

applied by certain actors. At the same time, a five-year perspective makes it possible to build a comprehensive picture of the situation when it comes to compliance (or non-compliance) with this obligation. The thesis underlying the article is that, contrary to some scholars' claims, the use of force and subsequent annexation of Crimea amounted to a gross violation of international law, and consequently, States are under an obligation not to recognize the illegal situation arising out of it, that is, not to recognize Crimea as part of the Russian Federation.[6]

In order to discuss the obligation of non-recognition arising out of the annexation of Crimea, some preliminary remarks on the scope and content of this obligation are necessary. With this aim, the article starts with a section which briefly defines the obligation of non-recognition, tracing its evolution and examining its content. The second and main part discusses the case of Crimea, highlighting the most important facts, discussing the statements on this case issued by the UN GA and the UN SC, and examining the stance adopted on this question by other international organizations and States.

1. Defining the Obligation of Non-Recognition

1.1. Evolution of the Obligation of Non-Recognition

Before analyzing the specific case of Crimea's annexation, a few general comments on the obligation of non-recognition are in order.

The obligation of non-recognition of illegal territorial acquisitions arising out of the use of force evolved alongside the prohibition of the use of force. As long as States had an unlimited right to wage wars, they could also recognize the territorial acquisitions seized during a war. When the first constraints on the right to wage war began to appear in legal instruments, the

---

[6] A State which has violated international law is further named as a "wrongdoing State." In this article, the phrase "obligation of non-recognition" refers to the obligation with regard to illegal territorial acquisitions arising out of the prohibited use of force.

obligation of non-recognition also began to crystallize. However, until the outbreak of World War II the obligation of non-recognition was not yet a customary norm, at least not of a general nature.[7] This state of law began to progressively change with the introduction of the prohibition on the use of force in Art. 2 (4) of the UN Charter in 1945.[8] Even though the Charter itself does not mention recognition or any obligation of non-recognition of illegal territorial acquisitions gained via a prohibited use of force, the obligation of non-recognition is nowadays considered a logical corollary to Art. 2 (4).[9] Since 1945 States have confirmed the binding force of the obligation of non-recognition with regard to territorial acquisitions arising out of the illegal use of force in numerous legal

---

[7] Alison Pert points out that a regional customary norm prohibiting recognition of illegal territorial acquisitions may have emerged in Latin America as early as the late 19th century; Pert, "Duty of Non-recognition," 52. For more on the practice of Latin American States, see Anti-War Treaty of Non-Aggression and Conciliation (Saavedra-Lamas Pact), signed on 10 October 1933, entered into force on 12 November 1935, available in English at http://avalon.law.yale.edu/20th_century/intam01.asp; Montevideo Convention on the Rights and Duties of States, signed on 26 December 1933, entered into force on 26 December 1934, available at http://avalon.law.yale.edu/20th_century/intam03.asp; and Declaration of Principles of Inter-American Solidarity and Cooperation, adopted on 21 December 1946, http://avalon.law.yale.edu/20th_century/intam07.asp.

[8] Article 2 (4): "All Members shall refrain in their international relations from the threat or use of force against the territorial integrity or political independence of any state, or in any other manner inconsistent with the Purposes of the United Nations"; Charter of the United Nations and Statute of the International Court of Justice, *United Nations Treaty Series* 16 (1946), 1.

[9] Dissenting Opinion of Judge Skubiszewski, East Timor (Portugal v. Australia), Judgment, I.C.J. Reports 1995, par. 125; Anne Lagerwall, *Le principe ex injuria jus non oritur en droit international* (Bruxelles: Bruylant, 2016), 149; Gowlland-Debbas, *Collective Responses to Illegal Acts*, 289; and Arcari, "Relocation of the US embassy," 5. However, interestingly, Vera Gowlland-Debbas looks for the Charter's grounds for the obligation of non-recognition also in art. 2 (5), which states that "All Members shall give the United Nations every assistance in any action it takes in accordance with the present Charter, and shall refrain from giving assistance to any state against which the United Nations is taking preventive or enforcement action"; Gowlland-Debbas, *Collective Responses to Illegal Acts*, 289–90.

acts and documents,[10] including also UN SC and UN GA resolutions.[11] In particular, in the aftermath of the Iraqi declaration on the "comprehensive and eternal merger" of Kuwait and its 1990 invasion,[12] the UN SC adopted Resolution 662, which stated that the annexation of Kuwait by Iraq "has no legal validity, and is considered null and void" (par. 1), and also called upon "all States, international organizations and specialized agencies not to recognize that annexation, and to refrain from any action or dealing that might be interpreted as an indirect recognition of the annexation" (par. 2).[13] Likewise, in resolution 661 the UN SC called upon all States "Not to recognize any regime set up by the occupying Power" (par. 9 (b)).[14] All these developments confirm that the obligation of non-recognition of illegal territorial acquisitions gained by the use of force is currently a customary norm.

One of the most important observations with regard to the obligation of non-recognition was made by the International Court of Justice (ICJ) in its Advisory Opinion on the Legal Consequences for States of the Continued Presence of South Africa in Namibia

---

[10] See UN GA Resolution 2625 of 24 October 1970, UN Doc. A/RES/25/2625; UN GA Resolution 2734 of 16 December 1970, UN Doc. A/RES/2734.; UN GA Resolution 3314 of 14 December 1974, UN Doc. A/RES/3314, Annex; Conference on Security and Co-operation in Europe Final Act, adopted on 1 August 1975, https://www.osce.org/helsinki-final-act?download=true; UN GA Resolution 42/22 of 18 November 1987, A/RES/42/22, Annex, par. 10.

[11] E.g. with regard to Southern Rhodesia—UN GA Resolution 3411D (XXX) of 28 November 1975, UN Doc. A/RES/3411(XXX)D, par. 3; UN SC Resolution 216 of 12 November 1965, UN Doc. S/RES/216, par. 1-2; bantustan Transkei —UN SC Resolution 402 of 22 December 1976, UN Doc. S/RES/402, par. 1; UN GA Resolution 31/6A of 26 October 1976, UN Doc. A/RES/31/6/A, par. 2-4; Turkish Republic of Northern Cyprus—UN SC Resolution 541 of 18 November 1983, UN Doc. S/RES/541; Israel and occupied territories—UN SC Resolution 2334 (2016) of 23 December 2016, UN Doc. S/RES/2334, par. 3.

[12] ILC, "Draft Articles on Responsibility of States for Internationally Wrongful Acts, With Commentaries," *Yearbook of the International Law Commission* II, Part Two (2001): par. 7.

[13] UN SC Resolution 662 of 9 August 1990, UN Doc. S/RES/662.

[14] UN SC Resolution 661 of 6 August 1990, UN Doc. S/RES/661.

(South West Africa) notwithstanding Security Council Resolution 276 (1970)[15] (hereinafter Namibia advisory opinion).

Given that by Resolution 276,[16] the UN SC declared that "the continued presence of the South African authorities in Namibia is illegal,"[17] the Court observed that "[a] binding determination made by an appropriate organ of the United Nations to the effect that a situation is illegal cannot remain without consequences." One such consequence is the obligation "especially upon members of the United Nations, to bring that situation to an end."[18] In addition, Member States are obliged to "recognize the illegality and invalidity of South Africa's continued presence in Namibia," and are also obliged to "refrain from lending any support or any form of assistance to South Africa with reference to its occupation of Namibia."[19]

The ICJ came to the conclusion that the exact content of the obligation of non-recognition should be determined by the "appropriate political organs of the United Nations"—in this case, the UN SC, which had already determined the allowed and prohibited measures in its Resolution 283. The Court decided that in this situation it could confine itself to enumerating five types of dealings with the Government of South Africa which were inconsistent with UN SC Resolution 276 (1970) "because they may imply a recognition that South Africa's presence in Namibia is legal." Thus, first, member States were obliged "to abstain from entering into treaty relations with South Africa in all cases in which the Government of South Africa purports to act on behalf of or concerning Namibia." Second, Member States were obliged not to apply the treaties concluded by South Africa "on behalf of or

---

[15] Legal Consequences for States of the Continued Presence of South Africa in Namibia (South West Africa) notwithstanding Security Council Resolution 276 (1970), Advisory Opinion, I.C.J. Reports 1971, par. 84-6. The ICJ mentioned the obligation of non-recognition also in the Legal Consequences of the Construction of a Wall in the Occupied Palestinian Territory, Advisory Opinion, I.C.J. Reports 2004, par. 87, 159.
[16] Namibia advisory opinion, par. 84-6.
[17] UN SC Resolution 276 (1970) of 30 January 1970, UN Doc. S/RES/276.
[18] Namibia advisory opinion, par. 117.
[19] Ibid., par. 119.

concerning Namibia." However, this rule could not be applied to general, multilateral conventions "of a humanitarian character" since their non-performance "may adversely affect people of Namibia." Third, States were obliged to "abstain from sending diplomatic or special missions to South Africa including in their jurisdiction the Territory of Namibia." Fourth, States should abstain "from sending consular agents to Namibia, and [...] withdraw any such agents already there." Fifth, States should have also made "it clear to the South African authorities that the maintenance of diplomatic or consular relations with South Africa does not imply any recognition of its authority with regard to Namibia."[20]

However, apart from determining the content of the obligation of non-recognition, the Court also established an exception to it, the so-called "Namibia exception."[21] The Court determined that:

> [i]n general, the non-recognition of South Africa's administration of the Territory should not result in depriving the people of Namibia of any advantages derived from international co-operation. In particular, while official acts performed by the Government of South Africa on behalf of or concerning Namibia after the termination of the Mandate are illegal and invalid, this invalidity cannot be extended to those acts, such as, for instance, the registration of births, deaths and marriages, the effects of which can be ignored only to the detriment of the inhabitants of the Territory.[22]

The obligation to protect the civilian population regardless of the obligation of non-recognition is reflected also in the European Court of Human Rights (ECHR) case law. In the case *Loizidou v. Turkey* the Court, agreeing with the arguments put forward by different bodies which called for non-recognition of the Turkish Republic of Northern Cyprus (TRNC), observed at the same time that "international law recognises the legitimacy of certain legal arrangements and transactions in such a situation, for instance as

---

[20] *Ibid.*, par. 122–23.
[21] This term is used by e.g. Arcari, "Relocation of the US Embassy," 10; UN Doc. A/CN.4/354, 49; and Ronen, "Status of Settler Implanted," 231 *et subsq.*
[22] Namibia advisory opinion, par. 125.

regards the registration of births, deaths and marriages,"[23] referring to the Namibia advisory opinion. In the case of *Cyprus v. Turkey* the ECHR observed that the advisory opinion in the Namibia case showed that even *de facto* authorities are obliged to ensure the protection, including the protection provided by the judicial system, to all residents. As a result, the Court "cannot simply disregard the judicial organs set up by the 'TRNC' in so far as the relationships at issue in the present case are concerned."[24]

1.2. Content of the Obligation of Non-Recognition

Given the above, the obligation of non-recognition consists of two parts. First and foremost, the obligation of non-recognition prohibits States from directly recognizing illegal territorial acquisitions as legal and obliges States to bring any such situation to an end. The second part of the obligation of non-recognition requires States to refrain from implied recognition of illegal situations.[25]

The obligations stemming from the prohibition of implied recognition are as follows: first, there is an obligation to refrain from providing support or any form of assistance in maintaining the illegal situation.[26] Such assistance could take the form of, for instance, "providing financial or technical aid in relation to the

---

[23] ECHR, Case of Loizidou v. Turkey (Application no. 15318/89) Judgment, 18 December 1996, par. 45.
[24] Case of Cyprus v. Turkey (Application no. 25781/94), Judgment, 10 May 2001, par. 96, 98. See also Grand Chamber Decision as to the Admissibility of Application nos. 46113/99, 3843/02, 13751/02, 13466/03, 10200/04, 14163/04, 19993/04, 21819/04 by Takis Demopoulos and Others, Evoulla Chrysostomi, Demetrios Lordos and Ariana Lordou Anastasiadou, Eleni Kanari-Eliadou and Others, Sofia (Pitsa) Thoma Kilara Sotiriou and Nina Thoma Kilara Moushoutta, Yiannis Stylas, Evdokia Charalambou Onoufriou and Others and Irini (Rena) Chrisostomou against Turkey.
[25] See Pert, "Duty of Non-Recognition," 67; and Talmon, "Duty Not to 'Recognize as Lawful'," 112.
[26] Likewise, Maurizio Arcari finds this obligation to be "corollary" to the obligation of non-recognition; Arcari, "Relocation of the US Embassy," 3.

seized territory," as well as many other forms;[27] a case-by-case analysis is always required.

Second, the consequences of the obligation of non-recognition also influence the treaty relations between the wrongdoing State and the rest of the international community.[28] Thus States should refrain from applying the treaties concluded with the wrongdoing State to the illegally acquired territory, and from concluding any new treaties with the wrongdoing State which would also be applicable to the illegally acquired territory. In particular, the prohibition against concluding new treaties with the wrongdoing State concerns any situation whereby a treaty could be deemed to recognize territorial acquisitions gained by the illegal use of force.[29]

Third, and what seems most vague, is the question of whether the obligation of non-recognition also covers diplomatic and consular relations with the wrongdoing State. In the most general sense, one could conclude that this component of the obligation of non-recognition requires States to not send their diplomatic and consular missions to the illegally-acquired territory as a part of their

---

[27] Pert, "Duty of Non-Recognition," 69.
[28] Jochen A Frowein, "Non-Recognition," *Max Planck Encyclopedia of Public International Law*, last updated December 2011, http://opil.ouplaw.com, par. 4; and Enrico Milano, "The Doctrine(s) of Non-recognition: Theoretical Underpinnings and Policy Implications in Dealing with De Facto Regimes," *ESIL Pre-2009 Conference Papers*, http://esil-sedi.eu/?page_id=62, 4.
[29] Stefan Kadelbach claims that since the prohibition of the use of force is a *jus cogens* norm, such treaty could be declared invalid by international tribunal; Stefan Kadelbach, "Jus Cogens, Obligations Erga Omnes and other Rules—The Identification of Fundamental Norms," in Tomuschat and Thouvenin, *Fundamental Rules of the International Legal Order*, 30. However, it should be observed that first, under art. 53 of the Vienna Convention on the Law of Treaties, "A treaty is void if, at the time of its conclusion, it conflicts with a peremptory norm of general international law," so it is void *ab initio*; Kirsten Schmalenbach, "Article 53," in *Vienna Convention on the Law of Treaties: A Commentary*, eds. Oliver Dörr and Kirsten Schmalenbach (Heidelberg/Dordrecht/London/New York: Springer, 2012), 925. Consequently, a treaty would not be invalid only from the moment it was declared as such by an international tribunal. Second, depending on the view one adopts regarding the peremptory character of the prohibition of the use of force, the same may be also applied to the prohibition of aggression.

diplomatic and consular relations with the wrongdoing State. However, it is easy to imagine that before the wrongdoing State illegally acquired territory that previously belonged to a different State, third States could have had their consular missions in that region, e.g. due to the fact that the region was inhabited by nationals of third States. In this context, Vera Gowlland-Debbas offers a reasonable solution, pointing out that the maintenance of consular offices should be distinguished from establishment of new consular relations, since the former does not imply recognition.[30] Even though such a flexible approach may be understood as at variance with some UN SC resolutions,[31] maintenance of such consular relations could be deemed part of the "Namibia exception" in the event that the circumstances of a given case require adopting such an approach.

These three obligations constitute the core components of the obligation of non-recognition. However, as the ICJ observed in the Namibia advisory opinion, the exact content of the obligation of non-recognition should be determined by "the appropriate organs." Analysis of the UN SC resolutions shows that this "organ" may establish the following additional obligations:

- the prohibition of import and export of commodities and products from or to the illegally acquired territories;
- the prohibition of the promotion of such import and export;
- the prohibition of making available any funds or any other financial or economic resources to the government of the wrongdoing State, or to any commercial, industrial, or public utility operating in the wrongdoing State or illegally acquired territories;

---

[30] Gowlland-Debbas, *Collective Responses to Illegal Acts*, 300.
[31] See UN SC Resolution 283 of 29 July 1970, UN Doc. S/RES/283. Also, UN SC 217 called upon all States "not to recognize this illegal authority and not to entertain any diplomatic or other relations with it" (par. 6); UN SC Resolution 217 of 20 November 1965, Un Doc. S/RES/217.

- an obligation to provide assistance to the government of the State injured by the illegal acquisition of territory;
- an obligation on the part of States to ensure that companies and other commercial and industrial enterprises owned by, or under their direct control, cease all dealings with respect to commercial or industrial enterprises or concessions in the illegally acquired territories;
- an obligation on the part of States to withhold from their nationals, and from companies of their nationality not under direct governmental control, all government loans, credit guarantees, and other forms of financial support that would be used to facilitate trade or commerce with the illegally acquired territories;
- an obligation to discourage the promotion of tourism and emigration to the illegally acquired territories;
- an obligation to ensure that any act performed by officials and institutions of the authorities of the illegally acquired territories shall not be accorded any recognition, official or otherwise, including judicial notice, by the competent organs of the State;[32] and:
- an obligation to interrupt any existing means of transportation to and from the illegally acquired territories.[33]

---

[32] With regard to Southern Rhodesia, Vera Gowlland-Debbas interprets this obligation by stating that obligation of non-recognition involves prohibition of "the granting of certain municipal law benefits to the régime which normally is discretionary, international law leaving it to the municipal law of States to determine." Such refusal involves "i) non-application of the laws or acts of an unrecognized government in municipal law; ii) denial of rights inherent in government status, i.e. right to sue or to sovereign and diplomatic immunity; iii) refusal of passports." Thus, the prohibition refers to all legislative, executive, and judicial acts; Gowlland-Debbas, *Collective Responses to Illegal Acts*, 302–03, 306.

[33] UN Doc. S/RES/661, par. 3, 4, 9a; UN SC Resolution 283, UN Doc. S/RES/283, par. 4-6, 11; UN SC Resolution 277 of 18 March 1970, S/RES/277, par. 1, 9b.

Consequently, these measures affect many aspects of the relations between States, starting from trade relations through to investments and financial relations, tourism, transport, and ending with the non-recognition of municipal acts of the authorities of the illegally acquired territories. Moreover, apart from the constraints imposed by the UN SC, other organs may also take appropriate steps. For instance, as Vera Gowlland-Debbas points out, the International Olympic Committee excluded Southern Rhodesia from the 20th Olympic Games.[34] Thus the restraints may also concern the domain of sport and other fields.

Among these measures one should distinguish one particular category, that is the steps concerning investment, financial, and export/import relations, which can be grouped together under the umbrella term "economic relations." Not only are these mentioned in the UN SC resolutions every time the Council adopts measures against illegally acquired territories, but they are also voluntarily undertaken by States, even without UN SC action, as will be demonstrated in section 2.3 of this article. Thus, one may conclude that, given the practice and *opinio juris* of States, obligation to restrain/suspense/rupture economic relations is a fourth component of the obligation of non-recognition.

Discussing the content of the obligation of non-recognition, one should also bear in mind the so-called "Namibia exception," which will be understood in this article as any exception to the obligation of non-recognition on "humanitarian" grounds. In general, the "Namibia exception" means that the obligation of non-recognition should be performed in a way that does not infringe human rights or the overall humanitarian situation of the individuals living in the illegally acquired territory.[35]

Two more remarks upon the content of the obligation of non-recognition are needed. First, one has to observe that some of the resolutions which introduce the measures to be taken in the event of illegal territorial acquisitions are grounded in Chapter VII of the

---

[34] Gowlland-Debbas, *Collective Responses to Illegal Acts*, 315.
[35] For more interpretations of the "Namibia exception" see Ronen, "Status of Settler Implanted," 233.

UN Charter. As a result, one may interpret them not as elements of the obligation of non-recognition but rather as sanctions established by the UN SC under art. 41 of the UN Charter. The doctrine of law endeavors to differentiate between the obligations stemming from sanctions and non-recognition in the case of illegal territorial acquisitions. With regard to consular relations between the wrongdoing State and third States, Vera Gowlland-Debbas claims, as mentioned above, that States are obliged only not to establish new consular relations, while the obligation of termination of existing consular relations would fall more under Art. 41 of the UN Charter.[36] On the other hand, Enrico Milano distinguishes three theories of non-recognition: "normativist," "communitarian," and "realist" (sanctions-based).[37] According to this latter theory, non-recognition as such is not mandatory; it becomes binding on States only in the event that the UN SC has sanctioned the illegal situation under Chapter VII of the UN Charter.[38]

This implies that the question of relations between the obligation of non-recognition and sanctions is inseparably linked with the existence and role of the "appropriate organ" to establish measures in the event that an illegal situation occurs. To put it differently, a question arises: is the obligation of non-recognition triggered only after an "appropriate organ," whichever it might be (the UN SC, the UN GA[39] or any other UN organ[40]), determines that

---

[36] Ibid., 300.
[37] Milano, "Non-recognition," 39–51.
[38] Ibid., 49.
[39] As Enrico Milano points out, if it is the UN GA that labels the situation as illegal, it may be considered even "more authoritative and representative" than in case of the Security Council since "the whole of the international community is there represented, had an opportunity to voice its views and to vote on the draft resolution"; ibid., 42.
[40] Judge Higgins observed that in case of the construction of the Wall in the Occupied Palestinian Territory it was not the UN SC that recognized the construction as illegal, but the ICJ in the advisory proceeding; nevertheless, as Judge Higgins claimed, the ICJ is one of the principal UN organs and the legal consequences of such finding are the same as if they were made by the UN SC; Separate Opinion of Judge Higgins, Legal Consequences of the Construction of a Wall in the Occupied Palestinian Territory, Advisory Opinion, I.C.J. Reports 2004, par. 38.

an illegal situation has occurred and that States are obliged to refrain from its recognition?[41] Or is it a self-executing obligation that does not require any particular action on the part of any particular international organ?[42] It has been claimed above that the obligation of non-recognition is a customary norm. If so, it is independent from the action of any international organ forming part of an international organization, since States are bound by the obligations arising from customary norms regardless of their membership in international organizations. Consequently, States are obliged to avoid treaty, diplomatic, consular, and economic relations with the wrongdoing State as soon as the illegal situation occurs: the UN organ (or other "appropriate" organ) only coordinates the effects of the obligation of non-recognition rather than establishing it.[43] At the same time, the UN SC may adopt a resolution and establish sanctions under Chapter VII of the UN Charter; these sanctions may tie in with the obligation of non-recognition, requiring some specific action on the part of States.

Last but not least, one should also mention the timeframe of the obligation of non-recognition: once the illegal situation has occurred, how long are States obliged to maintain non-recognition? Given the States' practice after 1945 so far, the answer should be: until the status *quo ante* has been restored. Stefan A. G. Talmon gives examples of situations recognized as illegal after 1945 and notes that in all these cases "collective nonrecognition has ended only with the establishment of the status *quo ante*."[44] Thus, since the obligation of non-recognition constitutes a response to a given factual situation, the international community needs to react to the changes in this factual situation: if the authorities established over

---

[41] E.g. Pert, "Duty of Non-Recognition," 63; and Gowlland-Debbas, *Collective Responses to Illegal Acts*, 319.

[42] See Talmon, "Duty Not to 'Recognize as Lawful'," 113; Dissenting Opinion of Judge Skubiszewski, East Timor (Portugal v. Australia), Judgment, I.C.J. Reports 1995, 90, par. 125; and Separate Opinion of Judge Onyeama, Legal Consequences for States of the Continued Presence of South Africa in Namibia (South West Africa) notwithstanding Security Council Resolution 276 (1970), Advisory Opinion, I.C.J. Reports 1971, 148.

[43] Talmon, "Duty Not to 'Recognize as Lawful'," 113.

[44] Ibid., 122–23.

illegally acquired territory continue to exercise their control over this territory and move to deepening, the international community should once again condemn it and continue to declare non-recognition. On the other hand, once the status *quo ante* has been restored, States should go back to their regular relations with the affected territories/wrongdoing State.

To conclude this part, the obligation of non-recognition, as a customary norm, consists of two components: 1) the prohibition of direct recognition of an illegal situation and the obligation to bring the illegal situation to an end; and 2) the obligation to refrain from implied recognition, which includes an obligation to refrain from offering support and assistance to the wrongdoing State, as well as to refrain from engaging in treaty, diplomatic, consular, and economic relations. At the same time, in exercising the obligation of non-recognition States are also obliged to take into account the "Namibia exception" which protects the fundamental rights of individuals from the negative consequences of the obligation of non-recognition.[45] The obligation of non-recognition is triggered by the sole occurrence of an illegal situation and not by the action of international organs which may only supplement the customary norm regulating the obligation.

2. The Case of Crimea

2.1. Background

The origins of the crisis in Ukraine date to November 2013, when the ruling authorities of Ukraine announced that they had suspended the preparations for the conclusion of an Association Agreement with the European Union—an announcement which triggered mass protests. Demonstrators soon started to demand not only integration with the EU, but also the deposition of President Viktor Yanukovych and the entire government. Even though the Ukrainian political leaders managed to come to an agreement, when President

---

[45] On three interpretations of the obligation of non-recognition see Ronen, "Status of Settler Implanted," 233–34.

Yanukovych left Kyiv on 22 February 2014, the Ukrainian parliament removed him from office and voted for Oleksandr Turchynov to become the new acting president of Ukraine. On 26 February 2014, a new government was formed.

The following day a group of armed men in plainclothes took over the governmental building in Simferopol in Crimea, including also the building of the local parliament. Even though the new Ukrainian authorities immediately announced that these were members of the Russian armed forces and paramilitary groups linked with Russia, the Russian Federation denied these allegations. In fact beginning in late February Russian armed forces began to support the Crimean separatists in taking over more and more locations in the Crimean Peninsula.[46] On 1 March 2014 President Putin submitted an appeal to the Federation Council of the Federal Assembly of the Russian Federation asking the Council "to use the Armed Forces of the Russian Federation on the territory of Ukraine until the social and political situation in that country is normalised."[47]

On 16 March 2014 the authorities of Crimea organized a referendum during which voters had to answer two questions: "Do you support reunifying Crimea with Russia as a subject of the Russian Federation?" and "Do you support the restoration of the 1992 Crimean constitution and the status of Crimea as a part of Ukraine?"[48] The referendum was declared illegal and invalid by many international institutions and States (see sections 2.2. and 2.3 below) for a number of reasons. First, the referendum was illegal

---

[46] P. Grzebyk, "The Annexation of Crimea in the Light of the Definition of Aggression. Does Prohibition of Aggression apply to Russia?" in *The Case of Crimea's Annexation Under International Law*, eds. Władysław Czapliński et al. (Warszawa: Scholar Publishing House, 2017), 137.

[47] "Vladimir Putin Submitted Appeal to the Federation Council," *President of Russia* website, 1 March 2014, http://en.kremlin.ru/events/president/news/20353.

[48] Translation of a ballot after "Crimea Referendum: What Does the Ballot Paper Say?" *BBC News*, 10 March 2014, https://www.bbc.com/news/world-europe-26514797.

under the Ukrainian constitution,[49] which states that "Ukraine is a unitary state," and that "[t]he territory of Ukraine within the limits of existent border is integral and inviolable" (Art. 2).[50] This is consistent with Article 134 which calls Crimea an "inalienable component part of Ukraine." Thus, since the referendum was aimed at disintegrating Ukraine and depriving it of Crimea, it was illegal. Moreover, in addition, to these provisions, one should also mention Article 138 of the Ukrainian Constitution which allows the Autonomous Republic of Crimea to organize and conduct referenda, but only "local referenda"—and certainly the referendum on "reunifying Crimea with Russia" exceeds the boundaries of being "local." On the other hand, any changes concerning the territory of Ukraine could be decided only by "all-Ukrainian referendum" (Article 73 of the Constitution). Secondly, the referendum failed to meet some international standards, which are included *inter alia* in Article 25 of the International Covenant on Civil and Political Rights and art. 3 of the First Protocol to the European Convention on Human Rights. These acts establish that any referendum should comply with the following principles: freedom, secrecy, equality, universality; questions asked in the referendum must be clear; and domestic and international observers must be present.[51] In the case

---

[49] Christian Marxsen, "The Crimea Crisis—An International Law Perspective," *Zeitschrift für ausländisches öffentliches Recht und Völkerrecht* 74 (2014): 380–81.

[50] All quotations from the Ukrainian Constitution come from the text of the Constitution available on the website of the US Department of Justice: https://www.justice.gov/sites/default/files/eoir/legacy/2013/11/08/constitution_14.pdf.

[51] Marxsen, "Crimea Crisis," 381–82. See also William W. Burke-White, "Crimea and the International Legal Order," *Research Paper* 14-24 (2014): 7–8. This analysis clearly shows that the referendum was illegal under Ukrainian law. The question remains whether it was also illegal under international law. It is beyond the scope of this article to discuss this problem in detail. However, it should be mentioned that the legality of such referenda remains doubtful under international law. Three different legal problems collide here: protection of territorial integrity of Ukraine; right to self-determination of people of Crimea; and the interference of Russia into the internal affairs of Ukraine. Russia claimed that people of Crimea have the right to self-determination, referring to "the well-known Kosovo precedent"; "Address by President of the Russian Federation", *President of Russia* website, 18 March 2014, http://en.kremlin.

of Crimea, the organizers of the referendum failed to meet these requirements.

Over 90% of voters who took part in the referendum supported Crimea's accession to the Russian Federation.[52] As a result, the Crimean authorities issued a declaration of independence, and on 18 March 2014 the Russian Federation and the Republic of Crimea signed an Agreement on the Accession of the Republic of Crimea into the Russian Federation and on Forming New Constituent Entities within the Russian Federation.[53] The Russian Duma ratified the agreement and on 21 March President Putin signed a law amending the Russian constitution to reflect the annexation.[54]

Russia claimed that what happened was not a case of aggression or the use of force since, as President Putin put it in his address to State Duma deputies, "I cannot recall a single case in history of an intervention without a single shot being fired and with no human casualties." Moreover, he claimed that:

> Armed Forces never entered Crimea; they were there already in line with an international agreement. True, we did enhance our forces there; however— and this is something I would like everyone to hear and know—we did not

---

ru/events/president/news/20603. However, on the other hand, the right to self-determination cannot be interpreted as allowing the dismembering of the existing State, especially upon outside interference; see Simone F. van den Driest, "Crimea's Separation from Ukraine: An Analysis of the Right to Self-Determination and (Remedial) Secession in International Law," *Netherlands International Law Review* 62 (3) (2015): 329–63; Anna Stepanowa, "International Law and Legality of Secession in Crimea," *Cambridge International Law Journal* 2014; Marxsen, "Crimea Crisis," 384–89; and Chris Borgen, "Can Crimea Secede by Referendum?" *Opinio Juris*, 3 June 2014, http://opiniojuris.org/2014/03/06/can-crimea-secede-referendum/.

[52] "Crimea Referendum: Voters 'Back Russia Union'," *BBC News*, 16 March 2014, https://www.bbc.com/news/world-europe-26606097.

[53] See "Agreement on the Accession of the Republic of Crimea to the Russian Federation Signed," *President of Russia* website, 18 March 2014, http://en.kremlin.ru/events/president/news/20604.

[54] "Crimea, Sevastopol Officially Join Russia as Putin Signs Final Decree," *RT*, 21 March 2014, https://www.rt.com/news/russia-parliament-crimea-ratification-293/.

exceed the personnel limit of our Armed Forces in Crimea, which is set at 25,000, because there was no need to do so.[55]

Likewise, the Russian representative in the UN SC highlighted the fact that President Putin's appeal to the Federation Council mentioned the use of the armed forces of the Russian Federation "on the territory of Ukraine" and not "against Ukraine," and that President Putin ultimately had not taken a decision on the use of armed forces on the territory of Ukraine.[56]

As mentioned above, not all scholars have declared the annexation of Crimea a violation of international law, even though some prominent commentators outside Russia entertained no doubts as to the fact that Russia had conducted an aggression (the use of force) against Ukraine.[57] As Antonello Tancredi has observed,

> the most reliable evidence of the occurrence of use of force in international relations, in addition to the classification given by Ukraine and other States, probably lies in the fact that Russia found it necessary to immediately provide a justification of the military operations carried out by its troops in the Crimea, resorting to classical arguments such as the consent of the local authorities and the necessity to protect its citizens abroad.[58]

Thus, despite Russia's justification, what actually took place was a "direct military intervention which resulted in the annexation of Crimea by Russia."[59]

---

[55] "Address by President of the Russian Federation."
[56] UN SC Provisional Records, Sixty-ninth year, 7124th meeting, 1 March 2014, UN Doc. S/PV.7124, 5.
[57] See e.g. Christian Henderson, *The Use of Force and International Law* (Cambridge: Cambridge University Press, 2018), 34, 220, 375; Christine Gray, *International Law and the Use of Force* (Oxford: Oxford University Press, 2018), 32; Veronika Bílková, "The Use of Force by the Russian Federation in Crimea," *Zeitschrift für ausländisches öffentliches Recht und Völkerrecht* 75 (2015): 30-7; and James A. Green, "Editorial Comment: The Annexation of Crimea: Russia, Passportisation and the Protection of Nationals Revisited," *Journal on the Use of Force and International Law* 1 no. 1 (2014): 5.
[58] Antonello Tancredi, "The Russian Annexation of the Crimea: Questions Relating to the Use of Force," *Questions of International Law: Zoom Out* I (2014): 7.
[59] Ibid., 10.

2.2. The Activity of the UN SC and UN GA

To sum up the events in Crimea, Russia used force against Ukraine, in consequence of which it annexed Crimea, thus flagrantly violating international law. Given the analysis set forth in the first part of this article, this illegal situation triggered the obligation of non-recognition on the part of other States. As has also been shown, in such a situation, international organs may determine the situation as illegal and establish some specific obligations on States which would further support the obligation of non-recognition. To find out whether such obligations were established in the case of Crimea, one has to analyze the actions of the UN SC and the UN GA with regard to the use of force by Russia and its annexation of Crimea.

On 15 March 2014, forty-two States submitted to the UN SC a draft resolution which in its preamble recalled:

> [the] obligation of all States under Article 2 of the United Nations Charter to refrain in their international relations from the threat or use of force against the territorial integrity or political independence of any state, and to settle their international disputes by peaceful means.[60]

The preamble also reaffirmed that "no territorial acquisition resulting from the threat or use of force shall be recognized as legal" and referred to the Helsinki Final Act. It further stated that "Ukraine has not authorized the referendum on the status of Crimea" (par. 4), and declared that:

> this referendum can have no validity, and cannot form the basis for any alteration of the status of Crimea; and calls upon all States, international organizations and specialized agencies not to recognize any alteration of the status of Crimea on the basis of this referendum and to refrain from any

---

[60] "Albania, Australia, Austria, Belgium, Bulgaria, Canada, Croatia, Cyprus, Czech Republic, Denmark, Estonia, Finland, France, Georgia, Germany, Greece, Hungary, Iceland, Ireland, Italy, Japan, Latvia, Liechtenstein, Lithuania, Luxembourg, Malta, Montenegro, Netherlands, New Zealand, Norway, Poland, Portugal, Republic of Moldova, Romania, Slovakia, Slovenia, Spain, Sweden, Turkey, Ukraine, United Kingdom of Great Britain and Northern Ireland and United States of America: draft resolution," 15 March 2014, UN Doc. S/2014/189.

action or dealing that might be interpreted as recognizing any such altered status (par. 5).

Interestingly, the resolution did not mention Russia at all, nor did it claim that Russia had illegally used force against Ukraine. On the other hand, it mentioned the obligation of non-recognition and in a general manner called upon States to "refrain from any action or dealing that might be interpreted as recognizing any such altered status of Crimea," without imposing on them any additional obligations. Even though the Russian veto to the resolution was anticipated, the final shape of the document was carefully worded (the British Ambassador to the UN called it "a deliberately reasonable text") since some of the UN SC members attempted to convince China to support the resolution, which would isolate the Russian position.[61]

During the debates within the UN SC held from 13 March, a number of States mentioned the obligation of non-recognition. Before the referendum in Ukraine was even held, the United States declared that it "cannot be recognized as legitimate, especially when carried out against the backdrop of a foreign military incursion."[62] The United Kingdom stated that the referendum in Crimea "will not be recognized by the international community."[63] Luxemburg also claimed with reference to the referendum that "the international community will in no way recognize its outcome."[64] During the debate over the draft resolution, the representative of France said that "The vast majority of Member States will prove, by their refusal to recognize the annexation of the Crimea, that they know that the territorial integrity of one of them is the guarantor of the territorial integrity of all."[65] The words of the fifth paragraph of the resolution

---

[61] Somini Sengupta, "Russia Vetoes U.N. Resolution on Crimea," *The New York Times*, 15 March 2014, https://www.nytimes.com/2014/03/16/world/europe/russia-vetoes-un-resolution-on-crimea.html.
[62] UN SC Provisional Records, Sixty-ninth year, 7134th meeting, 13 March 2014, UN Doc. S/PV.7134, 6.
[63] *Ibid.*, 8.
[64] *Ibid.*, 4.
[65] UN SC Provisional Records, Sixty-ninth year, 7138th meeting, 15 March 2014, UN Doc. S/PV.7138, 5.

were also repeated by the representative of Lithuania during the debate.⁶⁶ The representative of Australia called the referendum "dangerous and destabilizing" and "unauthorized and invalid," and asserted that "[t]he international community will not recognize the result nor any action taken on the basis of it."⁶⁷ In one of the further meetings of the UN SC, South Korea also declared that it would not recognize the referendum in Crimea or the annexation of Crimea by Russia.⁶⁸

Ultimately, the draft resolution was supported by 13 UN SC members, including the USA, France, and the UK. Russia voted against it and China abstained,⁶⁹ which means that under Art. 27 (3) of the UN Charter the resolution was not adopted due to the veto of Russia as the UN SC permanent member. However, as Enrico Milano observes, even if the resolution had been adopted by the UN SC it would not have been binding, since it was not adopted under Chapter VII (he claims it would be clearly adopted under Chapter VI).⁷⁰

Since the UN SC failed to adopt a resolution, on 27 March 2014 the UN GA voted for Resolution 68/262 titled "Territorial integrity of Ukraine." In the preamble, the UN GA recalled the obligations of States stemming from Art. 2 of the UN Charter, including the prohibition of the use of force. It referred to the Declaration of Principles of International Law and the principle contained therein, i.e. that "the territory of a State shall not be the object of acquisition by another State resulting from the threat or use of force," as well as the Helsinki Final Act. Next, it called upon "all States to desist and refrain from actions aimed at the partial or total disruption of the national unity and territorial integrity of Ukraine, including any

---

⁶⁶ Ibid., 6–7.
⁶⁷ Ibid., 9.
⁶⁸ UN SC Provisional Records, Sixty-ninth year, 7144th meeting, 19 March 2014, UN Doc. S/PV.7144, 11.
⁶⁹ UN Doc. S/PV.7138, 3.
⁷⁰ Enrico Milano, "The Non-recognition of Russia's Annexation of Crimea: Three Different Legal Approaches and One Unanswered Question," *Questions of International Law Zoom Out* I (2014): 51.

attempts to modify Ukraine's borders through the threat or use of force or other unlawful means" (par. 2), as well as appealing to:

> all States, international organizations and specialized agencies not to recognize any alteration of the status of the Autonomous Republic of Crimea and the city of Sevastopol on the basis of the above-mentioned referendum and to refrain from any action or dealing that might be interpreted as recognizing any such altered status (par. 6).

It also underscored the fact:

> the referendum held in the Autonomous Republic of Crimea and the city of Sevastopol on 16 March 2014, having no validity, cannot form the basis for any alteration of the status of the Autonomous Republic of Crimea or of the city of Sevastopol (par. 5).

Once again this resolution also did not mention Russia at all. The resolution was adopted with 100 votes in favor and 11 against, with 58 abstentions.[71]

During the debate on the resolution, the representative of the European Union stated that the EU "does not recognize the illegal referendum in Crimea, which is in clear violation of the Ukrainian Constitution. It strongly condemns the illegal annexation of Crimea and Sevastopol to the Russian Federation and will not recognize it."[72] The representative of Lichtenstein stated that it regarded the annexation of Crimea and Sevastopol as "null and void and will not recognize it or its consequences."[73] Canada also declared that the referendum in Crimea was "illegitimate and null and void," and that it "will not recognize its outcome."[74] A similar declaration was made by the representative of Georgia.[75] Turkey stated that "[t]he results of the illegal referendum held in Crimea on 16 March, in violation of the Ukrainian Constitution and international agreements, do not bear legal validity. Turkey does not recognize the de facto

---

[71] UN GA Official Records, Sixty-eighth session, 80th plenary meeting, 27 March 2014, UN Doc. A/68/PV.80, 17.
[72] Ibid., 4.
[73] Ibid., 7.
[74] Ibid., 9.
[75] Ibid., 11.

situation."[76] Norway asserted that it "does not recognize the illegal annexation of Crimea or Sevastopol."[77]

What conclusions can be drawn, then, from these developments within the UN SC and the UN GA? Neither of these organs explicitly declared that the annexation of Crimea was in fact illegal, nor that Russia had illegally used force against Ukraine. The most severe consequences of the situation in Crimea, as declared by the UN SC draft resolution and the UN GA resolution were connected with the referendum in Crimea, which was declared invalid. Thus, States were not called upon to not recognize the annexation, since it was illegal and prompted by the Russian aggression against Ukraine; rather, the obligation of non-recognition in both cases referred to the referendum. Moreover, neither of these acts mentioned any concrete obligations imposed upon States with regard to this illegal situation, as both these acts claimed only that States are obliged to "refrain from any action or dealing that might be interpreted as recognizing any such altered status." Thus, in very general terms both these resolutions prohibited direct or implied recognition of "alteration of the status of Crimea on the basis of this referendum."

To demonstrate that this is not always the case in similar situations, one may recall that when Iraq invaded and annexed Kuwait in 1990 the UN SC in its first resolution in this regard called the Iraqi action a "breach of international peace and security" (preamble)[78]; and in further resolutions established detailed obligations on the part of States so as not to imply recognition of the annexation (see section 1.1 above).

To do justice to the UN GA, it must be noted that it did go on to adopt four further resolutions with respect to the human rights situation in Crimea and the militarization of the peninsula. In Resolutions 71/205 and 72/190 the UN GA condemned "the ongoing temporary occupation of part of the territory of Ukraine—the Autonomous Republic of Crimea and the city of Sevastopol

---

[76] Ibid., 11.
[77] Ibid., 14.
[78] UN SC Resolution 660 of 2 August 1990, UN Doc. S/RES/660.

(hereinafter 'Crimea')—by the Russian Federation, and reaffirm(s) the non-recognition of its annexation."[79] Thus, the UN GA "reaffirmed" the non-recognition of annexation of Crimea even though in neither of its previous resolutions did it declare the annexation as illegal, nor did it explicitly declare that States should not recognize it. In two most recent resolutions of December 2018, the UN GA made much stronger statements regarding the situation in Crimea, *inter alia* "[a]ffirming that the seizure of Crimea by force is illegal and a violation of international law, and affirming also that those territories must be returned."[80] Again, neither of these resolutions established any measures which would support the "non-recognition of annexation" (instead, all four resolutions imposed some obligations on Russia with regard to the protection of human rights and demilitarization of Crimea). The UN SC has not adopted any resolution on the annexation of Crimea.

To sum up, while the annexation of Crimea could be considered one of the major examples of application of the obligation of non-recognition, as has been shown, the most important UN organs did not formulate States' obligations in this regard in a decisive and precise manner, perhaps because the drafters of the resolutions were endeavoring to convince as many States as possible to support the resolutions and hence came up with compromise texts. Thus, these examples also prove that the obligation of non-recognition should not be dependent on the determination of a situation as illegal by an international organ, but needs to be understood as triggered by the mere illegal actions of a wrongdoing State. On the other hand, the statements issued by multiple States during the UN GA and the UN SC debates demonstrate that the obligation of non-recognition is one of the most important consequences of the creation of an illegal situation, and one that States are aware of and generally comply with.

---

[79] UN GA Resolution 71/205 of 19 December 2016, UN Doc. A/RES/71/205, preamble; UN GA Resolution 72/190 of 19 December 2017, UN Doc. A/RES/72/190, preamble.

[80] UN GA Resolution 73/263 of 22 December 2018, UN Doc. A/RES/73/263, preamble; see also UN GA Resolution 73/194 of 17 December 2018, UN Doc. A/RES/73/194.

2.3. Reaction of the International Community outside the UN

Despite the vague position adopted by the UN GA and the UN SC, one may distinguish three types of reactions within the international community towards the use of force by Russia against Ukraine and annexation of Crimea.

The first group includes those actors which reacted to the annexation in the most harsh and decisive manner. Undoubtedly, the State that most powerfully proclaimed (and continues to proclaim) the illegality of the Crimean annexation is the United States.[81] In line with this approach, the US introduced sanctions against Russia, first established in the Presidential Executive Order of 6 March 2014. The sanctions were first and foremost targeted against persons responsible for or complicit in certain activities with respect to Ukraine, officials of the Government of the Russian Federation, persons operating in the arms or related materiel sector of the Russian Federation, as well as individuals and entities operating in the Crimea region of Ukraine. However, they also prohibited "the importation or exportation of goods, services, or technology to or from the Crimea region of Ukraine, as well as new investment in the Crimea region of Ukraine by a United States person, wherever located."[82] The US Department of State also issued the Ukraine Travel Advisory, which states: "Do not travel to Crimea due to (…) foreign occupation and abuses by occupation authorities." Moreover, the US government is warning its citizens that it is unable to provide emergency services to US citizens traveling in Crimea since US government employees are prohibited from traveling to Crimea.[83] However, at the same time, the US has

---

[81] See e.g. "Russia's Continued Illegal Occupation of Crimea," *U.S. Mission to the OSCE* website, 1 March 2018, https://osce.usmission.gov/russias-continued-illegal-occupation-crimea-2/.

[82] Department of the Treasury, Office of Foreign Assets Control, "Ukraine/Russia—Related Sanctions Program," Updated 16 June 2016, 3, https://www.treasury.gov/resource-center/sanctions/Programs/Documents/ukraine.pdf.

[83] US Department of State – Bureau of Consular Affairs, "Ukraine Travel Advisory," 10 January 2018, https://travel.state.gov/content/travel/en/travelad visories/traveladvisories/ukraine-travel-advisory.html#ExternalPopup.

also applied the "Namibia exception," allowing, under general license, such activities as: the exportation or reexportation of certain agricultural commodities, medicine, medical supplies, and replacement parts from the United States or by a US person, wherever located, to the Crimea region of Ukraine; the operation of certain accounts in a US financial institution for an individual ordinarily resident in the Crimea region of Ukraine; certain transactions with respect to the receipt and transmission of telecommunications and mail involving the Crimea region of Ukraine; and the exportation or reexportation of certain services and software from the United States or by a US person, wherever located, to the Crimea region of Ukraine.[84]

The US example also illustrates how highly politicized the policy of non-recognition is. At the beginning of July 2018 rumors began to appear that US President Donald Trump might recognize the Russian annexation of Crimea, since he reportedly said during the G7 summit that "Crimea is Russian because the population of the peninsula speaks Russian."[85] However, a few days later Michael R. Pompeo, the US Secretary of State, issued a statement titled "Crimea Declaration" in which he offered an assurance that "the United States reaffirms as policy its refusal to recognize the Kremlin's claims of sovereignty over territory seized by force in contravention of international law."[86]

No less decisive was the reaction of the European Union. The first EU organ to issue a statement on the annexation of Crimea was the European Council. The EU leaders discussed the annexation at a meeting on 20–21 March 2014, and the European Council declared in its "Conclusions" from the meeting that it "strongly condemned the annexation of Crimea and Sevastopol to the Russian Federation

---

[84] Department of the Treasury, Office of Foreign Assets Control, "Ukraine/Russia-Related Sanctions Program," 6.
[85] "Donald Trump's Talking Points on Crimea are the Same as Vladimir Putin's," *Washington Post* website, 3 July 2018, https://www.washingtonpost.com/news/democracy-post/wp/2018/07/03/donald-trumps-talking-points-on-crimea-are-the-same-as-vladimir-putins/?noredirect=on&utm_term=.5218fa84b8da.
[86] US Department of State, "Crimea Declaration," Press Statement, 25 July 2018, https://www.state.gov/secretary/remarks/2018/07/284508.htm.

and will not recognise it."⁸⁷ The EU further upheld this approach and repeated it on multiple occasions, declaring that the goal of the EU policy of non-recognition was "to demonstrate that the EU does not accept the illegal annexation, using tangible measures in addition to regular political and diplomatic action."⁸⁸ The measures adopted by the EU as a consequence of its non-recognition of the annexation of Crimea include, *inter alia*: the freezing of assets; visa bans which apply to 150 persons and 38 entities; a ban on imports of goods originating in Crimea or Sevastopol unless they have Ukrainian certificates; a prohibition on investment in Crimea; a ban on providing tourism services in Crimea or Sevastopol; a ban on making any payments to the Port Authority of Kerch or the Port Authority of Sevastopol; and a ban on the export of goods and technology for the transport, telecommunications, and energy sectors or for the exploration of oil, gas, and mineral resources to Crimean companies or for use in Crimea (including a ban on technical assistance, brokering, construction, and engineering services).

In addition, the EU issued guidelines recommending a common approach to be taken by Member States towards Russian passports issued in Crimea. The guidelines recommend non-recognition of Russian ordinary international passports issued by the Russian administrative authorities established in Crimea and Sevastopol after the illegal annexation of these territories, as well as Russian ordinary passports issued by Russian administrative authorities in the Russian Federation to residents of Crimea and Sevastopol after the illegal annexation of these territories, unless these persons held Russian citizenship prior to the annexation. At the same time however, this does not amount to a travel ban for those who have documents recognized by the EU Member States.⁸⁹ The latest development with regard to free movement between Crimea and the EU Member States was the passage of the Regulation

---

⁸⁷ European Council, "Conclusions," 21 March 2014, EUCO 7/1/14.
⁸⁸ "The EU Non-recognition Policy for Crimea and Sevastopol: Fact Sheet," 12 December 2017, https://eeas.europa.eu/headquarters/headquarters-Homepage/37464/eu-non-recognition-policy-crimea-and-sevastopol-fact-sheet_en.
⁸⁹ *Ibid.*

of the European Parliament and of the Council of 19 April 2017,[90] by which Ukraine was moved from Annex I of the Regulation (EC) No 539/2001 (countries whose nationals need a visa to enter the Schengen area) to Annex II (visa free countries). As a result, Ukrainian citizens with a biometric passport travelling to the EU for up to 90 days no longer need a visa. The regulation of 19 April 2017 does not mention any special status for Crimea with regard to visa liberalization; thus, all inhabitants of Crimea who possess Ukrainian biometric passports are included and may travel to the EU without a visa.[91]

One should also add that Crimean public entities are not eligible to participate in EU programs that Ukraine has joined, such as Creative Europe, Horizon 2020 and Erasmus+. Nevertheless, Crimean students who undertake studies in the EU can still apply for Erasmus Mundus Joint Master Degree scholarships.[92]

When it comes to the European States outside the EU, as early as on 18 March 2014, the Minister of Foreign Affairs of Norway declared that his State condemned Russia's annexation of Crimea, calling it a violation of international law, and stating that the use of military force by Russia was unacceptable.[93] Likewise, the Swiss Federal Council called the referendum of 16 March 2014 a "violation of the Ukrainian constitution and therefore illegal," and stated that the annexation of Crimea "contravenes international law and the principle of the territorial integrity of states." Moreover, Switzerland

---

[90] Regulation of the European Parliament and of the Council amending Regulation (EC) No 539/2001 listing the third countries whose nationals must be in possession of visas when crossing the external borders and those whose nationals are exempt from that requirement (Ukraine), 19 April 2017, PE-CONS 13/17.

[91] Loreline Merelle, Jean Comte, "EU Visa Waiver Looms for Russia-annexed Crimeans," *EU Observer*, 11 May 2017, https://euobserver.com/justice/137859.

[92] "The EU Non-recognition Policy for Crimea and Sevastopol: Fact Sheet."

[93] Ministry of Foreign Affairs, "Norway Condemns Russia's Annexation of Crimea," 18 March 2014, https://www.regjeringen.no/en/aktuelt/condemns_russia/id753260/.

established sanctions against Russia[94] (and subsequently extended them).[95]

In addition, the Parliamentary Assembly of the Organization for Security and Cooperation in Europe (OSCE) adopted, during its twenty-third annual session, a "Resolution on Clear, Gross and Uncorrected Violations of Helsinki Principles by the Russian Federation." This Resolution states that Russia "(...) since February 2014, violated every one of the ten Helsinki principles in its relations with Ukraine, some in a clear, gross and thus far uncorrected manner (...)"; and that it views "the 16 March 2014 referendum in Crimea as an illegitimate and illegal act, the results of which have no validity whatsoever" (par. 15). The Resolution also calls upon "all participating States to refuse to recognize the forced annexation of Crimea by the Russian Federation" (par. 16).

Since one of the major tasks of the OSCE Office for Democratic Institutions and Human Rights is to observe elections to assess the extent to which voting processes respect fundamental freedoms, the issue arose whether the OSCE should observe the voting procedures which take place in Crimea in the aftermath of the annexation. Starting from the referendum of March 2014, the OSCE ruled out such a possibility, since as the OSCE Chair stated, "the basic criteria for a decision in a constitutional framework was not met."[96] Likewise, the OSCE refused to send its observers to monitor the Russian presidential election in Crimea, which took place in March 2018.[97]

---

[94] "Switzerland Condemns Russia's Annexation of Crimea," *Kyiv Post*, 27 March 2014, https://www.kyivpost.com/article/content/ukraine-politics/switzerland-condemns-russias-annexation-of-crimea-341051.html.

[95] "Switzerland Steps Up Sanctions against Russia over Ukraine," *UNIAN*, 18 November 2015, https://www.unian.info/politics/1052853-switzerland-steps-up-sanctions-against-russia-over-ukraine.html.

[96] OSCE, "OSCE Chair says Crimean Referendum in its Current Form is Illegal and Calls for Alternative Ways to Address the Crimean Issue," 11 March 2014, https://www.osce.org/cio/116313.

[97] "OSCE, EU Refuse to Observe Russian Election in Crimea," *Ukrinform*, 25 December 2017, https://www.ukrinform.net/rubric-polytics/2371217-obse-i-es-otkazalis-nabludat-za-rossijskimi-vyborami-v-krymu.html. The same approach was also adopted by the EU ("EU Doesn't Recognize Russian Elections in Crimea—Mogherini," *UNIAN*, 16 March 2018, https://www.unian.info/politics/10045295-eu-doesn-t-recognize-russian-elections-in-crimea-mogherini.html.

Similarly, the Parliamentary Assembly of the Council of Europe stated, in a resolution of 9 April 2014, that "the so-called 'referendum'" in Crimea was unconstitutional. Its outcome and "the illegal annexation of Crimea by the Russian Federation therefore have no legal effect and are not recognised by the Council of Europe."[98] It should also be mentioned that the European Organisation for the Safety of Air Navigation has recommended that international operators avoid flying over Crimea and has called for non-recognition of air navigation services other than those provided by the Ukrainian authorities.[99]

Apart from the US and European examples, one may invoke the case of Australia which has prohibited the direct or indirect supply, sale, or transfer to Russia, for use in Russia, or for the benefit of Russia, of arms or related matériel, as well as some oil products. Australia has also prohibited the provision to Russia, or to a person for use in Russia, of technical advice, assistance, or training; financial assistance; financial service or another service if it assists with, or is provided in relation to a military activity or the manufacture, maintenance, or use of "arms or related materiel." In addition, Australia has banned certain financial transactions with entities listed with Autonomous Sanctions (Russia, Crimea and Sevastopol) Specification 2015. The Australian regulation does not mention any exceptions from the sanctions, although it does note that a sanctions permit may be granted in the event that the Minister for Foreign Affairs "is satisfied that it would be in the national interest to do so."[100]

Likewise, Canada prohibited any person in Canada and any Canadian outside Canada from, *inter alia*, making an investment in the Crimea region of Ukraine; providing or acquiring financial or

---

[98] "The Illegal Annexation of Crimea has No Legal Effect and is Not Recognised by the Council of Europe," *Parliamentary Assembly* website, 9 April 2014, http://assembly.coe.int/nw/xml/News/News-View-EN.asp?newsid=4975&cat=8.
[99] Milano, "Non-recognition," 37.
[100] Australian Government, Department of Foreign Affairs and Trade, "Sanctions Regime: Russia," https://dfat.gov.au/international-relations/security/sanctions/sanctions-regimes/Pages/russia.aspx; Autonomous Sanctions (Russia, Crimea and Sevastopol) Specification 2015, 9 August 2017, F2017C00697.

other related services to, from, or for the benefit of or on the direction or order of the Crimea region of Ukraine; transferring, providing, or communicating technical data or services to, from, or for the benefit of or on the direction or order of the Crimea region of Ukraine; as well as docking a cruise ship in the Crimea region of Ukraine. However, Canada also established exceptions to these rules, including, e.g., pension payments to any person in Canada or any Canadian outside Canada.[101] In addition, in March 2018 Canada stated that it would not recognize "the illegitimate extension of Russia's presidential elections to annexed Ukrainian territory."[102]

The second group of States comprises those which, even though they did not recognize Crimea as part of Russia and condemned the use of force against Ukraine and annexation of Crimea, nevertheless adopted a quite ambivalent attitude and failed to impose effective sanctions on Russia. This group of States includes Japan. On 18 March 2014, the Japanese Minister for Foreign Affairs issued a statement on "Measures against Russia over the Crimea referendum" in which it was declared, *inter alia*, that the referendum "has no legal effect and Japan does not recognize its outcome."[103] Immediately after annexation, Japan also decided to suspend talks on an investment pact and on the relaxation of visa requirements,[104] as well as banning certain financial transactions

---

[101] Government of Canada, "Canadian Sanctions Related to Ukraine," https://www.international.gc.ca/world-monde/international_relations-relations_internationales/sanctions/ukraine.aspx?lang=eng.

[102] "Statement by Minister of Foreign Affairs on Fourth Anniversary of Illegal Annexation of Crimea," 16 March 2018, https://www.canada.ca/en/global-affairs/news/2018/03/statement-by-minister-of-foreign-affairs-on-fourth-anniversary-of-illegal-annexation-of-crimea.html.

[103] Ministry of Foreign Affairs of Japan, "Statement by the Minister for Foreign Affairs of Japan on the Measures against Russia over the Crimea referendum," 18 March 2014, https://www.mofa.go.jp/press/release/press4e_000239.html. This position was further upheld e.g. in 2018; "Japan Refuses to Recognise Russian Election in Crimea: Report," *Radio Poland*, 23 March 2018, http://www.thenews.pl/1/10/Artykul/355364,Japan-refuses-to-recognise-Russian-election-in-Crimea-report.

[104] "Japan to Impose Sanctions on Russia for Crimea Move," *Reuters*, 18 March 2014, https://www.reuters.com/article/us-ukraine-crisis-japan/japan-to-impose-sanctions-on-russia-for-crimea-move-idUSBREA2H02T20140318.

with forty individuals. Nevertheless, these bans did not concern high-level officials, who allegedly visited Japan in the aftermath of annexation. Likewise, Japan never disclosed who was listed on the visa bans. Reportedly, the reason for Japanese abstinence is the Japanese–Russian territorial dispute over the Kuril Islands—Japan launched negotiations to settle the dispute in 2012 and it seeks to preserve the outcomes of these negotiations, which very restrictive sanctions would place in jeopardy.[105] Summing up, one may describe the Japanese sanctions as rather symbolic.[106]

In this context, one may also mention the attitude adopted by Turkey. On one hand, Turkey did not recognize the annexation of Crimea (the Turkish minister of foreign affairs reiterated this position in 2018),[107] and Turkey also supported the release of Ukrainians imprisoned in Russia after the annexation.[108] However, on the other hand, it seems that in recent years Turkey and Russia only tightened their relations. The biggest rupture in the ties between these two States occurred not after the annexation of Crimea but after Turkish fighter jets shot down a Russian Su-24 near the Syria-Turkey border in 2015.[109] Nevertheless, relations warmed up again after President Recep Tayyip Erdoğan apologized for this incident in 2016. It is estimated that since then Putin and Erdoğan have met around ten times.[110] Moreover, in 2017 Turkey signed an

---

[105] Maria Shagina, "Japan's Sanctions Policy vis-à-vis Russia. Implications for Western Sanctions Unity," *Sasakawa USA Forum* 15 (2018): 1-5.

[106] Daisuke Kitade, "Considering the Effects of Japanese Sanctions Against Russia," 7 July 2016, https://www.mitsui.com/mgssi/en/report/detail/1221522_10744.html.

[107] "Turkish FM: Turkey Not to Recognize Annexation of Crimea," *UNIAN*, 8 June 2018, https://www.unian.info/politics/10145702-turkish-fm-turkey-not-to-recognize-annexation-of-crimea.html.

[108] "Crimean Tatar Leader Says Turkey's Erdogan Promised 'To Talk To Putin' Regarding Ukrainians Jailed In Russia," *RadioFreeEurope*, 22 August 2018, https://www.rferl.org/a/crimean-tatar-leader-says-turkey-s-erdogan-promised-to-talk-to-putin-regarding-ukrainians-jailed-in-russia/29447062.html.

[109] See also Gareth Winrow, "Turkey and Russia: The Importance of Energy Ties," *Insight Turkey* 19 (1) (2017): 17.

[110] "Russia and Turkey in the Black Sea and the South Caucasus," *International Crisis Group*, 28 June 2018, https://www.crisisgroup.org/europe-central-asia/western-europemediterranean/turkey/250-russia-and-turkey-black-sea-and-south-caucasus.

agreement with Russia to purchase a Russian surface-to-air missile system.[111]

Finally, not all countries took the decision to not recognize the annexation of Crimea. Eight States[112] so far have supported the annexation: Cuba, Nicaragua, Venezuela, Syria, Afghanistan, North Korea, [113] Bolivia, [114] and Kyrgyzstan. [115] All these States have, in explaining their approach, repeated the Russian rhetoric about the persecution of the Russian minority in Crimea and the historical ties between Crimea and Russia. To legitimize their decision, they also referred to the outcome of the referendum of 16 March claiming that reunification with Russia was the result of "the free will of the Crimean people," which should be respected. [116] While all these States are outside Europe, there have recently been signals that the Russian annexation of Crimea may also find supporters within Europe, as the Serbian opposition Radical Party announced in June 2018 that it planned to put to a vote the question of recognition of

---

[111] Carlotta Gall and Andrew Higgins, "Turkey Signs Russian Missile Deal, Pivoting From NATO," *The New York Times*, 12 September 2017, https://www.ny times.com/2017/09/12/world/europe/turkey-russia-missile-deal.html.

[112] In addition, while Zimbabwe has not issued any official statement on recognition, the Zimbabwean Environment Minister Saviour Kasukuwere paid an official visit to Crimea in December 2014, an action which Ukraine interpreted as indicating "disregard on the part of Zimbabwe for current Ukrainian legislation, international law, the UN Charter"; "Ukraine Angry as Zimbabwe Minister Visits Crimea," *Crimean News Agency*, 23 December 2014, http://qha.com.ua/en/politics/ukraine-angry-as-zimbabwe-minister-visits-cri mea/132828/.

[113] "These are the 6 Countries on Board with Russia's Illegal Annexation of Crimea," *Business Insider Polska*, 31 May 2016, https://businessinsider.com.pl/internatio national/these-are-the-6-countries-on-board-with-russias-illegal-annexation-of-crimea/6wxsh1n.

[114] "Bolivia's Evo Morales Pledges to Recognize Crimea and Support 'Anti-Imperialist Russia'," *Fort Russ News*, 22 February 2018, https://www.fort-russ.com/2016/06/bolivias-evo-morales-pledges-to/.

[115] "Kyrgyzstan Says Crimea Referendum 'Legitimate'," *Radio Free Europe*, 20 March 2014, https://www.rferl.org/a/kyrgyzstan-recognition-crimea-referen dum-ukraine-russia/25304439.html.

[116] Matthew Rosenberg, "Breaking with the West, Afghan Leader Supports Russia's Annexation of Crimea," *The New York Times*, 23 March 2014, https://www.ny times.com/2014/03/24/world/asia/breaking-with-the-west-afghan-leader-supp orts-russias-annexation-of-crimea.html.

the Russian annexation of Crimea.[117] However, the Serbian government rushed to make assurances that Serbia would not recognize the annexation of Crimea, since this could be interpreted as amounting to support for the independence declared by Kosovo.[118]

To sum up, the majority of the international community have complied with the obligation of non-recognition vis-à-vis the annexation of Crimea. Despite the fact that some States have not adopted a uniform and consistent attitude, still, many States and international organizations have not only declared that they will not recognize the annexation, but have also introduced measures in order to fulfil their obligation of non-recognition, such as travel bans, termination of consular relations, and restraints on economic ties, thereby proving the content of the obligation of non-recognition as mentioned above.

Moreover, States undertook these measures despite the fact that neither the UN SC nor the UN GA explicitly declared the annexation of Crimea as illegal, which proves that there is no need for action on the part of any international organ in order to activate the obligation of non-recognition. On the other hand, the scope of the measures adopted both by the EU and the OSCE shows that the obligation of non-recognition may be proclaimed and enforced not only by UN organs, but also by regional organizations. Thus there is no fixed rule as what is the "appropriate organ" to declare a given situation illegal and impose consequences resulting therefrom. It is worthwhile to observe that the measures adopted by international organizations and States were comprehensive and covered all activities which could imply recognition, including also the observation of the Russian presidential election in Crimea. In addition, some actors, like the US, Canada, and the EU, have

---

[117] "112.ua: Serbian parliament to vote for recognition of referendum in Crimea," *Kyiv Post*, 14 June 2018, https://www.kyivpost.com/ukraine-politics/112-ua-serbian-parliament-to-vote-for-recognition-of-referendum-in-crimea.html?cn-reloaded=1.

[118] "Serbia Doesn't Recognize Crimea as Part of Russia, Won't Impose Sanctions on Russia," *Ukrinform*, 4 June 2018, https://www.ukrinform.net/rubric-polytics/2473315-serbia-doesnt-recognize-crimea-as-part-of-russia-wont-impose-sanctions-on-russia.html.

undertaken measures within the framework of a policy of non-recognition that have taken into account the "Namibia exception," so as not to affect the everyday life of ordinary people in Crimea.[119]

At the same time, only a few States have taken a different stand, and this also confirms the validity of the obligation of non-recognition, since they did not undermine the validity of this obligation as such. However, President Trump's recent statements prove that the obligation of non-recognition, as originating from the very discretional and highly politicized act of recognition, is also a matter of policy and may change, depending on political goals.

Ultimately, one must acknowledge that the policies which States have adopted towards the annexation of Crimea confirm the binding force of the obligation of non-recognition, and that its content includes far more than the sole obligation to withhold direct recognition of an illegal situation.

Conclusions

Contrary to some claims raised in the doctrine of law, the annexation of Crimea by Russia constituted a flagrant violation of international law, which activated the obligation of non-recognition on the part of other States. The attitude adopted by the majority of the international community towards the annexation proved that the obligation of non-recognition is a customary norm, as well as confirmed its scope as established in the first part of this article. In addition, States not only complied with the obligation of non-recognition itself but also applied the "Namibia exception," protecting individuals against the negative consequences of the obligation. The attitude of a few States that did not comply with the obligation of non-recognition does not undermine the significance of the obligation since these States referred to political objectives in

---

[119] One should also mention that not only third States, but also Ukraine adopted measures which are said to protect the basic rights of residents of Crimea, despite lack of recognition of Russian annexation; see e.g. Law of Ukraine "On Ensuring Civil Rights and Freedoms, and the Legal Regime on the Temporarily Occupied Territory of Ukraine," entered into force 27 April 2014, http://zakon1.rada.gov.ua/laws/anot/en/1207-18.

explaining their standpoints rather than denying the existence of such an obligation.

Despite these conclusions, it is important to observe that in the case of Crimea no State or international organization has managed to fulfil the most fundamental of all duties stemming from the obligation of non-recognition—that is, the duty to bring the illegal situation to an end. As a result, for now, Crimea remains under Russian control.

Russia's Legal Position on the Annexation of Crimea: A Critique[*]

Dasha Dubinsky and Peter Rutland

Abstract: *Russia's annexation of Crimea in 2014 is widely seen as a turning point in Russia's domestic politics and its relations with the international community, reflecting a new willingness to confront the West, with military means if necessary.*

Since 1991 Russia had gradually been drawn into the sphere of international commitments, as evidenced by its inclusion in the Council of Europe, the WTO, and other bodies. But Crimea seemed to represent a break with that trajectory, signaling a flagrant disregard for the norms of international law, notably sovereignty, territorial integrity, and the binding nature of international treaties.

Russian officials and academics deployed some spurious legal reasoning in trying to justify the annexation, including appeals to self-determination, historical legitimacy, the Kosovo precedent, the purported illegality of the Ukrainian government, and alleged threats to the security of Russians and Russian-speakers in Crimea. At the same time, however, Moscow declined to recognize the sovereignty of the self-proclaimed Donetsk and Luhansk People's Republics, and in annexing Crimea it tried to disguise its violation of international law (by avoiding casualties, by using "little green men," and by holding a referendum). A close study of the Crimean case can suggest ways in which international law could be strengthened with a view to deterring similar actions in the future.

Keywords: **Crimea, Russia, annexation, self-determination**

---

[*] An earlier version of this paper was presented at the British International Studies Association workshop "Narrating Russian and Eurasian security," King's College, London, 19 June 2018; and to the American Political Science Association convention, Boston, 1 September 2018. Thanks to Natasha Kuhrt, Tuomas Forsberg, Stephen Fortescue, Giulio Gallarotti, and the two anonymous reviewers for their comments.

Introduction

This paper examines the arguments used by the Russian leadership and academics as to the legality of the annexation of Crimea. It also discusses the role of international law in this conflict, and the implications for Russia's use of international law in the future. It finds Russia's arguments for the incorporation of Crimea wanting both in factual basis and in legal foundation, while noting that Russia made considerable efforts to defend their actions as conforming to international law.

After a short introduction, the article discusses the concept of self-determination, and then examines Russia's arguments regarding whether or not the Crimeans are a "people;" the history of Crimea's status within Ukraine; alleged threats to Russians living there; and the relevance of the Kosovo precedent. The next section examines arguments regarding the legality of Russia's use of force.

The annexation of Crimea in March 2014[1] came as a shock to most of the international community, which saw it a violation of the rules of international engagement that kept the peace between the great powers since 1945. Prior to the annexation of Crimea the Russian Federation, like the Soviet Union before it, had repeatedly stressed the importance of state sovereignty and territorial integrity. It fought two bloody wars to prevent the secession of Chechnya, in 1994–96 and 1999–2002. Even after Crimea, Russia's military intervention in Syria in 2015 to preserve the regime of President Assad was in part justified by reference to state sovereignty and territorial integrity.

Kadrii Idris makes the case in a recent report for the European Council on Foreign Relations:

> The EU and Russia have become locked in an open battle over the norms of international conduct. They disagree on some of the most fundamental normative elements of the post-cold war international order—its Western-led "unipolar" nature; its emphasis on human rights and democracy; and the idea that countries have the right to choose their own alliances and join once

---

[1] Russia officially refers to the action as "reunification," not annexation.

they qualify. ... This is a clash between liberal universalism and authoritarian statism; the liberal international order and realpolitik.[2]

The UN General Assembly promptly adopted a resolution stating that the annexation had no legal standing,[3] and only a small number of countries have accepted Russian sovereignty over Crimea.[4] For all intents and purposes, however, Crimea has been removed from Ukrainian hands. In May 2018 Russian occupancy was affirmed by the completion of an 18 km bridge (the longest in Europe) across the Kerch Strait linking Crimea to the Russian mainland. Russia began regulating the passage of ships under the bridge into the Sea of Azov, and in December 2018 seized three Ukrainian naval vessels making the journey.

Before we dismiss Russia as an outlaw, rogue state, it is worth remembering that Russia is a major world power, a founding member of the United Nations, and signatory to a dense network of international treaties governing trade, finance, political relations, and military operations. It is not in Russia's long-term national interest to see a breakdown of international law. Russia routinely relies on international legal institutions such as the Stockholm Arbitration Institute to defend its interests, even in dealings with strategic partners such as China.

Second, there are grounds for seeing Crimea as exceptional, a special case. Crimea is home to Russia's Black Sea Fleet (a force that played an active role in Russia's military intervention in Syria). European Russia lacks warm-water ports: the Baltic is easily closed by adversaries, and its Arctic ports are remote. None of the ports on the Russian portion of the Black Sea are suitable for a major naval

---

[2] Kadrii Idriis, "Winning the Normative War with Russia." European Council on Foreign Relations, 21 May 2018, http://www.ecfr.eu/publications/summary/winning_the_normative_war_with_russia_an_eu_russia_power_audit. Unless otherwise stated, all URLs cited below were accessible on 8 August 2018.

[3] UN General Assembly, *Territorial Integrity of Ukraine*, 27 March 2014, A/RES/68/262. 100 countries voted in favor, 11 against, and 58 abstained.

[4] In December 2017 the UN General Assembly passed a resolution condemning Russian actions in Crimea: 76 countries voted in support, 26 opposed, and 76 abstained; UN General Assembly, *Situation of Human Rights in the Autonomous Republic of Crimea and the City of Sevastopol, Ukraine*, 19 December 2017, A/RES/72/190.

base. Similarly, Ukraine as a whole has a unique place in Russia's strategic world view, given its size and location. Moscow views the prospect of Ukraine joining NATO and/or hosting US military bases as an existential threat to Russian security, and it saw the Maidan revolution that toppled President Viktor Yanukovych as a breakthrough event which set Ukraine on the path to closer Western integration.[5] Russia's adversaries are all too aware of the importance of Ukraine: Zbigniew Brzezinski famously opined: "Without Ukraine, Russia ceases to be an empire."[6]

Third, one should recognize that Russia is not unique: all of the great powers repeatedly violate international law when they see it in their national security interests to do so.[7] Neoliberal institutionalists and soft-power proponents decry this state of affairs, arguing that in an increasingly inter-dependent world all states benefit from rule-bound cooperation.[8] Even before President Trump, the US was a leading culprit, refusing to join the International Criminal Court and the UN Convention on the Law of the Sea (UNCLOS), and launching military operations from Kosovo to Iraq without UN authorization. The People's Republic of China likewise refuses to accept UNCLOS and has built bases on artificial islands to enforce its claims to the "nine dash line" in the South China Sea. The European Union is exceptional in its scrupulous respect for international law (as in the Idris quote above). However, as Robert Kagan and others have argued, the EU is only able to adopt this position because it has outsourced the dirty work of military

---

5   John Mearsheimer, "Why the Ukraine Crisis Is the West's Fault. The Liberal Delusions That Provoked Putin," *Foreign Affairs* (September/October 2014), https://www.foreignaffairs.com/articles/russia-fsu/2014-08-18/why-ukraine-crisis-west-s-fault.
6   Zbigniew Brzezinski, *Strategic Vision: America and the Crisis of Global Power* (New York: Basic Books, 2012), 95.
7   John Mearsheimer, *The Tragedy of Great Power Politics* (New York: W.W. Norton, 2014).
8   Robert Keohane, *After Hegemony: Cooperation and Discord in the World Political Economy* (Princeton, NJ: Princeton University Press, 2005); and Giulio Gallarotti, *Cosmopolitan Power in International Relations* (Cambridge: Cambridge University Press, 2010).

enforcement to the United States.[9] In confronting the West Russia finds itself facing the "good cop" EU and the "bad cop" US.

The Annexation of Crimea

In February 2014, following the flight of President Viktor Yanukovych from Ukraine, Russian forces moved out from their bases in Crimea and seized Ukrainian government buildings and military installations across the peninsula.[10] At the time Russia claimed that the soldiers —who wore Russian army-issue uniforms but had no identifying insignia—were Crimean self-defense groups. In the West they were dubbed "little green men," and in Russia "polite people" (*vezhlivye liudi*). Later, in 2015, President Putin acknowledged that they were in fact Russian soldiers.[11] The very fact that the Russians engaged in this subterfuge, and went to considerable lengths to avoid casualties,[12] indicates that they were aware of the shaky legal foundations of their actions and were striving to maintain a degree of "plausible deniability" if things went wrong (as they did in July 2014, with the shootdown of MH17 over Donbas, killing all 298 people on board). There is disagreement over the extent to which the annexation of Crimea was planned in advance. Mikhail Zygar reports that, at the Bucharest summit in 2008, Putin warned NATO that Ukraine would lose Crimea if it tried to join NATO.[13] On the other hand, in February 2014 the initial plan

---

[9]   Robert Kagan, *Of Paradise and Power. America and Europe in the New World Order* (New York: Vintage, 2004).

[10] Steven Fortescue, "Russia's Security-related Decision-making: The Case of Crimea," in *A Quarter Century of Post-Communism Assessed*, eds. M. Steven Fish, Graeme Gill, and Milenko Petrovic (London: Palgrave Macmillan, 2016), 295–314.

[11] Shaun Walker, "Putin Admits Russian Military Presence in Ukraine for First Time," *The Guardian*, 17 December 2015; https://www.theguardian.com/world/2015/dec/17/vladimir-putin-admits-russian-military-presence-ukraine.
See also Putin interviewed in the documentary film, "Crimea: The Way Home," directed by Andrei Kondrashov, March 2015, https://www.youtube.com/watch?v=3Mw4Y9jRwCQ.

[12] During the occupation of Crimea there was only one death: a Ukrainian officer was shot.

[13] Mikhail Zygar, *All the Kremlin's Men* (New York: Public Affairs, 2017), 154.

seemed to be for secession: the wording of the referendum was only changed to unity with Russia on 6 March.[14]

In the referendum on 16 March 2014 Crimeans were given two options: "Do you support reunifying Crimea with Russia as a subject of the Russian Federation?" and "Do you support the restoration of the 1992 Crimean constitution and the status of Crimea as a part of Ukraine?"[15] (The 1992 constitution asserted Crimea's autonomy within Ukraine.) No option was provided for maintaining existing Crimea's status, nor for an independent Crimea. Moscow dictated the terms of the referendum in accordance with the result they wanted. Official results reported 97% of Crimeans voting to join Russia, although Western countries questioned the validity of the referendum and its results.[16] Nevertheless, in Moscow "The Treaty on Accession of the Republic of Crimea to Russia" was signed just two days later, incorporating Crimea into the Russian Federation.[17]

The Concept of Self-Determination

> We did not annex [Crimea], we did not seize it, we gave people the opportunity to express themselves and make a decision and we treated that decision with respect.
> —Vladimir Putin[18]

Understanding the principle of self-determination is pivotal in assessing the legitimacy of Crimea's annexation. This principle has evolved over time and has expanded in its application, leading to confusion and debate about when it can be applied and by whom.

---

[14] Fortescue, "Russia's Security-related Decision-making," 284.
[15] "Crimea Referendum: What Does the Ballot Paper Say?" *BBC News*, 10 March 2014, http://www.bbc.com/news/world-europe-26514797.
[16] Ilya Somin, "The Dubious Crimean Referendum on Annexation by Russia," *Washington Post*, 17 March 2014, https://www.washingtonpost.com/news/volokh-conspiracy/wp/2014/03/17/the-dubious-crimean-referendum-on-annexation-by-russia/?utm_term=.foc3ed49605e.
[17] "Agreement on the Accession of the Republic of Crimea to the Russian Federation Signed," *Official Internet Resources of the President of Russia*, 18 March 2014, http://en.kremlin.ru/events/president/news/20604.
[18] "Seliger 2014 National Youth Forum," *Official Internet Resources of the President of Russia*, 29 August 2014, http://en.kremlin.ru/events/president/news/46507.

Yet it has long been a principle of international law.[19] In 1914, Vladimir Lenin published *The Right of Nations to Self-Determination*, in which he wrote "the self-determination of nations means the political separation of these nations from alien national bodies, and the formation of an independent national state."[20] In contrast, Woodrow Wilson imagined self-determination not as a national right but as a civil right for citizens to participate in their own government.[21] He pushed for this conception to be instated in the League of Nations and proposed it at the Paris Peace Conference in 1919.[22] It was ultimately rejected "due to inconsistences in its interpretation."[23] This is a problem that, as we will see, has not gotten much clearer in the subsequent 100 years.

The concept resurfaced in Article 1 of the UN Charter, which states that one of the purposes of the United Nations is to "develop friendly relations among nations based on respect for the principle of equal rights and self-determination of peoples."[24] But how self-determination is defined, who it applies to, and how it is be accomplished was left up to subsequent treaties, court decisions, and customary law.[25]

Yet, self-determination can only be exerted so long as it does not infringe upon the territorial integrity of a state. As Thomas D. Grant notes: "The international order that emerged after 1945... is,

---

[19] Hurst Hannum, *Autonomy, Sovereignty, and Self-determination: The Accommodation of Conflicting Rights*, (Philadelphia, PA: University of Pennsylvania Press, 2011), 473.
[20] Vladimir Lenin, "The Right of Nations to Self-Determination," *Marxists Internet Archive*, 395; https://www.marxists.org/archive/lenin/works/1914/self-det/index.htm.
[21] Trygve Throntveit, "The Fable of the Fourteen Points: Woodrow Wilson and National Self-determination," *Diplomatic History* 35, no. 3 (2011): 455–81.
[22] Sofia Cavandoli, "The Unresolved Dilemma of Self-determination: Crimea, Donetsk and Luhansk," *The International Journal of Human Rights* 20, no. 7 (2016): 875–92, 876.
[23] Ibid.
[24] Charter of the United Nations, Chapter I, Article 1(2) (1945).
[25] "Customary international law refers to international obligations arising from established state practice, as opposed to obligations arising from formal written international treaties"; *Legal Information Institute*; https://www.law.cornell.edu/wex/customary_international_law.

in short, an order of settled boundaries and enduring territorial settlements."[26] Without this consensus on preserving territorial integrity, none of the modern forms of international law that we are accustomed to could have come into being.

Following World War II, self-determination was largely seen in the context of decolonization. In 1960 the UN General Assembly adopted the Declaration on the Granting of Independence to Colonial Countries and Peoples, affirming that "All peoples have the right to self-determination;"[27] but like all documents relating to self-determination, it also states that this right must not interfere with territorial integrity. In the colonial context, territorial integrity was less of a problem, since most colonies already had internationally-recognized borders, and their independence did not threaten the sovereignty of the colonizing country. In 1966, the International Covenant on Economic, Social and Cultural Rights reaffirmed that self-determination is a right guaranteed to "all peoples" and "by virtue of that right they freely determine their political status and freely pursue their economic, social, and cultural development."[28]

The Helsinki Final Act, signed in 1975, gave an even more inclusive interpretation of self-determination: "By virtue of the principle of equal rights and self-determination of peoples, all peoples always have the right, in full freedom, to determine, when and as they wish, their internal and external political status, without external interference, and to pursue as they wish their political, economic, social and cultural development."[29] The Soviets had lobbied hard against this broader language.[30] As the right of self-determination began to apply beyond the colonial context, for

---

[26] Thomas D. Grant, *Aggression against Ukraine: Territory, Responsibility, and International Law* (New York: Springer, 2015), 4.
[27] UN General Assembly, *Declaration on the Granting of Independence to Colonial Countries and Peoples*, 14 December 1960, A/RES/1514(XV).
[28] UN General Assembly, *International Covenant on Economic, Social and Cultural Rights*, 16 December 1966, United Nations, Treaty Series, vol. 993, Article 1(1).
[29] Organization for Security and Co-operation in Europe (OSCE), *Conference on Security and Co-operation in Europe (CSCE): Final Act of Helsinki*, 1 August 1975.
[30] Boris Meissner, "The Right of Self-Determination after Helsinki and Its Significance for the Baltic Nations," *Case W. Res. J. Int'l L.* 13 (1981): 377–78.

example to secession movements within post-colonial states,[31] the focus on preserving territorial integrity and state sovereignty persisted. States were encouraged to give minority groups political autonomy within the existing state. This emphasized a difference between internal self-determination, defined as "the right of people to freely choose their own political, economic, and social system," and external self-determination, which is the right of a people "to constitute itself a nation-state or to integrate into, or federate with, an existing state."[32] Thus for example in *Reference re Secession of Quebec* (1998) the Supreme Court of Canada ruled that "a state whose government represents the whole of the people or peoples resident within its territory, on a basis of equality and without discrimination, and respects the principles of self-determination in its own internal arrangements, is entitled to the protection under international law of its territorial integrity."[33] That is, there is no unconditional right to secession under international law.[34]

However, "more recently the right to secede from a state has also been granted in situations where a people have been denied civil and political rights and subject to serious human rights abuses."[35] The case of Kosovo, which declared independence in 2008, is pivotal. Many countries, including Russia, saw Kosovo's independence as an infringement on Serbia's territorial integrity and the result of illegal use of force by NATO to assist the Kosovar Albanians.

It remains unclear who qualifies as a people capable of exercising self-determination. Former Judge Antonio Cassese, who served as the first president of the Yugoslav war crimes tribunal, writes: "Nowhere in international law can one find a definition of

---

[31] Examples include the 1960 Katanga and South Kasai secessions from the Republic of the Congo, and the 1967 Biafra secession from Nigeria. All three provinces were later reincorporated into their parent states.
[32] Salvatore Senese, "External and Internal Self-Determination," *Social Justice* 16, no. 1 (1989): 19–25, 19.
[33] Supreme Court of Canada, *Reference re Secession of Quebec*, 1998, 2 S.C.R. 217, para. 130.
[34] Roya M. Hanna, "Right to Self-Determination in In Re Secession of Quebec," *Md. J. Int'l L. & Trade* 23, no. 1 (1999): 214–46, 241.
[35] Cavandoli, "Unresolved Dilemma," 878.

the peoples enjoying the right at issue."[36] Christopher Borgen writes: "At various points in international legal history, the term 'people' has been used to signify citizens of a nation-state, the inhabitants in a specific territory being decolonized by a foreign power, or an ethnic group."[37] In 1989, UNESCO conducted a study aimed at understanding who a "people" refers to in the context of self-determination, but the results were far from conclusive.[38] They offered general criteria of a common historical tradition, cultural homogeneity, territorial connection, a common economic life, and a common consciousness.[39] Thus the legal concept of self-determination is very much a work in progress, evolving along with changes in international circumstances.

Russia's Arguments in Defense of Crimean Self-Determination

As a founding member of the United Nations and signatory to multiple international treaties, Russia is committed to the idea and practice of international law. Indeed, the Russian Constitution stipulates that international laws and international treaties to which Russia is a signatory take priority in cases where they are inconsistent with the domestic law of the Russian Federation.[40]

How, then, have they tried to justify the annexation of Crimea in terms of international law? One of their central arguments is that they were assisting the people of Crimea in exercising their right of self-determination.[41]

---

[36] Antonio Cassese, *Self-determination of Peoples: A Legal Reappraisal* (Cambridge: Cambridge University Press, 1995), 326–27.
[37] Christopher J. Borgen, "Law, Rhetoric, Strategy: Russia and Self-determination Before and After Crimea," *International Law Studies* 91, no. 1 (2015): 218–80, 225.
[38] UNESCO, *International Meeting of Experts on Further Study of the Concept of the Rights of Peoples*, 27 November 1989, SHS-89/CONF.602/7.
[39] Ibid., 22.
[40] Russia (Federation), *The Constitution of the Russian Federation* (adopted by referendum, December 1993), Article 15 (4).
[41] Anton Moiseienko, "What Do Russian Lawyers Say About Crimea?" *OPINIO JURIS*, 24 September 2014; http://opiniojuris.org/2014/09/24/guest-post-russian-lawyers-say-crimea/.

Are Crimeans a "People"?

Crimea has a distinct historical trajectory and its residents undoubtedly have a strong sense of regional identity, but it is not clear that they constitute a distinct "people" with the right to self-determination under international law. Nevertheless, Anatoly Kapustin, President of the Russian International Law Association, insists that the residents of Crimea constitute a "political-ethnic community" possessing the right to self-determine.[42] (Presumably, if the Crimeans had decided *not* to join Russia, Kapustin might have changed his opinion on this point.) In contrast Ukrainian law professor Oleksandr Merezhko writes "Officially the population of Crimea has never been considered a separate people, neither by Ukraine nor by Russia."[43]

The Crimean Tatars pose a particular problem for the Russian approach.[44] Bill Bowring argues that the Crimean Tatars are the only group that can be seen as a "people" with the right to self-determination, given their status as "indigenous people of Crimea." [45] Furthermore, they had faced significant persecution within the Soviet Union: they were deported to Central Asia in 1944 and they—alone among the deported peoples of 1944—were not rehabilitated after the death of Stalin. This adds validity to their claim as a self-determination unit. The Office of the United Nations High Commissioner for Human Rights reported that the majority of

---

[42] Anatoly Kapustin, "Crimea's Self-Determination In the Light of Contemporary International Law," *Heidelberg Journal of International Law* 75 (2015): 101–18, 115.
[43] Oleksandr Merezhko, "Crimea's Annexation by Russia—Contradictions of the New Russian Doctrine of International Law," *Heidelberg Journal of International Law* 75 (2015): 167–94, 183.
[44] Andrew Wilson, "The Crimean Tatar Question: A Prism for Changing Nationalisms and Rival Versions of Eurasianism," *Journal of Soviet and Post-Soviet Politics and Society* 3, no. 2 (2017): 2–45.
[45] Bill Bowring, "Who are the 'Crimea People' or 'People of Crimea'? The Fate of the Crimean Tatars, Russia & Legal Justification for Annexation, and Pandora's Box," in *The Use of Force against Ukraine and International Law*, eds. Sergey Sayapin and Evhen Tsybulenko (The Hague: Springer, 2018), 21–40, 21.

the Tatar community boycotted the referendum, with only about 1,000 out of about 300,000 Tatars choosing to participate.[46]

The Legal Status of Crimea within Ukraine

Even if one was to concede that Crimeans can be considered a "people" with a right for self-determination, it would still have to be proven that they had a legal right to secede from Ukraine. On this front the main Russian argument is the illegality of the Kyiv regime given the dramatic events of February 2014: the fall of the government, the flight of President Yanukovich, and the unconstitutional transfer of powers to a new acting president.[47] This holds no legal merit since a governmental transition or revolution does not invalidate the territorial integrity of the state[48] nor its legal continuity.[49] The Russians also suggest that self-determination was necessary because the autonomy of Crimea as a territory of Ukraine was at risk under the new leadership, but cannot point to any specific legislative or executive actions in support of that claim. The Russian position is undermined by the speed of their actions in Crimea: for example, they did not wait for the new presidential election, scheduled for 24 May 2014. In Ukraine, the government continued to function and exercised effective control of its territory apart from the secessionist regions; and most other countries recognized the interim Ukrainian government.[50]

A second line of argument used by Russia is that there was a deep historical connection between Crimea and Russia, and that the

---

[46] Office of the United Nations High Commissioner for Human Rights, *Report on the Human Rights Situation in* Ukraine, 15 April 2014, 4.
[47] Mikhail Deliagin, "Crimea: The First Step in Russia's Return to the World," *Russian Politics & Law* 53, no. 2 (2015): 6–31, 9.
[48] Merezhko, "Crimea's Annexation," 187; and Alexei Moiseev, "Concerning Certain Positions on the Ukrainian Issue in International Law," *Russian Politics & Law* 53, no. 2 (2015): 47–60, 50.
[49] Hans Kelsen, *Principles of International Law*, 2nd rev. edn. (New York: Holt, Rinehart and Wilson, 1966), 387.
[50] Christian Marxsen, "The Crimea Crisis—An International Law Perspective," *Heidelberg Journal of International Law* 74, no. 2 (2014): 367–91, 377.

incorporation of Crimea into Ukraine in 1954 was illegitimate.[51] Putin himself has said "In people's hearts and minds, Crimea has always been an inseparable part of Russia."[52] In his 18 March 2014 address to the State Duma on the incorporation of Crimea into the Russian Federation, Putin stated, "I heard residents of Crimea say that back in 1991 they were handed over like a sack of potatoes. This is hard to disagree with. And what about the Russian state? What about Russia? It humbly accepted the situation."[53] In 2015 the Russian Federal Assembly passed a bill annulling the Soviet Union's 1954 transfer of Crimea to Ukraine.[54] However, as Borgen points out, "International legal doctrines of sovereignty, effective dates of boundaries and non-intervention deliberately do not give weight to such historical grievances because almost every country can point to some past wrong and some previous territorial distribution that they believe is more just."[55]

In 1921 Crimea was formed as the Crimean Autonomous Socialist Soviet Republic within the Russian Soviet Federative Socialist Republic, and redesignated as the Crimean Oblast' of the RSFSR in 1945. Then in 1954, this oblast' was transferred to the Ukrainian Socialist Soviet Republic by the Presidium of the Supreme Soviet. Officially it was framed as a goodwill gesture, connected to the 300th anniversary of the Treaty of Pereiaslav, when the Cossack Hetman Bohdan Khmelnytsky swore allegiance to the Tsar.[56] At the

---

[51] Anatoly Kapustin, "Circular Letter to the Executive Council of the International Law Association," June 2014, http://www.ilarb.ru/html/news/2014/5062014.pdf.
[52] Vladimir Putin, "Address by President of the Russian Federation," *Official Internet Resources of the President of Russia*, 18 March 2014, http://en.kremlin.ru/events/president/news/20603.
[53] Ibid.
[54] "New Russian Bill Condemns 1954 Transfer of Crimea to Ukraine as 'Illegal,'" *Moscow Times*, 5 February 2015; https://themoscowtimes.com/news/new-russian-bill-condemns-1954-transfer-of-crimea-to-ukraine-as-illegal-43588.
[55] Borgen, "Law, Rhetoric, Strategy," 259.
[56] Mark Kramer, "Why Did Russia Give Away Crimea Sixty Years Ago?" *Wilson Center*, 19 March 2014; http://www.wilsoncenter.org/publication/why-did-russia-give-away-crimea-sixty-years-ago.

time of the transfer there were 268,000 Ukrainians and 858,000 ethnic Russians living in Crimea.[57]

Questions regarding the legal validity of Crimea's inclusion in Ukraine were raised during and after the break-up of the Soviet Union. It was argued that according to the RSFSR Constitution a territorial change could only be made by the entire RSFSR Supreme Soviet, not just the Presidium, and that the 1936 USSR Constitution stipulated that "the territory of a union republic may not be altered without its consent."[58] On 21 January 1991, the people of Crimea voted in a referendum to change Crimea's status from an oblast to an Autonomous Region (ASSR) within the USSR, which was granted by Kyiv in June 1991. After the failed August 1991 coup, in the Ukraine-wide independence referendum conducted on December 1, 1991, 54.2% of Crimeans voted affirmatively to the question "Do you support the Act of Declaration of Independence of Ukraine?"[59] This discredits Russia's claim that Crimea was forcibly seized by Ukraine in 1991. Kapustin admits that "international customary law does not grant a right of option to the inhabitants of a territory in the case of state succession."[60]

Yet, there were voices raised in protest in the early 1990s. In May 1992, the Crimean parliament voted to declare independence, contingent on a referendum. They passed a new constitution, which defined the "Republic of Crimea" as a state with sovereign powers, while simultaneously affirming it as a part of the Ukrainian state. Gwendolyn Sasse argues this constitution was used as a way to force Kyiv into negotiating a better deal for the region, which eventually

---

[57] Joshua Keating, "Khrushchev's Gift," *Slate*, 25 February 2014, http://www.slate.com/blogs/the_world_/2014/02/25/separatism_in_ukraine_blame_nikita_khrushchev_for_ukraine_s_newest_crisis.html.
[58] Evgenii Ambartsumov, interview in *Novoe vremia* 6 (1992): 18-20; and *1936 Constitution of the USSR* (adopted 5 December 1936), Article 18.
[59] Chrystyna Lalpychak, "Over 90% Vote Yes in Referendum; Kravchuk Elected President of Ukraine," *The Ukrainian Weekly*, 8 December 1991; http://www.ukrweekly.com/old/archive/1991/499101.shtml.
[60] Kapustin, "Crimea's Self-Determination," 111 footnote 35. State succession here is defined as the transition of the state from the Ukrainian SSR to Ukraine.

paid off.⁶¹ In 1994 a movement to reunite with Russia gained momentum, driven by economic weakness, ethnic resentment of the Crimean Tatars, and conflicts with Kyiv, rather than a perceived historical/cultural affinity with Russia.⁶² Consequently, the mobilization fell apart in the absence of any backing from Moscow.

Article 134 of the Ukrainian Constitution, passed in 1996, states "The Autonomous Republic of Crimea is an inseparable constituent part of Ukraine and decides on the issues ascribed to its competence within the limits of authority determined by the Constitution of Ukraine."⁶³ In 1998, a new Crimean Constitution was approved, which defined Crimea as an "inseparable constituent part of Ukraine."⁶⁴

The status of Crimea seemed to be resolved, both legally and in the eyes of its residents. Based on her fieldwork in Crimea in 2012-13, Eleanor Knott writes, "Including the minority of respondents who identified with Russia, and felt discriminated by Ukraine, none of my [Knott's] respondents supported secession from Ukraine: it just seemed unthinkable, if not farcical."⁶⁵ Similarly, surveys run by Grigore Pop-Eleches and Graeme Robertson found that although Crimeans were less likely than other regions to view Ukraine as their homeland, instead naming Crimea itself, only about 1% identified Russia as their homeland.⁶⁶ A 2013 Razumkov Center survey showed a majority of Crimeans opposing separation from Ukraine.⁶⁷ This evidence casts doubt on the validity of the March 2014 referendum.

---

61 Gwendolyn Sasse, *The Crimea Question: Identity, Transition, and Conflict* (Cambridge, MA: Harvard University Press, 2007), 146.
62 *Ibid.*, 172.
63 Ukraine (federation), *The Constitution of Ukraine*, (adopted 28 June 1996), Article 134.
64 Sasse, *Crimea Question*, 202.
65 Eleanor Knott, "Crimea before Annexation: Reflections on Writing a 'History of the Past,'" *Eleanor Knott* (blog), 29 September 2015; https://eleanorknott.wordpress.com/tag/russian-annexation-of-crimea/.
66 Grigore Pop-Eleches and Graeme Robertson, "Do Crimeans Actually Want to Join Russia," *Washington Post*, 6 March 2014; https://www.washingtonpost.com/news/monkey-cage/wp/2014/03/06/do-crimeans-actually-want-to-join-russia/?utm_term=.f2babf5780c5, Figure 1.
67 *Ibid.*

A yearning for self-determination that only begins *after* the use of force or intimidation by an outside power cannot hold weight under international law.

Furthermore, although Russia might speak of their historical ties with Crimea, legally the matter had been resolved when Russia vowed to respect Ukraine's territorial integrity in international agreements. The 1994 Budapest Memorandum stated that:

> The United States of America, the Russian Federation, and the United Kingdom, reaffirm their obligation to refrain from the threat or use of force against the territorial integrity or political independence of Ukraine, and that none of their weapons will ever be used against Ukraine except in self-defense or otherwise in accordance with the Charter of the United Nations.[68]

This was necessary to assure Ukraine of its security following its agreeing to give up nuclear weapons. A 1997 treaty between Russia and Ukraine confirmed the respect for each other's territorial integrity, and Ukraine granted Russia's Black Sea fleet a 20-year lease to use the facilities in Sevastopol.[69]

Although history shows a complicated path to internal autonomy for Crimea following the dissolution of the Soviet Union, these issues were resolved by the late 1990s. There is little evidence that Crimeans were politically oppressed, or aimed to secede from Ukraine, prior to the events of February 2014.

The Persecution of Russians

Russian legal theorist Anatoly Kapustin writes:

> In the Crimean situation, the physical existence of the people was at stake and therefore a secession from Ukraine was justified under the requirements of "remedial secession." Of course, compared to Bangladesh, Kosovo and

---

[68] General Assembly Security Council, *Memorandum on Security Assurances in Connection with Ukraine's Accession to the Treaty on the Non-proliferation of Nuclear Weapons*, 19 December 1994, A/49/765.
[69] "Treaty of Friendship, Cooperation, and Partnership between Ukraine and the Russian Federation" (signed 31 May 1997).

other examples of this kind, the situation in Crimea was different. In fact, there were no mass killings of civilians or full-scale military actions.[70]

There is no credible factual evidence to support Kapustin's view that "the physical existence of the people was at stake." Kapustin cites as evidence the clash in Odessa on 2 May 2014 that left 52 people dead after a building caught fire.[71] However, this happened two months *after* the Crimean referendum, and was the result of violence on both sides.

Moscow cites threats to Ukraine's Russian-speakers in support of Crimean self-determination. (A majority of Crimeans speak Russian at home.[72]) They point to a bill approved by the Verkhovna Rada on 27 February 2014 overturning a 2012 law that allowed for the use of more than one official language in regions where more than 10% of residents spoke a regional language.[73] The bill was approved a day after the vote to impeach President Yanukovych, but was vetoed by the acting president Turchynov on 1 March and never went into law.[74] In practice Ukraine was and is a multilingual society, with widespread use of Russian.[75] It is anyway not clear whether the Russian language in Ukraine is entitled to protection under international law. The European Charter for Minority Languages adopted by the Council of Europe in 1992, and

---

[70] Kapustin, "Crimea's Self-Determination," 117.
[71] Office of the United Nations High Commissioner for Human Rights, *Report on the Human Rights Situation in Ukraine*, 15 June 2014, 37–50.
[72] Pop-Eleches and Robertson, "Do Crimeans Actually Want to Join Russia," fig. 3.
[73] "Canceled Language Law in Ukraine Sparks Concern among Russian and EU Diplomats," *RT*, 28 February 2014; https://www.rt.com/news/minority-language-law-ukraine-035/. Thirteen of Ukraine's 27 regions then adopted Russian as a second official language, and two Western regions introduced Romanian and Hungarian as official languages.
[74] "Ukraine's 2012 Language Law to Stay Until New Bill Ready—Turchynov," *Sputnik International*, 3 March 2014; https://sputniknews.com/world/20140 303188063675-Ukraines-2012-Language-Law-to-Stay-Until-New-Bill-Ready--Tu rchynov/. A law mandating Ukrainian as the sole official language and language of instruction in schools from 5th grade on was passed in September 2017.
[75] Volodymyr Kulyk, "Shedding Russianness, Recasting Ukrainness," *Post-Soviet Affairs* 34, no. 2–3 (2016): 119–38; and Aleksei Stoliarenko, "Vse pro status russkogo iazyka," *Ukrainskaia pravda* 13 March 2014, https://www.pravda.com. ua/rus/columns/2014/03/13/7018654/.

ratified by Ukraine in 1993, is aimed to protect "minority languages" which are under threat of extinction, and not the rights of ethnic minorities to speak a certain language.[76]

The UN human rights report released on 15 April 2014 stated in regard to Crimea:

> Although there was no evidence of harassment or attacks on ethnic Russians ahead of the referendum, there was widespread fear for their physical security. Photographs of the Maidan protests, greatly exaggerated stories of harassment of ethnic Russians by Ukrainian nationalist extremists, and misinformed reports of them coming armed to persecute ethnic Russians in Crimea, were systematically used to create a climate of fear and insecurity that reflected on support to integration of Crimea into the Russian Federation.[77]

Thus it was the media climate and propaganda surrounding the referendum that created a fear of persecution, and not real threats. Many Russian media perpetuated claims of Ukrainian extremists oppressing ethnic Russians in Crimea through videos and images that were later discredited.[78] As the International Court of Justice emphasized in the Western Sahara Advisory Opinion, "the application of the right of self-determination requires a free and genuine expression of the will of the peoples concerned." [79] Furthermore, although little evidence was found in the UN Human Rights Report relating to persecution of Russians, there were multiple cases of harassment of people in Crimea seen as opposing the referendum.[80]

---

[76] Lada Kolomiyets, "From Mistranslation of the European Charter for Regional or Minority Languages to the Halt of Minsk II," Association for Study of Nationalities, Columbia University, 3 May 2018; and Council of Europe, *European Charter on Regional and Minority Languages* (1992), https://www.coe.int/en/web/european-charter-regional-or-minority-languages.

[77] *Report on the Human Rights Situation in Ukraine*, 15 April 2014, para. 89.

[78] Oleg Shynkarenko, "Putin's Crimea Propaganda Machine," *Daily Beast*, 3 March 2014; https://www.thedailybeast.com/putins-crimea-propaganda-machine.

[79] International Court of Justice (ICJ), *Western Sahara, Advisory Opinion*, I.C.J. Reports 16 October 1975, General List No. 61, para. 55.

[80] *Report on the Human Rights Situation in Ukraine*, 15 April 2014, para. 6, 84.

The Kosovo Precedent

The Kosovo case was pivotal in changing understanding of how to apply the principle of self-determination, opening the door to a looser interpretation of territorial integrity.[81] However, Russia's use of Kosovo as justification for its actions in Crimea ignores critical disparities between the two cases.

Long-standing dissatisfaction with Kosovo's status within Yugoslavia intensified after Slobodan Milosevic took over the Serbian presidency in 1989. Seeing NATO intervene in Bosnia in 1995 emboldened Kosovo nationalists and led to the creation of the Kosovo Liberation Army (KLA) in 1996. Conflict between the KLA and Serbian forces led NATO to launch a 78-day bombing campaign in 1998, without UN approval and over Russian objections. Milosevic eventually withdrew his troops, but a decade of negotiations failed to produce agreement over the status of Kosovo (and the Serbia minority still living there). Kosovo declared independence in April 2008 and won recognition from 106 states by 2018, but has not gained entry to the UN.[82] "The recognition and non-recognition of Kosovo has, however, demonstrated a level of inconsistency and arbitrariness that understandably has given rise to questions about the role of international law in the recognition process—and indeed led some to ask whether international law has any role to play at all."[83]

In its 2010 Advisory Opinion on *Accordance with International Law of the Unilateral Declaration of Independence in Respect to Kosovo*, the International Court of Justice found that the Kosovo declaration of independence was not illegal, "because international law does not prohibit declarations of independence."[84] Beyond that,

---

[81] K. William Watson, "When in the Course of Human Events: Kosovo's Independence and the Law of Secession," *Tulane Journal of International and Comparative Law* 17, no. 1 (2008): 269–74, 272.
[82] Kosovo Thanks You; https://www.kosovothanksyou.com/.
[83] John Dugard, *The Secession of States and Their Recognition in the Wake of Kosovo* (Leiden: Brill, 2013), 43.
[84] *Accordance with International Law of the Unilateral Declaration of Independence in Respect of Kosovo* (Request for Advisory Opinion), para. 83; and Curtis Doebbler, "The ICJ Kosovo Independence Opinion: Uncertain

however, the court failed to answer key questions such as "whether Kosovo was a state; whether recognition of Kosovo was lawful; whether Kosovo Albanians are a people for the purpose of self-determination or even whether they have a right to 'remedial secession.'"[85] It thus missed an opportunity for further clarification of the principle of self-determination, to the annoyance of many on both sides.[86]

Although Russia opposed Kosovo's decision to secede and has still not recognized Kosovo as an independent state, they seem to rely on this case as precedent for Crimea. Putin stated: "We keep hearing from the United States and Western Europe that Kosovo is some special case. What makes it so special in the eyes of our colleagues? [...] According to this logic, we have to make sure every conflict leads to human losses."[87]

However, Kosovo had a history of denial of autonomy and repression by Yugoslavia, culminating in a massive campaign of ethnic cleansing in 1998. None of this is true for Crimea. Also, Kosovo unlike Crimea sought independence, not incorporation into a neighboring state.

Summary

Self-determination is not an easy concept to understand or to actualize. While it is a right granted to all people, it is simultaneously curtailed by territorial integrity.

None of the arguments presented by Russia justify Crimean secession under the principle of self-determination. They ignore the core modern view of self-determination as a right that must be pursued internally, except for rare cases when internal autonomy is

---

Precedent," *Jurist*, 23 July 2010, http://www.jurist.org/forum/2010/07/the-icj-kosovo-independence-ruling-an-uncertain-precedent.php.

[85] Jure Vidmar, "Unilateral Secession and Multilateral State-making," in *Kosovo: A Precedent? The Declaration of Independence, the Advisory Opinion and Implications for Statehood, Self-Determination and Minority Rights*, ed. James Summers (Leiden: Brill, 2011), 143–78, 152.

[86] Thomas Burri, "Kosovo Opinion and Secession: The Sounds of Silence and Missing Links," *German Law Journal* 11 (2010): 881–90, 886.

[87] Putin, "Address by President of the Russian Federation."

not granted or when a people are subject to persecution. As recently as 2009, Russia itself was still citing the traditional focus on internal-self-determination in the Kosovo case, arguing that, "all efforts should be taken in order to settle the tension between the parent State and the ethnic community concerned within the framework of the existing State."[88]

The Use of Force

Russia must not only justify the secession of Crimea, but also their use of military force in the region to ensure its secession. The UN Charter states, "All members shall refrain in their international relations from the threat or the use of force against the territorial integrity or political independence of any state, or in any other manner inconsistent with the Purposes of the United Nations."[89] Use of force is only allowed for self-defense, or with authorization from the Security Council.[90]

Like most principles in international law, the interpretation of self-defense has varied widely over time. The original test for self-defense comes from the 1837 *Caroline* case, involving a British attack on an American ship carrying supplies to Canadian rebels. The court decided that the threat would have to be "instant, overwhelming, leaving no choice of means, and no moment of deliberation."[91] Although Article 51 states "self-defense if an armed attack occurs," some argue it can be invoked in cases of "anticipatory self-defense against an imminent danger of attack."[92] Israel used it to justify

---

[88] "Written Statement by the Russian Federation," *Accordance with International Law of the Unilateral Declaration of Independence in Respect of Kosovo* (Request for Advisory Opinion), 16 April 2009, 31–32.

[89] Charter of the United Nations, Chapter I, Article 2 (4) (1945).

[90] Raymond John Vincent, *Nonintervention and International Order* (Princeton, NJ: Princeton University Press, 2015), 14; and Agatha Verdebout, "The Contemporary Discourse on the Use of Force in the Nineteenth Century: A Diachronic and Critical Analysis," *Journal of the Use of Force and International Law* 1, no. 2 (2014): 223–46, 227.

[91] Daniel Webster, "Letter to Sir Henry Stephen Fox," *The Papers of Daniel Webster: Diplomatic Papers* 1 (1983): 1841–43.

[92] Peter Malanszuk, *Akehurst's Modern Introduction to International Law* (London: Routledge, 2012), 311.

bombing an Iraqi nuclear reactor in 1981, and the US in bombing Libya in 1986.[93] Another contentious form of self-defense is the armed protection of nationals abroad. Most scholars agree that it does not justify the use of force against a sovereign state, but in some instances, this form of intervention has "met a relative lack of condemnation by organs of the United Nations, although they have not been approved as being lawful."[94]

A more recent justification for the use of force is the concept of Responsibility to Protect, or R2P. As its originator Gareth Evans explained:

> The emergence of the "Responsibility to Protect" (R2P) was a response to a real international problem: the continuing inability of the international community, notwithstanding the embrace of the Genocide Convention and many other new international human rights standards after World War II, to effectively prevent or halt mass atrocity crimes—viz. genocide, ethnic cleansing and other major crimes against humanity and war crimes—occurring behind sovereign state borders.[95]

The idea gained strength following the genocides in Rwanda and Bosnia in 1994–95. In 2011, the UN Security Council used R2P to justify intervention in Libya, but it has not yet reached a standard of customary international law.[96]

In some cases a state projects military force into another without directly deploying its own troops. In the 1986 *Nicaragua* case, the International Court of Justice ruled that if the US had "effective control" over the operation of Contra guerrillas operating in Nicaragua they could be held legally responsible for them.[97] In the former Yugoslavia, the ICTY did not agree with this narrow

---

[93] Ibid., 313.
[94] Ibid., 316.
[95] Presentation by Gareth Evans to China Institute of International Studies (CIIS) Conference on *Responsible Protection: Building a Safer World*, Beijing, 17 October 2013; http://www.gevans.org/speeches/speech535.html.
[96] Alex J. Bellamy, "The Responsibility to Protect—Five Years On," *Ethics & International Affairs* 24, no. 2 (2010): 143–69, 144.
[97] International Court of Justice (ICJ), *Case Concerning Military and Paramilitary Activities In and Against Nicaragua (Nicaragua v. United States of America)*, I.C.J. Reports, 27 June 1986, General List No. 70, para.115.

definition of control and, in the *Tadic* case, chose instead the looser criterion of "overall control." The court stated, "It must be proved that the State wields overall control over the group, not only by equipping and financing the group, but also by coordinating or helping in the general planning of its military activity."[98]

What Constitutes Russia's Use of Force in Crimea?

The actions of Russian troops in Crimea meet the minimum requirements for the threat or use of force.[99] There is also the question of whether Moscow had effective or overall control over the Crimean self-defense forces, making Russia legally accountable for their actions as well.[100] In November 2016 the International Criminal Court classified the situation in Crimea as an international armed conflict between Ukraine and Russia.[101] Article 2 of the Geneva Conventions specifically states that armed conflicts include "all cases of partial or total occupation of the territory of a High Contracting Party, even if the said occupation meets with no armed resistance."[102]

Russia's Arguments in Defense of the Use of Force

Russian government officials and scholars have presented multiple arguments defending the use of force, with some denying it entirely and others bringing in multiple different approaches to persuade the world that the use of force was legal.

---

[98] International Criminal Tribunal for the former Yugoslavia (ICTY), *Prosecutor v. Dusko Tadic (Appeal Judgement)*, IT-94-1-A, 15 July 1999.

[99] Gary Wilson, "Secession and Intervention in the Former Soviet Space: The Crimean Incident and Russian Interference in Its 'Near Abroad,'" *Liverpool Law Review* 37, no. 3 (2016): 153–75, 166.

[100] William Burke-White, "Crimea and the International Legal Order," *Survival* 56, no. 4 (2014): 65–80, 69.

[101] International Criminal Court, Office of the Prosecutor, "Report on Preliminary Examination Activities 2016," 14 November 2016.

[102] International Committee of the Red Cross (ICRC), *Convention (I) for the Amelioration of the Condition of the Wounded and Sick in Armed Forces in the Field*. Geneva, Article 2, 12 August 1949.

In 1997 Russia and Ukraine signed three treaties related to the status of the Black Sea Fleet. These agreements were extended these agreements through 2042 by the 2010 Kharkhiv Pact. The treaties set a limit of 25,000 troops and Russia pledged to "respect the sovereignty of Ukraine, honor its legislation and preclude interference in the internal affairs of Ukraine."[103] Russian forces could operate "beyond their deployment sites" only after "coordination with the competent agencies of Ukraine."[104] In February 2014 these troops operated beyond these limits, and were joined by additional soldiers later admitted to have been sent from Russia.

On 1 March 2014 deposed president Yanukovych, in exile in Russia, issued a statement: "I therefore appeal to the President of Russia, V.V. Putin, to use the armed forces of the Russian Federation to restore law and order, peace and stability and to protect the people of Ukraine."[105] UN ambassador Vitalii Churkin also stated "Mr. Aksyonov, Prime Minister of Crimea, went to the President of Russia with a request for assistance to restore peace in Crimea. According to available information, the appeal was also supported by Mr. Yanukovych, whose removal from office, we believe, was illegal."[106] This is reminiscent of the Soviet invasion of Czechoslovakia in 1968, when Moscow published a letter from (at the time unnamed) members of the Czechoslovak government requesting fraternal assistance.[107]

The request from Crimea's prime minister, against the wishes of the Ukrainian government, does not attribute legality to their intervention. In the *Nicaragua* case, the ICJ stated: "It would certainly lose its effectiveness as a principle of law if intervention were to be justified by a mere request for assistance made by an

---

[103] Spencer Kimball, "Bound by Treaty: Russia, Ukraine and Crimea," *Deutsche Welle*, 11 March 2014, http://www.dw.com/en/bound-by-treaty-russia-ukraine-and-crimea/a-17487632.
[104] Ibid.
[105] United Nations Security Council, 7125th meeting, 3 March 2014, UN S/PV/. 7125, 3–4.
[106] United Nations Security Council, 7124th meeting, 1 March 2014, UN S/PV/. 7124, 5.
[107] Kieran Williams, *The Prague Spring and its Aftermath: Czechoslovak Politics 1968–1970* (Cambridge: Cambridge University Press, 1997).

opposition group in another State."[108] Yanukovych's statement makes no reference to the secession of Crimea. Furthermore, even if the initial intervention had been supported by Yanukovych's appeal, the annexing of territory, without the permission of the Ukrainian state, would be an illegal use of force. Yanukovych's statement does not justify the secession of Crimea.

The Need for Self-Defense

Article 51 of the UN Charter allows for the use of force in cases of self-defense. Since there was no threat to the sovereignty of the Russian state, self-defense could have been invoked in order to protect Russian nationals abroad. On 18 March 2014 Putin stated "Russia has not introduced troops into Crimea but merely strengthened its grouping there without exceeding the limit on the number of troops set by international agreement" for the purpose of protecting "the lives of citizens of the Russian Federation, our compatriots, and personnel of the military contingent of the armed forces of the Russian Federation deployed on the territory of Ukraine in accordance with international agreement."[109]

The use of self-defense to protect a state's nationals abroad is a slippery issue. *Akehurst's Modern Introduction to International Law* explains that "most states and most writers agree that attacks on a state's national residents abroad do not entitle the state to use force in order to defend its nationals without the consent of the foreign government."[110] However, some scholars argue that such protection should fall under the authorization for self-defense.[111] The problem in Crimea was that Russia was extending protection not just to Russian citizens but also to ethnic Russians living in the area and even to all Russian-speakers. An additional problem is that the "protection" ended up with the annexation of Ukrainian

---

[108] ICJ, *Nicaragua v. United States of America*, para. 246.
[109] Moiseev, "Concerning Certain Positions," 52.
[110] Malanszuk, *Akehurst's Modern Introduction*, 315.
[111] Ibid., 316.

The problem in Crimea was that Russia was extending protection not just to Russian citizens but also to ethnic Russians living in the area and even to all Russian-speakers. An additional problem is that the "protection" ended up with the annexation of Ukrainian territory. Under no circumstances can self-defense be used to claim the territory of another state. Relatedly, there is little factual evidence to show that ethnic Russians or Russian nationals were being harmed to an extent that would require intervention from the Russian state, or were in danger of such imminent harm as to justify pre-emptive intervention.

The Responsibility to Protect

R2P, as a fairly new concept in international law, has not been fully accepted or clarified. It can be understood primarily as a way to prevent tragic losses of human life from occurring, in cases where the Security Council chooses not to act. It initially faced criticism from the Russian government. In 2000, Minister for Foreign Affairs Igor Ivanov stated, "We should not rule out that use of different doctrines of humanitarian intervention can destabilize international order to the point which would be dangerous even for those would like to appropriate the 'right' to hold military actions."[112] In 2008, however, Russia used R2P argumentation to justify its intervention in South Ossetia;[113] and again with respect to Crimea,[114] where even less evidence to support an R2P claim existed. Although R2P seeks to prevent human rights abuses, these have actually increased in Crimea since the annexation.[115]

---

[112] Igor' Ivanov, "Verzhovenstvo prava v mezhdunarodnykh otnoshenii," *Moscow Journal of Internal Law* 1 (2001): 7.
[113] Emma Gilligan, "Redefining Humanitarian Intervention: The Historical Challenge of R2P," *Journal of Human Rights* 12, no. 1 (2013): 21–39, 32.
[114] Kapustin, "Crimea's Self-Determination," 117.
[115] "UN Human Rights Office: Russia Violating Int'l Law in Crimea," *ABC News*, 25 September 2017, http://abcnews.go.com/amp/International/wireStory/human-rights-office-russia-violating-intl-law-crimea-50070627.

Implications for Russia and the International Legal System

> While it is clear that force persists and that international law can go further to restrain the use of force, it is not true that law has not and cannot have an impact.
> —Mary Ellen O'Connell[116]

Examination of the Crimean case points to the illegality of Russia's actions and the weakness of their arguments in terms of factual basis and interpretation of the law.

Are we to see Crimea as a one-time departure from international law, or is this the beginning of a new trend that states will cite to shape the future of international law? Chief legal advisor to the President of Georgia, Anna Dolidze, argues that historically Russia has oscillated between two approaches to the language of international law: as an estranged foreigner or a multilingual non-native speaker attempting to shape and control the interpretation of international law.[117] So, having violated international law in the Crimean case, will Russia swing back towards international legality in the future?

Why Follow the Law?

Yale law professor Harold Koh offers five possible explanations for why nations might obey international law: "power, self-interest or rational choice; liberal explanations based on rule-legitimacy or political identity; communitarian explanations; and legal process explanations at the state-to-state level and from the international-to-national level."[118] The power argument suggests that states are coerced by other states to obey the law. Russia has indeed been penalized for annexing Crimea, from economic sanctions to

---

[116] Mary Ellen O'Connell, "Enforcing the Prohibition on the Use of Force: The UN's Response to Iraq's Invasion of Kuwait," *Southern Illinois University Law Journal* 15 (1990): 453–86, 457.

[117] Anna Dolidze, "The Non-Native Speakers of International Law: The Case of Russia," *Baltic Yearbook of International Law Online* 15, no. 1 (2016): 77–103.

[118] Harold Hongju Koh, "How is International Human Rights Law Enforced," *Ind. Lj* 74 (1998), 1401.

expulsion from the G7. The communitarian explanation sees state leaders as embedded in an international society. Between 1996–98, Russia was admitted to the Council of Europe; joined the G7 political forum, turning it into the G8; and ratified the European Convention on Human Rights and the Law of the Sea Convention. Although the Soviet Union's approach to international law continues to influence Russia,[119] there has been a definite shift, evidenced by the new engagement of Russia in multiple international organizations[120] and by the increasing adoption of international law language in Russian politics and scholarship.[121]

As a self-serving, realist power, Russia is currently much more likely to pursue something out of self-interest and rational choice analysis than out of the fear of another state or out of communal bonds. Yet, in a world increasingly prone to globalization, rational choice calculations must include the responses of other states.[122] Although Russia stepped outside the bounds of the law in Crimea, it is against Russia's long-term interests to allow this case to serve as a precedent that weakens the concept of territorial integrity. "In terms of the hierarchy of principles Russians continue to give priority to the principle of state sovereignty," writes Lauri Mälksoo.[123] Arguably, it is in Russia's vital interests to make what happened in Crimea an outlier of state practice and to follow and accept laws in the future, but it has long been recognized that "states will refuse to follow international law when vital interests are at stake."[124]

---

[119] Mälksoo, *Russian Approaches*, 9.
[120] Valerie Sperling, *Altered States: The Globalization of Accountability* (Cambridge: Cambridge University Press, 2009), 325, 330–31.
[121] Dolidze, "Non-Native Speakers," 98.
[122] Andrew T. Guzman, *How International Law Works: A Rational Choice Theory* (Oxford: Oxford University Press, 2008), 211.
[123] Mälksoo, *Russian Approaches*, 141.
[124] David W. Ziegler, *War, Peace, and International Politics* (New York: Little, Brown and Company, 1987), 168.

Global Response and the Power of Non-Recognition

The majority of the international community expressed disapproval for Russia's actions in Crimea and denied recognition of the incorporation of Crimea into Russia. The European Union, the United States, and several other countries imposed economic sanctions both against Russian individuals and against certain sectors of the economy. On 27 March 2014 the UN General Assembly adopted a resolution on the "Territorial Integrity of Ukraine," "calling on States, international organizations and specialized agencies not to recognize any change in the status of Crimea or the Black Sea port city of Sevastopol, and to refrain from actions or dealings that might be interpreted as such."[125]

However, four years later, Russia remains adamant that it will not countenance giving up control over Crimea. The Kosovo case normalized and expanded the concept of remedial secession in cases of extreme oppression and the denial of internal self-determination. In contrast, the non-recognition of Crimea instead shows the failings of an annexation that circumvented generally accepted norms of the law.

There have been multiple cases, such as East Timor, North Cyprus, and Western Sahara, where the international community did not accept a change in a territory's status even after it was occupied for considerable periods of time.[126] Annexations have happened infrequently over the last century, and recognition of these annexations has been even rarer (see Table 1 below).

---

[125] 68th General Assembly, "General Assembly Adopts Resolution Calling upon States Not to Recognize Changes in Status of Crimea Region," *United Nations Meetings Coverage and Press Releases*, 27 March 2014, https://www.un.org/press/en/2014/ga11493.doc.htm.

[126] Wilson, "Secession and Intervention in the Former Soviet Space," 169. East Timor was treated as a case of decolonization under Chapter 7 of the UN charter, accepted by China and Russia; Natasha Kuhrt, "'Parallelism' and Constructive Ambiguity in Understandings of Self-determination, Sovereignty and Statehood after Kosovo," paper presented at "Narrating Russian and Eurasian security," BISA Workshop, King's College London, 18–19 June 2018.

Table 1. Annexations.

Territory	Annexed by	Year of Annexation	Reversal?	Recognized Today
Crimea	Russia	2014	No	No
Kuwait	Iraq	1990	Yes, 1991	No
Golan Heights	Israel	1981	No	No
East Timor	Indonesia	1975	Yes, 2002	No
Western Sahara	Morocco	1975	No	No
Sikkim	India	1975	No	Yes
Western New Guinea	Indonesia	1962	No	Yes
Goa	India	1961	No	Yes
Kuril Islands	Soviet Union	1945	No	No
Baltic states	Soviet Union	1940	Yes, 1991	No
Sudetenland, Austria, etc.	Nazi Germany	1938	Yes, 1945	No
Ethiopia	Italy	1936	Yes, 1941	No
Svalbard Islands	Norway	1925	No	Yes
Korea	Japan	1910	Yes, 1945	No
Hawaii	United States	1898	No	Yes

Counter-Arguments on the Impact of Crimea

Territorial integrity and the prohibition on the use of force are the most fundamental building blocks of international law. Although Russia might have chosen to circumvent them in this instance, there is no reason to believe that Russia wants to shift the balance towards self-determination beyond the case of Crimea.[127] Even if we accept the concept of creating two divided languages of international law, it is hard to see a legal coalition forming around use of force to violate territorial integrity. Even key Russian allies such as China, Belarus, and Kazakhstan did not vote for recognizing the annexation

---

[127] Mälksoo, *Russian Approaches*, 141.

of Crimea. Furthermore, there are crucial weaknesses in Russia's legal arguments that would not hold up in other cases. Russia used multiple arguments for both self-determination and the use of force because it hoped that one of them would stick, or at least could be used rhetorically fend off its critics. Whether or not the rest of the world accepted these arguments or whether they were valid, it remains case that Putin and other government officials attempted to convey a respect and appreciation for international law. It would be naïve to deduce that this symbolizes an inherent love for the law. Clearly a line was crossed and President Putin recognized that he crossed it. Yet, it also shows that Moscow recognizes the importance of staying within some passable version of the law so as to limit the negative impact on Russia's place in the international community. It is unclear whether the Russian authorities truly believed that the world would accept their legal arguments, or it was just a calculated effort to minimize the costs while regaining a vital territory. Either way, in the long term it does not serve Russia's interests to repeat a similar operation outside of the law, both because of the severity of the reaction to the Crimea situation, and because of Russia's own self-interest in preserving territorial integrity and restrictions on the use of force. As Karagiannis writes, "Blatant disregard of international law has not been common in Russian diplomacy. Like most (if not all) great powers, Russia prefers to reinterpret and redefine legal rules to serve national interests."[128]

The Cases of Georgia and Donbas

To help illustrate Russia's view and usage of the law, it is worth briefly considering Russia's actions in two other cases that have certain similarities to Crimea, but that symbolize a more careful approach to the law from the Kremlin.

When the two provinces of Abkhazia and South Ossetia tried to break away from Georgia in the early 1990s, elements in the Russian government and Russian society offered them military, political, and economic support. The Russian government inserted

---

[128] Karagiannis, "Russian Interventions," 401.

a peacekeeping force under the Commonwealth of Independent States, with the agreement of the Georgian government, but refused to recognize the sovereignty of the break-away provinces. (Likewise, Russia has declined to recognize the independence of the province of Transnistria, which broke away from Moldova—with Russian military help—in 1992.) But in August 2008 Georgian forces attacked South Ossetia, triggering a military response from Russia. Russia went on to recognize the independence of Abkhazia and South Ossetia—citing the Kosovo precedent. Russia stated that its motivation was protecting Russian citizens, including the CIS peacekeepers, but Georgia's decision to pursue NATO membership significantly contributed to Russia's opposition to the incorporation of South Ossetia and Abkhazia back into Georgia. President Medvedev declared, "we were invariably guided by the recognition of Georgia's territorial integrity," but went on to say "Saakashvili opted for genocide to accomplish his political objectives. By doing so he himself dashed all the hopes for the peaceful coexistence of Ossetians, Abkhazians, and Georgians in a single state."[129] The language here mirrors the language of the secession of Kosovo; it incorporates the expanded understanding of external self-determination in the face of oppression and human rights abuses by the parent state.

Arguably, the legal argumentation around the Georgian cases shows a careful fusion and balance of the principles of territorial integrity and self-determination, in a way that served to maximize Russia's interests.[130] In Crimea, the bounds were more clearly broken. It remains to be seen whether Russia will revert to a more respectful approach to international law, leaving Crimea as an outlier. Russia's continuing support for the insurrectionists in Donbas does not augur well.

---

[129] Dmitri Medvedev, "Medvedev's Statement on South Ossetia and Abkhazia," *New York Times*, 26 August 2008, http://www.nytimes.com/2008/08/27/world/europe/27medvedev.html.

[130] Thomas Hodson, "Verbal Strategies from Kosovo to Crimea. Part One," *Institute of Modern Russia*, 6 February 2018, https://imrussia.org/en/law/2910-verbal-strategies-from-kosovo-to-crimea.

Unlike the relatively peaceful and fast transition in Crimea, the Ukrainian government was not going to let Donetsk and Lugansk secede without a fight, and Russia did not have bases in the area from which thousands of troops could be deployed, presenting Kyiv with a *fait accompli*. The war which broke out in April 2014 has resulted in some 10,000 deaths and 1.7 million people displaced.[131] Russia supports the desire of the Luhansk and Donetsk regions to gain more autonomy from Kyiv, and provides the economic and military assistance that enables them to defy the Ukrainian government. But Russia is not ready to acknowledge the republics as independent from Ukraine, still less annex them to Russia. While the Russian government accepts official documents issued to residents by the republics of Donetsk and Lugansk,[132] it has not granted Donbas residents Russian passports en masse, as it had in Abkhazia, South Ossetia, and Crimea.[133]

Conclusion

The law does not exist in a vacuum. Andrew Guzman, dean of USC Gould School of Law, states, "International law has the potential to influence state behavior, but always does so in a political context."[134]

If international law is indeed a guiding force or at least a limit for state actions, and if it is beneficial for countries to stay within the bounds of the law to secure their own interests, then the next question becomes how to strengthen principles of the law to prevent reinterpretations that violate international standards. Powerful countries can use the language of the law but twist it to produce readings that are much more favorable for the actions they want to take. The United States has been known to reinterpret and

---

[131] Julian Coman, "On the Frontline of Europe's Forgotten War in Ukraine," *The Guardian*, 12 November 2017, https://www.theguardian.com/world/2017/nov/12/ukraine-on-the-front-line-of-europes-forgotten-war.

[132] Wojciech Górecki, "Russia Recognizes Donbas Separatists' Documents," *Osrodek Studiow Wschodnich*, 22 February 2017, https://www.osw.waw.pl/en/publikacje/analyses/2017-02-22/russia-recognises-donbas-separatists-documents.

[133] Ibid.

[134] Guzman, *How International Law Works*, 217.

circumvent international laws, for example the decision to classify people as "enemy combatants" in order to circumvent "prisoner of war" rights guaranteed under the Geneva Conventions during the "war on terror."[135]

As the world's largest country, with a number of secessionist movements and disputed borders, it is in Russia's interest that the norm of territorial integrity be respected. The annexation of Crimea was a striking departure from international law, and a violation of Ukraine's territorial integrity. It is important to search for ways to minimize the risk that situations like Crimea will recur. Maintenance of non-recognition is making Russia pay a price for its actions, and shows that the annexation of a territory without permission of the parent state will not be normalized. Likewise, international courts have an important role to play in clarifying the definitions of legal principles, thus making it harder for countries to offer a wide range of interpretations. Cavandoli is correct in arguing "that the current law of self-determination needs a clearer and more consistent approaching order to avoid posing a serious threat to the stability of the existing state system."[136] Similar ambiguity surrounds the concept of self-defense.[137]

Arguably, Crimea was a deviation that was not in line with Russia's long-term approach to international law. Still, Crimea shows us that it is imperative to enforce stricter definitions and clearer applications of the law and to maintain a united, global front in condemning violations when they occur, in order to limit future breaches.

Much of the popular debate over Crimea is conducted through the prism of moral condemnation and political calculation: it often seems irrelevant whether it was legal or not. Russia is treated as a pariah state that cannot be expected to follow the law. However, Russia's convoluted attempts at defending their actions in Crimea can help us understand the complexities of the current legal norms

---

[135] Ingrid Detter, "The Law of War and Illegal Combatants," *Geo. Wash. L. Rev.* 75, no. 6 (2006): 1049–1104.
[136] Cavandoli, "Unresolved Dilemma," 876.
[137] McCormack, *Self-Defense*, 240.

and their potential for change. Furthermore, they suggest the possibility of a greater Russian regard for the law than one would initially presume.

We tend to think of an enforcement system as a powerful entity punishing those who disobey, similar to the domestic legal system in which the state enforces its laws. Such a system does not work in international law, where every state has sovereignty and is unlikely to give up its independence and submit to some type of supreme enforcer. But this does not mean that there is no enforcement whatsoever. If we accept that the law does have relevance, then there is some incentive to follow it and to abide by it. The difficulty is in making sure that in the state's calculations of self-interest, obeying the law outweighs breaching it. While Crimea will in all probability never be returned to Ukraine, it can still serve as a warning and help limit future circumventions of the law.

Business as Usual: Sanctions Circumvention by Western Firms in Crimea[*]

Maria Shagina

Abstract: *Despite the ongoing sanctions regime, many foreign companies continue their operations in Crimea without any legal repercussions. The purpose of this article is to highlight the common patterns of sanctions circumvention used by Western firms in order to keep their businesses in Crimea. By juxtaposing the companies' justifications and their behavior, this article assesses the companies' activities vis-à-vis the sanctions' legal framework. The article reveals the weaknesses within the sanctions regime and makes policy recommendations for the enhancement of the effectiveness of sanctions.*

Keywords: sanctions, Crimea, Ukraine, Russia, compliance

Introduction

In 2014, the United States and the European Union imposed sanctions on Russia in response to its annexation of Crimea and hybrid war in Eastern Ukraine. March 2018 marked four years since Russia's violation of fundamental principles of international law. Reaffirming its Ukraine policy, in July 2018 the United States issued the Crimea Declaration stating that the US "rejects Russia's attempted annexation of Crimea and pledges to maintain this policy

---

[*] This research was financially supported by the Japan Society for the Promotion of Science. Special thanks also go to Professor Mika Hayashi, Kobe University, who helped me during the writing of this article.

until Ukraine's territorial integrity is restored."[1] The European Union also recently reiterated its position that it does not recognize Russia's illegal annexation and it continues to condemn Russia's violation of international law.[2] As part of the US and EU non-recognition policies, the Crimea sanctions, which ban trade, investment, finance, and shipping services, remain in place.

Due to the comprehensive sanctions regime, it is now mostly Russian companies that are actively operating in Crimea. The majority of investment in Crimea comes from the Russian budget and is directed to infrastructure, tourism, and agriculture.[3] In 2014–2017, Russian federal spending on Crimea amounted to 350 billion rubles ($5.2 billion).[4] Another 300 billion rubles ($4.4 billion) from the budget were spent on the construction of the Kerch Bridge that physically connects Crimea with the Russian mainland.[5] Both the US and the EU condemned those involved in the building of the bridge, stating that it represents "an attempt by Russia to solidify its unlawful seizure and its occupation of Crimea."[6]

However, it is not only Russian businesses who are eager to stay in Crimea. According to Sergey Aksenov, Crimea's self-proclaimed prime minister, nearly 3,000 foreign firms, including

---

[1] US Department of State, "Crimea Declaration," *US Department of State official website*, 25 July 2018, https://www.state.gov/secretary/remarks/2018/07/284508.htm. All URLs cited in this article were accessible on 31 August 2018.

[2] European Council, "Ukraine: EU adds six entities involved in the construction of the Kerch Bridge connecting the illegally annexed Crimea to Russia to sanctions list," *European Council official website*, 31 July 2018, https://www.consilium.europa.eu/en/press/press-releases/2018/07/31/ukraine-eu-adds-six-entities-involved-in-the-construction-of-the-kerch-bridge-connecting-the-illegally-annexed-crimea-to-russia-to-sanctions-list/.

[3] "Kto investiruet v Krym," *Vedomosti*, 16 March 2018, https://www.vedomosti.ru/economics/articles/2018/03/16/753933-investiruet-krim.

[4] Ibid.

[5] "Kak stroiat Krymskii most," *Vedomosti*, 10 June 2018, https://www.vedomosti.ru/realty/galleries/2016/06/10/644809-kak-stroyat-kerchenskii-most.

[6] US Department of State, "The Opening of the Kerch Bridge in Crimea," *US Department of State official website*, 15 May 2018, https://www.state.gov/r/pa/prs/ps/2018/05/282116.htm.

European companies, are currently working on the peninsula.[7] Aksenov has encouraged foreign companies to invest in Crimea, pointing out that there are ways to circumvent sanctions and to conceal companies' identities.[8] Indeed, despite the sanctions, European and American companies such as Visa, Mastercard, Volkswagen, Auchan, DHL, Adidas, Metro Cash&Carry and others continue operating in Crimea.[9] In spite of the prohibitions, in 2015 the number of EU-registered ships calling at sanctioned Crimean ports grew by 23.4%—89 calls more than in 2014. Ships with links to Germany, Italy, Greece, and Bulgaria were the most frequent ones.[10]

In 2017, the Siemens scandal offered a vivid illustration of such sanctions breaches, highlighting problems with compliance and enforcement. In summer 2015, it was alleged that Siemens, a German engineering corporation, had supplied gas turbines for the construction of a power plant in Crimea. Siemens representatives refuted this allegation, stating that the company "has not delivered turbines to Crimea and complies with all export control restrictions."[11] They asserted that the supplied turbines had been destined for a power plant in Russia's Taman under their contract with a Russian firm, Technopromexport. As more light was shed on the deal, more questions appeared about Siemens' due diligence process.[12] Eventually ceding to international pressure, in July 2017

[7] "Nearly 3,000 Foreign Firms Working in Crimea Despite Sanctions," *RT*, 30 March 2018, https://www.rt.com/business/422790-sanctioned-crimea-thousands-foreign-investors/.
[8] "Aksenov soobshchil o vozmozhnosti dlia zarubezhnogo biznesa rabotat' v Krymu v obkhod sanktsii," *Kommersant*, 4 November 2017, https://www.kommersant.ru/doc/3459822.
[9] "Ne smeshite nashi magaziny. Kak obkhodiat sanktsii v Krymu," *Novaia gazeta*, 31 January 2018, https://www.novayagazeta.ru/articles/2018/01/31/75337-ne-smeshite-nashi-magaziny?utm_source=push.
[10] Lloyd's List, "Out of Sight, Out of Mind. Are Shipping Companies Violating Sanctions in Crimea?" *The Intelligence*, January 2016, 13.
[11] Anton Zverev, Anastasia Lyrchikova, and Gleb Stolyarov, "Exclusive: Siemens Turbines Delivered to Crimea Despite Sanctions—Sources," *Reuters*, 6 July 2016, https://www.reuters.com/article/us-ukraine-crisis-crimea-power-exclusive-idUSKBN19Q26I.
[12] Alya Shandra, "How Siemens Chose to Ignore the Obvious. An Investigation into the Crimean Sanctions Break," *Euromaidan Press*, 24 July 2017,

the company acknowledged that their gas turbines had in fact been transferred to Crimea, but claimed that this had been done without Siemens' knowledge or consent. Siemens emphasized that they prohibited the delivery of the gas turbines to Crimea and that their Russian partners breached "delivery contracts, trust and EU regulations."[13] Next, Siemens brought lawsuits to the Moscow Arbitration Court to invalidate the transactions and to force these companies to return the gas turbines to their original destination outside Crimea. Predictably, these lawsuits were rejected by the Moscow Arbitration Court.[14]

The infamous Siemens case does not appear to have acted as a deterrent to others. Recent reports reveal that there are still a number of foreign companies which fail to conduct thorough due diligence and/or are willing to circumvent sanctions.[15] Shifting the focus from the Siemens case, the main purpose of this article is to examine the loopholes within US/EU sanctions and to analyze how Western firms are exploiting the gaps to avoid or evade sanctions. Consequently, the focus is on Western companies rather than on Russian ones. Russian companies' desire to circumvent sanctions is understandable. "Economic warfare inevitably promotes economic crime"[16]: it is not surprising that, in order to adapt to this situation,

---

http://euromaidanpress.com/2017/07/24/how-siemens-chose-to-ignore-the-obvious-crimea-turbines/.

[13] Official statement regarding turbines to Crimea, *Siemens Press Release*, 21 July 2017, http://sie.ag/2tPhIge.

[14] "Arbitration Court Denies Siemens Appeal to Return Gas Turbines Delivered to Crimea," *TASS*, 14 December 2017, http://tass.com/economy/980866; and "Siemens unterliegt in der Krim-Affäre," *NZZ*, 11. Januar 2018, https://www.nzz.ch/wirtschaft/siemens-unterliegt-in-der-krim-affaere-ld.1346447.

[15] See, for example, Alya Shandra, "How Siemens Chose to Ignore the Obvious. An Investigation into the Crimean Sanctions Break," *Euromaidan Press*, 24 July 2017, http://euromaidanpress.com/2017/07/24/how-siemens-chose-to-ignore-the-obvious-crimea-turbines/; Tatiana Guchakova and Andrii Klymenko (eds), *"The Gray Zone." Occupied Crimea: Sanctions Violations in 2017. Monitoring Results* (Kyiv: The Black Sea Institute of Strategic Studies, 2018); and Aleksandr Golubov, "Narushyteli sanktsii: kak evropeiskie kompanii vedut biznes v Krymu," *Krym.Realii*, 11 July 2018, https://ru.krymr.com/a/29357169.html.

[16] Richard Naylor, *Economic Warfare: Sanctions, Embargo Busting, and Their Human Costs* (Boston: Northeast University Press, 2001), 4.

the targeted Russian entities would be willing to engage in sanctions-busting. However, a sanctions-busting scheme usually needs facilitators and enablers in the West—whenever there is a sanctions breach orchestrated by a Russian firm, there is a Western firm at the other end of this transaction. Although Western companies should be under closer scrutiny and show more integrity, the breaching of sanctions compliance still happens. By distinguishing between sanctions avoidance and sanctions evasion, this article provides a legal assessment of Western companies' activities in Crimea.

This article has the following structure. First, it will review the previous studies conducted on this topic from the perspectives of international law and international relations (IR). Second, it will examine the international sanctions regime vis-à-vis Crimea. In particular, the restrictive measures adopted by the US and EU will be discussed and their differences and weaknesses will be analyzed. Third, five sanctions compliance cases involving Western firms will be examined. Juxtaposing companies' justifications and behavior with the legal provisions, the cases will be classified as instances of sanctions avoidance or evasion. The final part will draw conclusions, highlighting the common practices in sanctions circumvention, and will make policy recommendations aimed at improving the effectiveness of the sanctions regime.

Literature Review

The vast majority of the academic literature on sanctions concentrates on their effectiveness. In particular, the scholarship tends to focus on evaluating the effects of a fully-fledged sanctions policy on its target. On the whole, the scholarly view on the effectiveness of sanctions as a foreign policy tool for changing a target's behavior is pessimistic.[17] However, with the arrival of so-

---

[17] See, for example, Robert A. Pape, "Why Economic Sanctions Do Not Work," *International Security* 22, no. 2 (1997): 90–136; Richard Haass, "Economic Sanctions: Too Much of a Bad Thing," *Brookings*, 1 June 1998, https://www.brookings.edu/research/economicsanctions-too-much-of-a-bad-thing/; Kimberly A. Elliott and Gary C. Hufbauer, "Same Song, Same Refrain?

called "smart sanctions," the discussion has shifted to examine the conditions under which sanctions are effective (e.g. the regime type, the salience of the issue, the timing of the imposition, the costs for the target, etc).[18]

Studies on the EU's autonomous sanctions gained their momentum after restrictive measures became an essential tool of the Common Foreign and Security Policy, established in 1992 by the Maastricht Treaty. Following the EU's development as a new sanctioning actor, scholars examined the effectiveness of the EU sanctions.[19] In particular, Anthonius W. De Vries and Hadelwych Hazelzet analyzed the EU's sanctions strategy at various stages of the decision-making, including the enforcement, monitoring, and planning stages. They concluded that at all three stages, the EU is heavily reliant on its member states. To ensure the effectiveness of sanctions, member states are obliged to pass legislation on penalties. However, while some member states pass permanent legislation on the penalties, the majority of states ratify separate legislation related directly to the EU Council Decision. Due to the lengthiness of this process, the effectiveness of sanctions is affected.

Economic Sanctions in the 1990's," *American Economic Review* 89, no. 2 (1999): 403–408; and Gary C. Hufbauer, Jeffrey J. Schott, Kimberly A. Elliott, and Barbara Oegg, *Economic Sanctions Reconsidered*, 3rd ed. (Washington, DC: Peterson Institute for International Economics, 2007).

[18] See, for example, Daniel Drezner, *The Sanctions Paradox* (Cambridge: Cambridge University Press, 1999); Risa A. Brooks, "Sanctions and Regime Type: What Works, and When?" *Security Studies* 11, no. 4 (2002): 1–50; Daniel Drezner, "Sanctions Sometimes Smart: Targeted Sanctions in Theory and Practice," *International Studies Review* 13, no. 1 (2003): 96–108; Adrian Ang and Dursun Peksen, "When Do Economic Sanctions Work? Issue Salience, Asymmetric Perception, and Outcomes," *Political Research Quarterly* 60, no. 1 (2007): 135–45; Navin Bapat and Clifton Morgan, "Multilateral versus Unilateral Sanctions Reconsidered: A Test Using New Data," *International Studies Quarterly* 53, no. 4 (2009): 1075–94; and Thomas Biersteker and Peter A.G. van Bergeijk, "How and When Do Sanctions Work?: The Evidence," in *On Target?: EU Sanctions as Security Policy Tools*, eds. Iana Dreyer and José Luengo-Cabrera (Paris: EU Institute for Security Studies, 2015).

[19] See, for example, Mikhael Eriksson, "EU Sanctions: Three Cases of Targeted Sanctions," in *International Sanctions: Between Words and Wars in the Global System*, eds. P. Wallensteen and C. Staibano (London, Frank Cass, 2005); and Clara Portela, "The EU's Use of Targeted Sanctions. Evaluating Effectiveness," *CEPS Working Documents*, no. 391 (March 2014): 1–44.

It creates a window of opportunity for the targets to shift their capital and payments to a country where the legislation is absent or weaker.[20] The more complex the sanctions regime, the more difficult it is to control the movements of capital and payments. The EU lacks sufficient resources to ensure compliance, while the member states do not have an effective monitoring system. The cooperation of the private sector, largely arising out of its fear of heavy fines, proves to be a crucial element for the effectiveness of EU sanctions regimes.[21]

Violations and breaches of international sanctions have mostly been discussed in the scholarship as part of the examination of the effectiveness of sanctions. Bringing the study of sanctions and transnational crime together, Richard Naylor and Peter Andreas analyzed the criminalizing effects of sanctions in the targeted country.[22] In particular, Andreas demonstrated how sanctions paradoxically contribute to the emergence of a sanctions-busting economy, including organized crime syndicates and shadowy commercial clans, leading to the spread of smuggling networks even to the neighboring countries.[23] Analyzing third-party spoilers, Bryan R. Early distinguished between profit-seeking and politically motivated sanctions-busting behavior. He examined how third-parties contribute to the mitigation of the effectiveness of the US sanctions and what might be done to counteract this.[24]

A lot of the sanctions-busting research is done by international organizations, NGOs, think tanks, and the media. Within the UN framework, the Stockholm Process (2003)

---

[20] Anthonius W. De Vries and Hadelwych Hazelzet, "The EU as a New Actor on the Sanctions Scene," in *International Sanctions. Between Words and Wars in the Global System*, eds. Peter Wallensteen and Carina Staibano (London: Frank Cass, 2005), 99.
[21] Ibid., 101–03.
[22] Richard Naylor, *Economic Warfare: Sanctions, Embargo Busting, and Their Human Costs* (Boston, MA: Northeast University Press, 2001); Peter Andreas, "Criminalizing Consequences of Sanctions: Embargo Busting and Its Legacy," *International Studies Quarterly* 49, no. 2 (2005): 335–60.
[23] Ibid., 345.
[24] Bryan R. Early, *Busted Sanctions. Explaining Why Economic Sanctions Fail* (Stanford, CA: Stanford University Press, 2015).

introduced good practices for sanctions implementation and monitoring to counter sanctions evasion, while in 2014 the Financial Action Task Force proposed recommendations for the implementation of targeted financial sanctions to stop proliferation finance.[25] Several reports about targets' tactics and techniques for circumventing sanctions were produced by the UK's Royal United Services Institute (RUSI) and the Asan Institute for Policy Studies with a particular focus on North Korea and Russia. To adapt, sanctioned individuals and entities in North Korea and Russia used complex front companies and intermediaries to muddy their transactions and activities. Targeting the weakest links in the sanctions chain, Russians and North Koreans sought countries or sectors with few resources for monitoring, poor implementation, and/or low awareness of the sanctions threat.[26] For example, in the maritime transportation, employing a combination of legal and technical loopholes, North Korean ships bypassed sanctions to obtain an illegal amount of oil and gas from Russia.[27] Highlighting the differences between US and EU sanctions, the *Economist* investigated how Russian businesses find loopholes in the complex legislation and change their corporate structures to stay afloat.[28]

Following the general trend, the analysis of US/EU sanctions towards Russia over the Ukraine crisis to date has likewise been predominantly framed from the point of view of their effectiveness. The evaluation of sanctions' economic impact and their ability to coerce Russian policy change has often prevailed. Various authors have examined whether US/EU sanctions have worked and what impact they had on Russia's economy and, vice versa, how Russia's

---

[25] FATF Targeted Financial Sanctions Experts' Meeting, 22 June 2014.
[26] Tom Keatinge, Emil Dall, Aniseh Bassiri Tabrizi and Sarah Lain, "Transatlantic (Mis)alignment. Challenges to US-EU Sanctions Design and Implementation," *RUSI Occasional Paper*, July 2017, 21; and Emil Dall and Tom Keatinge, "Underwriting Proliferation. Sanctions Evasion, Proliferation Finance and the Insurance Industry," *RUSI Occasional Paper*, July 2018, 1.
[27] The Asan Institute for Policy Studies, "The Rise of Phantom Traders: Russian Oil Exports to North Korea," *Asan Report*, July 2018, 7.
[28] "Fancy Footwork: How Businesses Linked to Blacklisted Oligarchs Avoid Western Sanctions," *Economist*, 12 February 2015, https://www.economist.com/business/2015/02/12/fancy-footwork.

counter-sanctions affected US/EU economic performance. The studies concurred that although the economic costs incurred have been considerably larger for the EU than for the US, the EU appears to have managed the burden, in part due to EU emergency funds, trade redirection, and increased purchasing power.[29] Embracing the multifaceted nature of sanctions, several studies focused on their political component.[30] The US/EU sanctions have been the most effective in sending a clear and strong signal and in constraining Russia's aggression in Eastern Ukraine.[31] Other studies narrowed down their focus to the EU-country and firm-level analysis or to particular sectors. The sanctions costs hit the EU members disproportionately, but pain from economic sanctions appeared to have no correlation with countries' sanctions positions. Surprisingly, countries that suffered the most proved to be the most hawkish in their attitudes towards Russia.[32] Bearing the main costs,

[29] See, for example, Erica Moret and Maria Shagina, "The Impact of EU-Russia Tensions on the Economy of the EU," in *Damage Assessment: EU-Russia Relations in Crisis*, eds. Lukasz Kulesa, Ivan Timofeev, and Joseph Dobbs (London: European Leadership Network, 2017), 17–24; Erica Moret, Francesco Giumelli and Dawid Bastiat-Jarosz, "Sanctions on Russia: Impacts and Economic Costs on the United States," Geneva: Graduate Institute of International and Development Studies, 20 March 2017; Daniel Gros and Mattia Di Salvo, "Revisiting Sanctions on Russia and Counter-Sanctions on the EU: The Economic Impact Three Years Later," *CEPS Commentary*, 13 July 2017; Austrian Institute of Economic Research (WIFO), "Disrupted Trade Relations between the EU and Russia: The Potential Economic Consequences for the EU and Switzerland," 2015; Daniel Gros and Federica Mustilli, "The Economic Impact of Sanctions Against Russia: Much Ado About Very Little," *CEPS Commentary*, 23 October 2015; and Michael Emerson, "The EU-Ukraine-Russia Sanctions Triangle," *CEPS Commentary*, 13 October 2014.

[30] See, for example, Ernest Wyciszkiewicz, "Crime Brings Punishment: The Importance of Sanctioning Russia," in *A Successful Failure: Russia After Crime(a)*, eds. Olga Irisova et al. (Warsaw: The Centre for Polish-Russian Dialogue and Understanding, 2017), 33–46; Erica Moret et al., "The New Deterrent? International Sanctions against Russia over the Ukraine Crisis: Impacts, Costs and Further Action," Geneva: Programme for the Study of International Governance, Graduate Institute, 12 October 2016; and Viljar Veebel and Raul Markus, "Lessons from the EU-Russia Sanctions 2014-2015," *Baltic Journal of Law & Politics* 8, no. 1 (2015): 165–94.

[31] Moret et al., "The New Deterrent?" 11.

[32] See, for example, Francesco Giumelli, "The Redistributive Impact of Restrictive Measures on EU Members: Winners and Losers from Imposing Sanctions on

the private sector was significantly hit by the sanctions and incurred collateral damage on its business activities.³³ In the energy sector, the collateral damage proved to be triggered by financial and technology-oriented sanctions.³⁴

The second strand of literature analyzes the sanctions from Russia's perspective, examining how Russia responded and adapted to them. In an attempt to shield itself from the external threats, Russia moved to "securitize" its economic policy, by enhancing its economic sovereignty and by pivoting to Asia.³⁵ Scholars are divided, however, on the question of the sanctions' outcome: while some argue that sanctions triggered consolidation around the Kremlin regime,³⁶ others show that sanctions failed to cause a "rally-around-the-flag" effect and put an enormous strain on Russia's balance of power, fostering a divide within the elites.³⁷ Meanwhile, analysis of the implementation and enforcement of US and EU sanctions in Russia has been rare. Although the importance of

---

Russia," *Journal of Common Market Studies* 55, no. 5 (2017): 1062–1080; and Maria Shagina, "Friend or Foe? Mapping the Positions on EU Member States on Russia Sanctions," London: European Leadership Network, 28 June 2017.

33 See, for example, Matthieu Crozet and Julian Hinz, "Collateral Damage: The Impact of the Russia Sanctions on Sanctioning Countries' Exports," *CEPII Working Paper*, Paris: Research and Expertise on the World Economy, June 2016.

34 See, for example, Tatiana Mitrova, "Shifting Political Economy of Russian Oil and Gas," Washington, DC: Center for Strategic and International Studies, March 2016; and Bud Coote, "Impact of Sanctions on Russia's Energy Sector," *Atlantic Council*, March 2018.

35 See, for example, Richard Connolly and Philip Hanson, "Import Substitution and Economic Sovereignty in Russia," *Chatham House*, June 2016; and Richard Connolly, *Russia's Response to Sanctions. How Western Economic Statecraft is Reshaping Political Economy in Russia* (Cambridge: Cambridge University Press, 2018).

36 See, for example, Anastasia Kazun, "Framing Sanctions in the Russian Media: The Rally Effect and Putin's Enduring Popularity," *Demokratyzatsiya: The Journal of Post-Soviet Democratization* 24, no. 3 (2016): 327–50.

37 See, for example, Timothy Frye, "Economic Sanctions and Public Opinion: Experiments from Russia," *Comparative Political Studies*, November 2018; and Maria Snegovaya, "Tensions on the Top. The Impact of Sanctions on Russia's Poles of Power," Washington, DC: Center for European Policy Analysis, July 2018.

transatlantic unity is broadly acknowledged,[38] the examination of sanctions coordination and emerging loopholes with particular focus on Crimea is non-existent.

This article will contribute to the body of literature on this topic in the following ways. Moving beyond the question of the effectiveness of sanctions, this article brings in a criminological perspective to the study of sanctions. Looking at the cases of sanctions compliance, it will examine the patterns of sanctions-busting. Second, while most of the studies look at the targeted country and its adaptation strategy, this article will focus on the practices of sanctions circumvention by commercial actors in the country-sender. Finally, this article will introduce a legal aspect into the IR studies, by providing a legal assessment of Western firms' activities. It will juxtapose companies' justification for their behavior with the legal framework.

International Sanctions Regime vis-à-vis Crimea

The international community strongly opposed Crimea's illegal referendum in 2014 and its subsequent annexation by Russia. The annexation, together with further Russian military involvement in Eastern Ukraine, is a violation of the international norms, including the UN Charter's norm on the prohibition of use of force. While the right to self-determination is guarded by international law, scholars agree that such a right cannot automatically justify foreign military involvement or intervention.[39]

---

[38] See, for example, Simond de Galbert, "Transatlantic Economic Statecraft. Building a Balanced Transatlantic Sanctions Policy between the United States and the European Union", Economic Statecraft Series, Center for Strategic & International Studies/Center for a New American Security, 21 June 2016; and Tom Keatinge and Emil Dall, "Consensus for Action: Towards a More Effective EU Sanctions Policy," Perspectives on Sanctions Series, New York: Center for Global Energy Policy, November 2018.

[39] See, for example, Peter Hilpold, "Self-Determination and Autonomy: Between Secession and Internal Self-Determination," in *Autonomy and Self-Determination: Between Legal Assertions and Utopian Aspirations*, ed. Peter Hilpold (Cheltenham: Edward Elgar, 2017), 42.

Accordingly, Russia's aggressive actions were seen as one of the most serious threats to the rule-based international order since the end of the Cold War. Following the US' strong response, EU and Canada expressed condemnation of Russia's unilateral change of borders. Other US and EU allies such as Australia, Japan, Switzerland, and Norway joined in stating their disapproval of Russia's change of the status quo by force. A series of diplomatic and restrictive measures were introduced by Western allies. However, a number of countries did not support the United Nations resolution 68/262 on the invalidity of the Crimean referendum: 58 countries abstained from the voting (e.g. Brazil, China, India, Vietnam), while 11 countries rejected the resolution altogether (e.g. Belarus, Bolivia, Nicaragua, North Korea, Syria, Venezuela). Despite the support for the UN resolution, South Korea, Singapore, and Turkey opted for a non-confrontational policy and imposed no sanctions against Russia.[40]

US Sanctions

The US sanctions have the broadest application of the sanctions regimes, constituting a comprehensive ban on any transactions and activities in Crimea. The purpose of the Crimea-related sanctions is to increase the diplomatic and financial costs of Russia's aggressive actions in Ukraine and to send a powerful signal about the scale of the consequences for the Russian government. On 6 March 2014, President Barack Obama declared a national emergency related to the undermining of Ukraine's sovereignty and territorial integrity and the Russian occupation of Crimea. Executive Order 13660 authorized sanctions on individuals and entities belonging to those who were responsible for the situation in Crimea. Expanding the scope of the national emergency, three other Executive Orders 13661, 13662, and 13685 were issued, condemning Russia's "purported

---

[40] United Nations, "General Assembly Adopts Resolution Calling upon States Not to Recognize Changes in Status of Crimea Region," *Meeting Coverage and Press Releases*, 27 March 2014.

annexation of Crimea and its use of force in Ukraine."[41] Executive Order 13685 defined a set of specific measures with respect to Crimea. First, the US prohibited new investment by US citizens, including in the energy sector. Under Directive 4, Russia-related sanctions prohibited the provision, export, or re-export of goods, technology, and services for Russia's deepwater, Arctic offshore, and shale oil exploration and production projects. The provision referred to Russia or any other maritime area claimed by Russia and extending from its territory, *de facto* including the Black Sea shelf area extending from Crimea.[42]

The second measure barred the importation and exportation of any goods, technology, or services, directly or indirectly, into or from the US. Later, Export Administration Regulations were amended, with an extra-territorial effect: the export or re-export of items to Crimea was banned even for non-US citizens.[43]

Finally, the Executive Order banned any approval, financing, facilitation, or guarantee by a US or foreign person of a transaction. Section 6 of the Executive Order 13685 stipulated that any transaction that "has the purpose of evading or avoiding, causes a violation" and thus is prohibited.[44] To minimize the negative effects for the civilian population, certain transactions were allowed under General Licenses, including agricultural products, medicine,

---

[41] US Department of the Treasury, "Blocking Property of Additional Persons Contributing to the Situation in Ukraine," Executive Order 13662, *Federal Register* 79, FR 13491, 20 March 2014, https://www.federalregister.gov/documents/2014/03/10/2014-05323/blocking-property-of-certain-persons-contributing-to-the-situation-in-ukraine.

[42] US Department of the Treasury, "Blocking Property of Certain Persons and Prohibiting Certain Transactions With Respect to the Crimea Region of Ukraine," Executive Order 13685, *Federal Register* 79, FR 77257, 19 December 2014, https://www.federalregister.gov/documents/2014/12/24/2014-30323/blocking-property-of-certain-persons-and-prohibiting-certain-transactions-with-respect-to-the-crimea.

[43] Bureau of Industry and Security, Commerce, "Russia Sanctions: Licensing Policy to the Crimea Region of Ukraine," *Federal Register* 80, FR 4776, 29 January 2015, https://www.federalregister.gov/documents/2015/01/29/2015-01638/russian-sanctions-licensing-policy-for-the-crimea-region-of-ukraine.

[44] US Department of the Treasury, "Blocking Property of Certain Persons and Prohibiting Certain Transactions with Respect to the Crimea Region of Ukraine," Executive Order 13685, 19 December 2014.

medical supplies, personal remittances, and software.[45] In August 2017, the Countering America's Adversaries Through Sanctions Act (CAATSA) introduced sanctions with respect to certain transactions with foreign sanctions evaders, namely, with any person who "materially violates, attempts to violate, conspires to violate, or causes a violation" or "facilitates a significant transaction". [46] Criminal penalties for breaching US sanctions include fines of up to $1 million and twenty years' imprisonment. Administrative penalties for each violation are $250,000. Breaching US sanctions may also lead to the offender being included on the sanctions list.[47]

EU Sanctions

In accord with the US, in March 2014 the EU strongly condemned "the unprovoked violation of Ukrainian sovereignty and territorial integrity" and called on Russia to immediately withdraw.[48] The EU leaders agreed to suspend the negotiations on visa liberalization and Russia's participation in the G8. Later, the European Council introduced additional restrictive measures, including travel bans and asset freezes vis-à-vis 33 Russian and Ukrainian officials who

---

[45] US Department of the Treasury, "Authorizing the Exportation or Reexportation of Agricultural Commodities, Medicine, Medical Supplies, and Replacement Parts," General License Number 4, *US Department of the Treasury official website*, 19 December 2014, https://www.treasury.gov/resource-center/sanctions/programs/documents/ukraine_gl4.pdf; and US Department of the Treasury, "Authorizing Certain Activities Prohibited by Executive Order 13685 of December 19, 2014 Necessary to Wind Down Operations Involving the Crimea Region of Ukraine," General License Number 5, *US Department of the Treasury official website*, 30 December 2014, https://www.treasury.gov/resource-center/sanctions/Programs/Documents/ukraine_gl5.pdf.

[46] US Department of the Treasury, "Countering America's Adversaries Through Sanctions Act," Section 228, Public Law 115-44, *US Department of the Treasury official website*, 2 August 2017, https://www.treasury.gov/resource-center/sanctions/Programs/Pages/caatsa.aspx.

[47] Lloyd's List, "Out of Sight, Out of Mind," 17.

[48] European Council, "Statement of the Heads of State and Government on Ukraine," *European Council official website*, 6 March 2014, https://www.consilium.europa.eu/media/29285/141372.pdf.

supported the annexation of Crimea.[49] From 23 June 2014, as part of the EU's non-recognition policy, a certificate from the Ukrainian authorities was required in order to import goods originating from Crimea and Sevastopol.[50] After the downing of the Malaysian Airlines flight MH17 in July 2014, further trade and investment restrictions in certain sectors such as transport, telecommunications, and energy, including the exploration and production of oil, gas, and minerals, were imposed.[51] In response to the lack of progress in implementing the Minsk Protocol, in December 2014 the EU substantially expanded its Crimea-related sanctions. European or EU-based companies were prohibited from acquiring or investing in real estate or entities in Crimea and Sevastopol and from supplying related services. The provision of financial and technical assistance, brokering, construction, and engineering services related to the infrastructure projects in Crimea were banned, as was the supply of key equipment and technology for the exploration of natural resources. European Union operators were prohibited from offering tourism services, while the ship cruising services were not allowed to call at any port on the Crimean Peninsula other than in the event of an emergency. This measure applied to all vessels owned by EU nationals or registered under EU

---

[49] Council of the European Union, "EU Adopts Restrictive Measures against Actions Threatening Ukraine's Territorial Integrity," *Official Journal of the European Union*, 17 March 2014, https://eur-lex.europa.eu/legal-content/EN/TXT/PDF/?uri=CELEX:32014R0269&from=GA; Council of the European Union, "Implementing Decision 2014/145/CFSP concerning Restrictive Measures in respect of Actions Undermining or Threatening the Territorial Integrity, Sovereignty and Independence of Ukraine," *Official Journal of the European Union*, 21 March 2014, https://eur-lex.europa.eu/legal-content/EN/TXT/PDF/?uri=CELEX:32014D0145&from=CS.

[50] Council of the European Union, Council Decision 2014/386/CFSP of 23 June 2014 concerning restrictions on goods originating in Crimea or Sevastopol, in response to the illegal annexation of Crimea and Sevastopol, *Official Journal of the European Union*, 23 June 2014, https://eur-lex.europa.eu/legal-content/EN/TXT/?uri=CELEX%3A32014D0386.

[51] Council of the European Union, Council Decision 2014/507/CFSP of 30 July 2014 amending Decision 2014/386/CFSP concerning restrictions on goods originating in Crimea or Sevastopol, in response to the illegal annexation of Crimea and Sevastopol, *Official Journal of the European Union*, 30 July 2014, https://eur-lex.europa.eu/legal-content/EN/TXT/PDF/?uri=CELEX:32014D0507&rid=1.

jurisdiction. Contracts signed prior to 20 March 2015 were exempted from the regulation.⁵²

In November 2016, the EU introduced restrictive measures against six Crimean individuals who became members of the Russian State Duma as a result of the elections in Crimea in September 2016. ⁵³ In August 2017, 3 Russian nationals and 3 companies were added to the list due to their involvement in the transfer of the Siemens gas turbines to Crimea. In June 2018, the EU added another six Russian entities to the sanctions list over their involvement in the construction of Kerch Bridge. The EU claimed that through their actions the companies had "supported the consolidation of Russia's control" over Crimea which in turn contradicted EU's non-recognition policy.⁵⁴

While the Crimea-related sanctions imposed by other allies are open-ended, the EU extends its restrictive measures each year. At the time of writing, [August/2018], the sanctions are in place until 31 July 2019. As the implementation and enforcement is the responsibility of the national governments of the member states, penalties for the violation of sanctions vary. For example, the UK's newly established Office of Financial Sanctions Implementation issues a monetary penalty up to 1 million pounds or 50% of the estimated value of funds involved in a transaction. Criminal penalties include a prison sentence of up to seven years. In Germany,

---

52 Council of the European Union, Council Decision 2014/933/CFSP of 18 December 2014 amending Decision 2014/386/CFSP concerning restrictive measures in response to the illegal annexation of Crimea and Sevastopol, *Official Journal of the European Union*, 18 December 2014, https://eur-lex.europa.eu/legal-content/EN/TXT/PDF/?uri=CELEX:32014D0933&from=NL.

53 Council of the European Union, "Russia: EU adds 6 members of the State Duma from Crimea to sanctions list over actions against Ukraine's territorial integrity," *Council of the European Union official website*, 09 November 2016, https://www.consilium.europa.eu/en/press/press-releases/2016/11/09/sanctions-list-over-actions-against-ukraines-territorial-integrity/.

54 Council of the European Union, "Ukraine: EU Adds Six Entities involved in the Construction of the Kerch Bridge connecting the Illegally Annexed Crimea to Russia to Sanctions List," *Council of the European Union official website*, 31 July 2018, https://www.consilium.europa.eu/en/press/press-releases/2018/07/31/ukraine-eu-adds-six-entities-involved-in-the-construction-of-the-kerch-bridge-connecting-the-illegally-annexed-crimea-to-russia-to-sanctions-list/.

under the Foreign Trade and Payments Act violation of the UN or EU sanctions carries a prison sentence from one to ten years.[55]

Weaknesses within and across Sanctions Regimes

The international sanctions regimes put in place in response to Russia's wrongdoings in Ukraine contain various kinds of weaknesses and loopholes. While one kind of weaknesses stems from sanctions design and internal decision-making, others are a result of a lack of coordination between allies.

In comparison with the US, the EU sanctions regime is weaker and less flexible. In order to initiate, maintain, or adapt sanctions, the EU has to obtain the unanimous consent of all 28 member states. The EU's requirement of unanimity shapes the design of sanctions to a great degree. It is the EU member states who decide whether sanctions are imposed, what type, and to what extent.[56] Due to diverging national security issues and economic interests within the EU, its sanctions list includes more individuals than businesses, including those on the sectoral list.[57] As the EU's economic dependency on Russia is higher than that of the US, the EU does not target the gas sector or key persons associated with the Putin regime. In addition, the EU sanctions include a so-called grandfather clause which validates pre-existing contracts, allowing European companies to do business with sanctioned entities.[58]

Second, the peculiarities of the EU's decision-making make its sanctions regime less flexible. As each member state has the right to veto sanctions, this considerably limits the EU's ability to act.[59] Although member states should act "in a spirit of loyalty and mutual solidarity," the EU is not eager to additionally test its fragile

---

[55] Federal Ministry of Economic Affairs and Energy, "Foreign Trade and Payments Act," *Federal Law Gazette*, 6 June 2013.
[56] De Vries and Hazelzet, "The EU as a New Actor on the Sanctions Scene," 98.
[57] Daniel P. Ahn and Rodney D. Ludema, "Measuring Smartness: Understanding the Economic Impact of targeted Sanctions," US Department of State, *Working Paper* 2017-01, 28–29.
[58] Jack Farchy, "EU's Russia Sanctions Fail to Dent Oil Deals," *Financial Times*, 14 July 2015, https://www.ft.com/content/21d66e58-10ef-11e5-8413-00144feabdc0.
[59] Keatinge, Dall, Tabrizi and Lain, "Transatlantic (Mis)alignment," 8.

unanimity.⁶⁰ The perilous process of reaching a unanimous decision is also time-consuming. The EU's inability to react swiftly delays implementation and gives targets ample time to adjust and to find alternative solutions. The EU's slow decision-making is also more likely to be affected by companies' lobbying which can hamper the sanctions' effectiveness.⁶¹

In contrast to the EU, the US approach has proved to be more hawkish and agile. In response to Russia's evasive practices, the Office of Foreign Assets Control (OFAC) updated the legislation and closed off loopholes on several occasions. For example, in July 2015 OFAC designated additional individuals and entities as a reaction to assets being shifted from sanctioned targets to their family members and friends.⁶² In August 2017, the CAATSA officially extended restrictive measures to blacklisted persons' relatives, including spouses, children, siblings, and parents.⁶³

Another weakness derives from the EU's enforcement mechanism. Although the EU's Ukraine/Russia sanctions were designed and agreed upon unanimously at the European level, they are implemented and enforced at the level of individual member states. Due to the different capabilities of the member states, including intelligence capacities and enforcement mechanisms, and their different degrees of willingness, the implementation varies in practice.⁶⁴ For example, overseas branches of some sanctioned Russian banks were exempted from sanctions in Austria, Germany, Cyprus, and France, as it was feared that the sanctions could lead to a negative systemic effect on the EU's banking sector.⁶⁵

---

60   European Union, Treaty of Nice, Amending the Treaty on European Union, the Treaties Establishing the European Communities and Certain Related Acts, *Official Journal of the European Communities*, 10 March 2001.
61   De Vries and Hazelzet, "The EU as a New Actor on the Sanctions Scene," 99.
62   US Department of the Treasury, "Treasury Sanctions Individuals and Entities Involved in Sanctions Evasion Related to Russia and Ukraine," *US Department of the Treasury official website*, 30 July 2015. https://www.treasury.gov/press-center/press-releases/Pages/jl0133.aspx.
63   US Department of the Treasury, "Countering America's Adversaries Through Sanctions Act," Public Law 115-44, 2 August 2017.
64   Iana Dreyer and José Luengo-Cabrera, "Introduction," in *On Target?*, eds. Dreyer and Luengo-Cabrera, 10.
65   Keatinge, Dall, Tabrizi and Lain, "Transatlantic (Mis)alignment," 8.

The legal contradictions within the sanctions regimes itself create another opportunity for the private sector to bypass sanctions. For example, the Kerch Commercial Sea Port became a convenient excuse for companies to exploit the legal inconsistencies. No transactions or activities are allowed with this port, which is a sanctioned entity on both the US and EU sanctions lists. However, in order to ship goods to Ukrainian ports in the Sea of Azov, transit dues and an obligatory pilotage fee must be paid to this port. As an unintended consequence, trading vessels destined for the Sea of Azov face a double risk—they can be fined either for breaching Western sanctions, or for violating the Ukrainian maritime law. Unintended by design, this provision remains unresolved.[66]

The loopholes that have emerged due to the lack of coordination between the senders also facilitate the circumvention of sanctions. In contrast to the US, EU, Canada, Australia, Switzerland, and Norway, Japan opted for only symbolic measures vis-à-vis Russia. Despite Japan's strong condemnation of Russia's change of the status quo by force,[67] Tokyo imposed light sanctions on Crimea. Although the Japanese government introduced an approval system for the import of goods from Crimea and Sevastopol, the export of goods, technology, and services was not targeted.[68] The exemption of exports became a loophole for the Crimean authorities. In 2014–2017, Toyota Camry and Toyota Land Cruisers were bought by the Crimean government, including the Prosecutor's Office.[69] Although the deal strictly speaking did not

---

[66] Lloyd's List, "Out of Sight, Out of Mind," 16.
[67] Ministry of Foreign Affairs of Japan, "Statement by the Minister of Foreign Affairs of Japan on the Measures against Russia over the Crimea Referendum," *Ministry of Foreign Affairs of Japan official website*, 18 March 2014, https://www.mofa.go.jp/press/release/press4e_000239.html.
[68] Ministry of Foreign Affairs of Japan, "Measures to Freeze Assets of Those Who Are Considered to Be Directly Involved in "Annexation" of the Autonomous Republic of Crimea and the City of Sevastopol or Destabilization of Eastern Part of Ukraine," *Ministry of Foreign Affairs of Japan official website*, 5 August 2014, https://www.mofa.go.jp/press/release/press4e_000387.html.
[69] "Toyota Bypassing Sanctions to Sell Cars in Crimea," *Hromadske International*, 20 July 2017, https://en.hromadske.ua/posts/toyota-bypassing-sanctions-to-sell-cars-in-crimea.

violate Japan's sanctions, it certainly breached the spirit of the Western sanctions.

Typology of Sanctions Circumvention

Sanctions circumvention refers to legal or illegal ways of avoiding compliance with rules or restrictions. In contrast, compliance means that "one consents to act in conformity or in accordance with some specific desire, request, condition, or direction." [70] In international law, compliance means that an actor is willing to accept international rules, regulations, and principles as binding constraints in its interactions with other actors. [71] Based on the motivational postures, voluntary and enforced compliance can be distinguished. In the case of voluntary compliance, actors approve punitive measures and indicate a desire to voluntarily commit to sanctions which are seen as a moral law and as fair punishment for the target. Enforced compliance occurs when actors disagree with measures but give in due to the risk of penalties. [72] Sanctions circumvention can thus be prompted by disagreement with the measures and/or by the authorities' inability to enforce and monitor compliance. Based on the theory of tax evasion, this article distinguishes between two types of sanctions circumvention behavior:

- *sanctions avoidance* as a legal activity within the legal framework, whereby the actor probes for loopholes within the sanctions regime with a view to reducing exposure to sanctions compliance. [73] In the case of sanctions avoidance, no rules are broken and no fraudulent transactions are undertaken. Sanctions

---

[70] Christopher C. Joyner, "Sanctions, Compliance and International Law: Reflections on the United Nations' Experience against Iraq," *Virginia Journal of International Law* 32, no. 1 (1991): 1.

[71] Ibid., 1.

[72] Erich Kirchler and Ingrid Wahl, "Tax Compliance Inventory: TAX-I Voluntary Compliance, Enforced Compliance, Tax Avoidance, and Tax Evasion," *Journal of Economic Psychology* 31, no. 3 (2010): 5.

[73] Doreen McBarnet, "Legitimate Rackets: Tax Evasion, Tax Avoidance, and the Boundaries of Legality," *The Journal of Human Justice* 3, no. 2 (Spring 1992): 60.

avoidance escapes administrative or criminal punishment and any risk of stigma.[74] From a *moral* standpoint, however, sanctions avoidance creates a schism between the letter and the spirit of the law. As it violates the intent of the law and ethical obligations, it represents a breach of the spirit;[75]

- *sanctions evasion* as an illegal activity that represents a violation of the law. The underlying motivation here is "deceit, misrepresentation and concealment." [76] The actor's motivation is to hide his/her activities from the authorities and to refrain from compliance with the sanctions regime. An actor that engages in evasive practices is liable to administrative and criminal penalties and carries a risk of criminal stigma.[77]

The two types of behavior reflect the interaction between actors' approval of sanctions and authorities' capacity to monitor. Sanctions avoidance occurs when actors have incentives to search for legal loopholes within the brackets of the law but are deterred from illegal actions due to effective monitoring and enforcement. Evasion occurs when the law is ignored or broken and the authorities lack power to monitor and enforce.[78]

In practice, however, the difference between avoidance and evasion is not as sharp as in the legal textbooks and the boundaries between the two may fall into the gray area. The term *avoision* has been coined to refer to cases which do not have clear or distinct boundaries and which generally shade from one to the other.[79]

---

[74] McBarnet, "Legitimate Rackets," 61.
[75] Graham Mansfield, "Five Ways Out of Tax: An Analysis of Avoidance Devices," *Journal of Financial Regulation and Compliance* 2, no. 2 (January 1994): 133.
[76] McBarnet, "Legitimate Rackets," 61.
[77] Agnar Sandmo, "The Theory of Tax Evasion: A Retrospective View," *National Tax Journal* LVIII, no. 4 (December 2005): 645.
[78] Kirchler and Wahl, "Tax Compliance Inventory," 3–5.
[79] Arthur Seldon, "Prologue to Avoision: The Moral Blurring of a Legal Distinction Without an Economic Difference," in *Tax Avoision: The Economic, Legal and Moral Inter-relationship between Avoidance and Evasion*, ed. Alfred Roman Ilersic (London: Institute of Economic Affairs, London, 1979), 51-70.

Actors practicing avoision use law and legal definitions as "a vehicle for exploitation" to serve their own interests and to disguise evasion as avoidance.[80] "Getting it wrong is not of itself an indication of evasion if you can provide evidence that you tried to get it right."[81] Indeed, through the provision of evidence actors try to ensure their compliance in form but not in substance.[82]

Following this typology, the next part will evaluate Western companies' practices in circumventing sanctions. Drawing on practical cases, the article will illustrate the techniques employed by the private sector to circumvent sanctions and will explore the boundaries between law-breaking and law-abiding activities.

Sanctions Circumvention: Practices and Cases

Over the last four years, the media has often reported on cases of sanctions breaches by Western firms. In many cases, the verdict—that the sanctions regime had been violated—was reached based on the spirit of the law rather than the letter. The purpose of this part is to provide a legal assessment of the cases where Western firms were involved. Juxtaposing companies' business activities in Crimea to the legal framework of sanctions, the article labels the individual cases as instances of sanctions evasion, sanctions avoidance, or the gray area, avoision, where the boundaries are less clear. The cases discussed below are arranged in order of importance.

Sanctions Avoision Case I: Shipping Companies

Context: despite Western restrictions on shipping activities in Crimea, a number of vessels docked in Crimea in violation of the sanctions. In 2014 the number of vessels dropped to 2,002, but in 2015 it expanded by 50%, equating to roughly the same number of ship calls as in 2013—prior to the sanctions. In particular, the number of ships with links to the EU grew by 23.4% for the year of

---

[80] Mansfield, "Five Ways Out of Tax," 133.
[81] McBarnet, "Legitimate Rackets," 66.
[82] Ibid., 67.

2015, with German-, Italian-, and Greek-registered vessels featuring most frequently. Similarly, the number of US-linked vessels increased from 18 in 2014 to 21 in 2015.[83]

Technique: foreign ships use a combination of manipulative techniques to avoid sanctions. First, the ship owners use "flags of convenience," a common practice in the maritime industry whereby vessels are re-registered with a country different to that of the ship owner. The vessels are usually registered under fictitious names and change operating companies frequently. The most common flags of convenience that enter Crimea are Russian, Togolese, and Panamanian. As ships are bound to adhere to the rules of their country of registration, it is convenient for the ship owner to register with a country which did not impose sanctions. Next, to hide the trail, various deceptive techniques are employed, ranging from switching off the radar from the Automatic Identification System (AIS) navigation system, loitering, routing to non-sanctioned ports, and transshipment in open waters.[84]

As a *Black Sea News* investigation revealed, in November–December 2017 two German shipping companies and a Norwegian mining company became involved in an illegal scheme involving the supply of ilmenite (titanium) ore to the Kerch port of Kamysh-Burun. On 3–6 November 2017, the German bulk ship HHL MISSISSIPPI, which belongs to German Hansa Heavy Left GmbH, received ten thousand tonnes of ilmenite in the Norwegian port of Jøssingfjorden, one of the largest titanium mines in Western Europe which belongs to Norway's Titania Kronos. After a brief stop in the Dutch port of Ijmuiden where it uploaded construction materials, HHL MISSISSIPPI set course for the Romanian port of Constanza. After offloading the materials, on 22 November the German cargo ship entered the Russian port of Kavkaz under the Liberian flag and stayed until 5 December. Because of a low bridge, the German ship could not enter the port and had to dock at the Kavkaz roadstead.

---

[83] Lloyd's List, "Out of Sight, Out of Mind," 13.
[84] Oleksandr Humeniuk, Maksym Kytsiuk, Olena Loginova and Andrii Ianitskyi, "International Trade with Crimea Ongoing despite Sanctions," *Organized Crime and Corruption Reporting Project*, 15 August 2015, https://www.occrp.org/en/investigations/5553-international-trade-with-crimea-ongoing-despite-sanctions.

During this stay, a Russian cargo ship NEFTERUDUVOZ-2 approached HHL MISSISSIPPI at least three times to receive the transshipment of ilmenite on the open sea. The Russian vessel then allegedly delivered the HHL MISSISSIPPI's cargo to the Kerch port of Kamysh-Burun. The same scheme was later used by the German cargo ship Callisto owned by German Heinz Corleis Reederei KG. It is believed that both deliveries were meant for the sole buyer of ilmenite in Crimea, the plant Titan which belongs to the Ukrainian oligarch Dmytro Firtash.[85]

Justification: Both German companies use the same justification for their activities and claim to have no knowledge about the final destination. Heinz Corleis KG does not accept responsibility for the violation: "We confirm that in 2017 Callisto fulfilled a transportation order from Norway to Kavkaz. As for where the cargo was transported after the end of the contract, we have no knowledge and it's outside of our responsibility."[86] Similarly, Hans-Joerg Simon from Hamburger Hansa Heavy Lift does not acknowledge any violation of the sanctions regime, and points out that the company performed an embargo check in line with the German export control instructions before the delivery. "This ilmenite is not subjected to any restrictions vis-à-vis Russia at least. We did not go to Crimea and we did not know that the end user is in Crimea."[87] He argues that the company could not know about the final destination based on the sole fact that the ship was supposed to return after a couple of hours. Jan Larsen, a Titania Kronos director, asserted that the company had "no direct sales" to Crimea and that it was currently clarifying the issue with the Ministry of

---

[85] "German Ship Delivers 10,000 Tons of Ilmenite from Norway to the Occupied Crimea's Titan Plant—A BSNews Investigation," *Black Sea News*, 27 December 2017, https://www.blackseanews.net/en/read/137635.

[86] Sabine Adler, "Deutsche Firmen des EU-Sanktionsbruchs verdächtigt," *Deutschlandfunk*, 6 July 2018, https://www.deutschlandfunk.de/verbotene-lieferungen-auf-die-krim-deutsche-firmen-des-eu.724.de.html?dram:article_id=422056.

[87] Ibid.

Foreign Affairs. He declined to comment on the identity of the end buyer of ilmenite or on why the ships sailed to the Kerch Strait.[88]

Legal assessment: According to the EU Council Regulation 825/2014, the export supply of titanium ore to Crimea and Sevastopol is strictly forbidden, including to Kamysh-Burun, an EU-sanctioned port.[89] Moreover, in June 2014 the Ukrainian authorities closed all the Crimean ports, so any ship docking in Crimea would be in violation of the Ukrainian law. Norway fully aligned with EU's Crimea sanctions and banned the sale, delivery, transport, or export of goods, including minerals.[90] Under the current legislation, both European and Norwegian companies are obliged to conduct due diligence to establish the end buyer and the final destination of the goods. It is companies' direct responsibility to make sure that the goods do not end up in Crimea.[91] In addition, the EU does not condone the participation of EU companies in activities whose purpose is to circumvent sanctions, regardless of the location—either in Crimea or anywhere else, including Russia. The EU's position on this rule is unambiguous: EU companies must not "participate, knowingly or intentionally, in activities the object or effect of which is to circumvent the prohibitions."[92] However, EU regulation includes a provision which reads that if the party "did not know, and had no reasonable cause to suspect that their actions would infringe the measures set out in the Regulation," then the party would be able to rely on this defense.[93] For example, this provision may work if the cargo was loaded in an intermediate port

---

[88] Nina Berglund, "UD Probes Possible Sanctions Violation," *News in English.no*, 31 January 2018, http://www.newsinenglish.no/2018/01/31/ud-probes-possible-sanctions-violation/.

[89] Council Regulation No 825/2014, 30 July 2014.

[90] Ministry of Foreign Affairs of Norway, "Norway to Implement New Restrictive Measures against Russia," *Government.no*, 11 August 2014, https://www.regjerin gen.no/en/aktuelt/Norway-to-implement-new-restrictive-measures-against-Russia/id765675/.

[91] Council Decision 933, 18 December 2014.

[92] *Ibid.*

[93] "Maritime Legal Issues arising out of Trading to Ukraine/Crimea. New EU Sanctions and Ukraine Directive," *Ince & Co*, 21 July 2014, https://www.incelaw.c om/en/knowledge-bank/maritime-legal-issues-arising-out-of-trading-to-ukrai ne-crimea.

and the party had no control over it. This get-out clause is significant, as it underlines the importance of due diligence, but also indicates a potential loophole. As long as the company can prove that enough screening was done and that it did not know that it was violating the sanctions, the case would be likely to be judged as a matter of sanctions avoidance, but not sanctions evasion.

Nevertheless, evaluating German companies' activities and justifications, it is hard to agree that sufficient due diligence was performed. The claim that the delivery was destined to Russia has no real support. According to Andrii Klymenko, a *Black Sea News* activist, Russia does not need to import ilmenite, as the country produces its own supply in the Urals. The only buyer of ilmenite in the vicinity is the Crimean plant Titan.[94] Moreover, both companies showed a lack of vigilance and a failure to consult adequately with the German government authorities for export control. Given the proximity of the Russian port of Kavkaz to the Crimean coast (a distance of only 20 km), it would be reasonable to expect from the companies to conduct a thorough due diligence.

Currently, the activities of both the German and Norwegian companies are under investigation. This illegal scheme of export supply clearly borders on sanctions evasion. The final decision on whether the companies in question breached sanctions will be judged by the degree of their due diligence.

Sanctions Avoision Case II: Bridge Constructors

Context: in May 2018, Russia completed the construction of the Kerch bridge connecting Crimea and the Russian mainland. In 2017, there were reports that two Dutch companies, Dematec Equipment and Bijlard Hydrauliek, were providing machines, machine parts, and other services for the construction of this bridge.[95] In the wake of the media allegation, Lilianne Ploumen, the Dutch Minister for Foreign Trade and Development Cooperation, reiterated the

---

[94] Adler, "Deutsche Firmen des EU-Sanktionsbruchs verdächtigt."
[95] "Obkhodnye puti," *Kommersant*, 14 September 2017, https://www.kommersant.ru/doc/3410460.

government's non-recognition policy of Crimea and that it "does not in any way stimulate activities that contribute to the normalization of the situation."[96] Eventually, the Dutch Public Prosecutor launched an investigation against seven Dutch companies believed to be involved in the bridge's construction.[97] In June 2017, the EU added six Russian companies involved in the construction of the Kerch Bridge.[98]

Technique: the two Dutch companies used different techniques to enable the delivery of the prohibited goods. Dematec Equipment, which was responsible for a hydraulic impact hammer, shipped the equipment to Russia in early 2016. The equipment was assembled on Russian territory. In the case of Bijlard Hydrauliek, an intermediary company was used. The Dutch company built an important part of the hammer and delivered it to a customer in the Netherlands.

Justifications: the two companies deny that their activities constitute a violation of the sanctions regime. Derk van den Heuvel, director of Dematec Equipment opined that "the sanctions had not been breached because the equipment was assembled on Russian territory."[99] He emphasized that "EU sanctions state that we are not allowed to work in Crimea, but we can in Russia."[100] The second company Biljard Hydrauliek "was unaware that its parts would be used to build the bridge."[101] In particular, Marcel Biljard claimed that "We simply supplied to a customer in the Netherlands. That's all."[102]

---

[96] "Scandal as Dutch Companies Help Build Bridge to Occupied Crimea, Violating Sanctions," *Euromaidan Press*, 6 September 2017, http://euromaidanpress.com/2017/09/06/dutch-government-to-investigate-companies-helping-russia-build-bridge-to-occupied-crimea/.

[97] "Krim-Brücke: Ermittlungen gegen niederländische Firmen," *ORF.at*, 4 May 2018, https://orf.at/stories/2436740/.

[98] Council of the European Union, "Ukraine: EU Adds Six Entities involved in the Construction of the Kerch Bridge Connecting the Illegally Annexed Crimea to Russia to Sanctions List," *Press Release*, 31 July 2018.

[99] "Dutch Companies Investigated for Supplying Equipment for Russian Bridge," *Dutchnews.nl*, 4 September 2017, https://www.dutchnews.nl/news/2017/09/dutch-companies-investigated-for-supplying-equipment-for-crimean-bridge/.

[100] Ibid.

[101] Ibid.

[102] Ibid.

Legal assessment: Council Regulation 825/2014 prohibits the sales and provision of key equipment and technology in the infrastructure sector to persons in Crimea or for use in Crimea. Dematec Equipment's justification that EU sanctions allow them to work in Russia refers to only part of the provision. The same article in the Council Regulation continues to argue it is "prohibited to participate, knowingly or intentionally, in activities the object or effect of which is to circumvent the prohibitions."[103] Since it was assisting in the construction of the bridge, the company could hardly claim that it did not know about the nature of the project.

In the case of Bijlard Hydrauliek, the legal assessment should be made based on the degree of due diligence. By claiming that it was not aware of the final destination for its goods, the company is attempting to use the get-out clause. If the company can prove that an intermediary company, which the equipment was sold to, had no prior public record of exporting goods to Russia, this justification may be sufficient and the case can be classified as avoidance. However, if the intermediary company was used as a cover-up and Bijlard Hydrauliek knew about the final destination, this would be an illegal activity aimed at sanctions evasion. The main problem here is defining what level of due diligence is sufficient to prove the company's justification. The legal boundaries between evasion and avoidance will likely be context-specific.

Another exploitation of the legal boundaries of the sanctions regimes is the location of the bridge. Being located outside the Crimean peninsula in the sea, the bridge does not strictly fall under the Crimea sanctions. However, the purpose of the bridge contradicts the EU sanctions at its core. By physically connecting Crimea with the mainland Russia, the bridge consolidated Russia's control over the peninsula and further undermined Ukraine's territorial integrity. As Ploumen rightly stressed, "even if laws were

---

[103] Council of the European Union, "Council Regulation No 825/2014 amending Regulation (EU) No 692/2014 concerning restrictions on the import into the Union of goods originating in Crimea or Sevastopol, in response to the illegal annexation of Crimea and Sevastopol," *Official Journal of the European Union*, 30 July 2014, https://eur-lex.europa.eu/legal-content/EN/TXT/?uri=uriserv:OJ.L.2014.226.01.0002.01.ENG.

not formally broken, the Dutch government expects companies to conduct socially responsible behaviour."[104]

Sanctions Avoision Case III: Credit Card Companies

Context: in April 2014, the US expanded its sanctions, blacklisting Russian individuals and entities from Putin's financial circle. This included Bank Rossiya and Sobinbank, linked to Yurii Kovalchuk, as well as SMP Bank and InvestCapitalBank, associated with Arkadii and Boris Rotenberg.[105] Both Visa and MasterCard, the world's largest US-based credit and debit card companies, suspended their services in Crimea and blocked the blacklisted Russian banks from using their payment system. "Due to the latest U.S. sanctions imposed against Crimea by Executive Order 13685 of December 19, 2014, Visa is now prohibited from offering Visa-branded products and services to Crimea. This means that we can no longer support card issuing and merchant/ATM acquiring services in Crimea," the Visa statement read.[106] MasterCard followed and also withdrew from the region due to the sanctions.[107] However, in early 2016 the media reported that Visa and MasterCard were back on the Crimean market.[108] Crimean Visa and MasterCard holders were able to make transactions and withdrawals from their accounts again as long as they were inside Russia.

Technique: in May 2014, the Russian government passed a new law "On the National Payment Card System." The purpose of the new law was to mitigate the harm inflicted on Russia's banking

---

[104] "Scandal as Dutch Companies Help Build Bridge."
[105] Peter Baker, "U.S. Expands Sanctions, Adding Holdings of Russians in Putin's Financial Circle," *The New York Times*, 28 April 2014, https://www.nytimes.com/2014/04/29/world/asia/obama-sanctions-russia.html.
[106] Andrey Ostroukh, "Visa Suspends Operations in Crimea," *The Wall Street Journal*, 26 December 2014, https://www.wsj.com/articles/visa-suspends-operations-in-crimea-1419609876.
[107] "MasterCard vsled za Visa prekratila obsluzhivat Krym," *BBC*, 26 December 2014, https://www.bbc.com/russian/rolling_news/2014/12/141226_rn_mastercard_crimea.
[108] "Visa, MasterCard Cards to Resume Functioning in Crimea in April," *Russia Beyond*, 6 February 2015, https://www.rbth.com/news/2015/02/06/visa_mastercard_cards_to_resume_functioning_in_crimea_in_april_43497.html.

sector by Western sanctions. According to the new legislation, credit institutions wishing to keep their business in Russia should move their transactions to the new system. The law required the credit card companies to pay interim contributions quarterly to the Central Bank of Russia, which amounted to 25% of their average daily turnover.[109] If Visa and MasterCard did not fulfill the requirements, they would have paid a huge security deposit.[110]

By the end of 2014, Visa and MasterCard agreed to gradually move the processing of the US companies' transactions within Russia under the roof of Russia's national payment system. They were obliged to transfer their traffic by 31 March 2015. As sole owner of the payment system, the Central Bank of Russia acted as a settlement office. All international transactions were to be cleared through the Russian banking center before the data were transmitted to the US. For that purpose, the National Payment Card System "cracked" the files of Visa and MasterCard.[111] Transactions would usually omit any references to Crimea but indicate "Russia" as the place of operation. "All transactions will be processed by our center. America won't even see and will not be able to block anything. Russian bank cards, Ukrainian, German, American, Japanese—any [cards], there will be no problem with that," explained Anatolii Aksakov, deputy head of the State Duma's financial committee.[112]

As the Ukrainian banks have left the peninsula and the major Russian banks feared international sanctions, less known Russian banks, usually with shady corporate structures, replaced Sberbank, VTB, and others. The Russian National Commercial Bank (RNKB) and Genbank became the main banking institutions to quickly expand their branches. Later, both Genbank and RNKB were added

---

[109] "National Russian Card Payment System Established," *RT*, 5 May 2014, https://www.rt.com/business/156912-russian-putin-card-payment/.
[110] Andrei Ostroukh, "Russia Launches Local Electronic Payment System," *The Wall Street Journal*, 15 December 2015, https://www.wsj.com/articles/russia-launches-local-electronic-payment-system-1450195940.
[111] "Novaia kartochka Kryma. Poluostrov podkliuchilsia k Visa," *Kommersant*, 21 January 2016, https://www.kommersant.ru/doc/2901471.
[112] "Visa, MasterCard Cards to Resume Functioning in Crimea in April," *Russia Beyond*, 6 February 2015.

to the OFAC blacklist and Visa and MasterCard blocked their operations. Until August 2018, Genbank was the only bank issuing new credit cards. However, in August 2018, the bank announced its decision to stop issuing new cards and to switch to the Russian-based payment card "Mir."[113]

Justification: from the standpoint of Visa and MasterCard, the companies were outwitted by the Russian government and were *de facto* forced to partake in sanctions circumvention. According to a source familiar with the situation, when the National Payment Card System was created, the companies were compelled to transfer all their Russian operations, including the Crimean ones, for the processing. Their withdrawal from the Russian market would mean a substantial loss in the market share. The companies claim that *de jure* they adhere to the sanctions, but *de facto* they have no control over transactions.[114]

Legal assessment: although the credit card companies did not directly violate any Western sanctions, they breached the spirit of the sanctions. Ceding to the request of the Russian authorities to transfer the traffic, both companies facilitated the circumvention of the US sanctions. Once the US financial institutions discovered deceptive practices employed in order to obfuscate Crimea-related transactions, the case started to border on sanctions evasion. In August 2015, OFAC issued a new clarification of the "misunderstood" nature of the embargo on US businesses, stating that: "The evasive practices identified by OFAC include the omission or obfuscation of references to Crimea and locations within Crimea in documentation underlying transactions involving U.S. persons or the United States. These practices apply to a range of activities involving both the financial services and international trade sectors."[115] OFAC stated that it had became aware of the seemingly

---

[113] "BBC soobshchila o prekrashchenii vypuska kart Visa i MasterCard v Krymu," *RBC*, 14 August 2018, https://www.rbc.ru/finances/14/08/2018/5b7310769a7947c21493bc52.

[114] "Ne smeshite nashi magaziny. Kak obkhodiat sanktsii v Krymu," *Novaia gazeta*, 31 January 2018.

[115] US Department of the Treasury, "Crimea Sanctions Advisory. Obfuscation of Critical Information in Financial and Trade Transactions Involving the Crimean

established practice of omitting the originator or beneficiary address from SWIFT messages. These obfuscation patterns were viewed by OFAC as an activity aimed at circumventing sanctions compliance.[116]

Sanctions Avoidance Case I: Retail Companies

Context: despite the EU sanctions, the French and German supermarket chains Auchan and Metro Cash&Carry continue to carry out their business activities in Crimea. Their products are visible on the shelves of the two German and one French stores that remain in operation in Crimea. The goods are shipped via the Kerch port from the Russian mainland, despite the fact that it is prohibited for the EU companies to deal with this EU-sanctioned entity. Both companies seem to be aware of this and do not contest the fact that they are using the EU-blacklisted port for their delivery.[117]

In August 2017, the Ukrainian Prosecutor General's Office launched a criminal investigation of Auchan in connection to the latter's violation of the Ukrainian border. The criminal investigation was aimed at establishing whether the deliveries of goods carried out by the French company were in line with the Ukrainian legislation.[118] However, the investigation had no legal consequences for the company.[119]

Technique: through the re-registration of their Crimean entities, both Metro Cash&Carry and Auchan were able to legally operate on the peninsula. According to the official documentation, the Metro stores in Crimea are owned by Moscow-based "Retail Property 5" LLC and "Retail Property 6" LLC. Ninety percent of the

---

Region of Ukraine," *OFAC*, 30 July 2015, https://www.treasury.gov/resource-center/sanctions/programs/documents/crimea_advisory.pdf.
[116] *Ibid.*
[117] Anton Zverev, Gleb Stolyarov, and Olga Sichkar, "Exclusive: How EU Firms Skirt Sanctions to Do Business in Crimea," *Reuters*, 21 September 2016, https://www.reuters.com/article/us-ukraine-crisis-crimea-sanctions-insig/exclusive-how-eu-firms-skirt-sanctions-to-do-business-in-crimea-idUSKCN11R1AN.
[118] "French Giants Auchan, Peugeot Face Prosecution in Ukraine over Work in Crimea," *TASS*, 28 April 2017, http://tass.com/economy/943725.
[119] "Ne smeshite nashi magaziny."

latter belongs to Metro Group Retail Real Estate GmbH and ten percent to Metro Holding Properties GmbH. Both companies are registered in Germany. In the case of Auchan, there are even fewer layers in their corporate structure: registered in Russia, Auchan LLC belongs directly to its French parent company.[120]

Both retail companies contract third-party transport companies to load up goods at distribution centers in southern Russia and then ship the trucks via ferry through the Kerch port. Later, the trucks disembark in Kerch and deliver the products to the stores in Crimea. The subcontractors are instructed not to use any sanctioned entities while delivering the goods to Crimea. However, it is not clear how the Russian subsidiaries monitor this.[121]

Justification: both retailers claim that they are not violating the EU sanctions, as their business activities in Crimea are conducted by Russian subsidiaries, which are not targeted. Auchan Holding's press office explained that the Russian retailers using the franchise are subject to Russian and not EU legislation. Antoine Pernod, senior vice-president for communication at Auchan Holding, justifies the company's decision to remain with the desire to alleviate the humanitarian situation there: "We have decided that we will continue to offer some vital products for the local population in Crimea, in particular foodstuffs, also we will not reduce the number of jobs."[122] Similarly, Metro Cash&Carry argues that their business in Crimea is run by Russian subsidiaries which are not liable to EU sanctions. The parent company claims to be not involved in the local operational activities in Crimea and that most of the products come from Russian suppliers.[123]

Legal assessment: this is a clear case of sanctions avoidance. According to EU sanctions, the export of goods to Crimea is limited to certain sectors, while Russian subsidiaries are not subjected to restrictive measures. This case illustrates that the EU sanctions are not fully comprehensive; certain activities are still legal under the

---

[120] Viktoriia Veselova, "Sekrety krupnogo biznesa: kak torguiut v Krymu Auchan i Metro," *Krym.Realii*, 10 October 2016, https://ru.krymr.com/a/28044057.html.
[121] Ibid.
[122] "Ne smeshite nashi magaziny."
[123] Zverev, Stolyarov, and Sichkar, "Exclusive: How EU Firms Skirt Sanctions."

sanctions regime. As an EU official acknowledged, the companies' business activities are in breach of the EU sanctions' spirit, but "in the absence of a trade embargo, there is always a fine line between compliance and non-compliance."[124] As the sanctions enforcement falls under the member states' regulations, it is for the German and French authorities to launch criminal investigations. However, no law suits are currently filed at the national levels.

Another loophole is the relationship between the parent company and the subcontractors. The transfer of goods to Crimea is a gray area, as the legal boundaries between the parent company and its subcontractor are hard to define.[125] In general, EU-based parent companies can be held liable "if they have instructed their local unit to act in violation of the sanctions," explained Artem Zhavoronkov, partner at law firm Dentons.[126] By creating complex corporate structures, both Metro Cash&Carry and Auchan intended to distance themselves from their Russian subsidiaries. With the re-registration of their businesses with Russian subcontractors, the German and French companies found a loophole in the EU sanctions regime that does not target Russian subsidiaries.

The way the German and French retailers justify their activities in Crimea is particularly interesting. The companies could have used the argument that selling foodstuffs in Crimea is not prohibited under the EU sanctions. However, as the goods are transported via a ferry that serves the EU-sanctioned Kerch port, the companies were in need of further justification, namely that it is the Russian subsidiaries that conduct business in Crimea. By distancing themselves, the German and French companies were able to shift the liabilities to their Russian counterparts (including for the violation of the Kerch port usage) and avoid the reputational risk associated with doing business in Crimea that could damage their international standing.

---

[124] Ibid.
[125] "Grauzone Krim-Sanktionen—Metro im Zweilicht?," *Medianet*, 22 September 2016, https://medianet.at/news/retail/grauzone-krim-sanktionen-metro-im-zwielicht-10623.html.
[126] Zverev, Stolyarov, and Sichkar, "Exclusive: How EU Firms Skirt Sanctions."

Sanctions Avoidance Case II: Car Dealers

Context: after the Crimea sanctions were put in place, Western automobile companies left the peninsula. However, soon afterwards, the media reported sightings on the streets of Crimea of new foreign cars by Volkswagen, Mercedes-Benz, Audi, BMW, Nissan, Peugeot, Toyota, Mitsubishi, and Kia Motors. In 2015–2016, it was revealed that the senior management of the "Crimean Federal University," former Taurida National University, and the Prosecutor's Office in Crimea had bought a Toyota Camry and a Toyota Land Cruiser for their own usage.[127] In 2018, it was reported that 15 Toyota Camry and 2 Mercedes-Benz had been subleased to the self-proclaimed Crimean government.[128] Ukraine's Ministry of Foreign Affairs issued a statement condemning Western car dealers for violating the sanctions regime and appealed to the relevant authorities to take the necessary measures.[129] Legal procedures have been initiated against several German companies, including Volkswagen.[130]

Technique: in July 2016, Crimea was officially incorporated into Russia's Southern Federal District. This allowed foreign automobile companies to use their network of official dealer offices on the Russian mainland effectively in order to conduct business in Crimea. As the Ukrainian car dealers are no longer present in

---

[127] "Toyota Bypassing Sanctions to Sell Cars in Crimea," *Hromadske International*, 20 July 2017, https://en.hromadske.ua/posts/toyota-bypassing-sanctions-to-sell-cars-in-crimea; and Aleksandr Alikin, "Krym prodolzhaet poluchat importnoe oborudovanie v obkhod sanktsii," *Eurasianet*, 21 February 2017, https://russian.eurasianet.org/node/65154.

[128] Viktoriia Veselova, "'Sanktsionnyi avtopark'. kak pravitelstvo Kryma zakupaet vonye inomarki," *Krym.Realii*, 23 January 2018, https://ru.krymr.com/a/2899 2306.html.

[129] Ministerstvo z pytan tymchasovo okupovannykh terytorii Ukrainy ta vnutrishnio peremishchenykh osib Ukrainy, "Vyiavleno fakty vykorystannia torgovykh marok avtomobilnykh brendiv na tymchasovo okupovanii terytorii Ukrainy," 27 December 2017, https://mtot.gov.ua/fakty_vykorystannia_torgov yh_marok.

[130] Matthias Beermann, "Moskau ist an einer Lösung nicht interessiert," *Rheinische Post Online*, 2 February 2018, https://rp-online.de/politik/ausland/ukrainischer-aussenminister-pawlo-klimkin-moskau-ist-an-einer-loesung-nicht-interessiert_aid -18877381.

Crimea, the car brands were delivered via sublease from Russia's nearest cities such as Krasnodar, Novorossiisk, and Nizhnii Novgorod. The financial partners in wire-transactions are the Russian banks operating in Crimea—Genbank and RNKB. While the vehicles are bought from the mainland in Russia, the technical services are performed in official distribution offices in Krasnodar.[131] Another technique used was to deliver the vehicle direct from the EU. Using a series of Russian and Austrian middlemen, Skoda Octavias were shipped to Crimea via the Kerch port without any legal repercussions.[132]

Justification: Western car manufacturers are unanimous in claiming that they have not violated the sanctions regime and that they have no official representation in Crimea. Natalia Kostyukovitch, communications officer at Volkswagen Group Russia, denied allegations that the company had circumvented the prohibitions.[133] Daimler acknowledged that it knows about the existence of gray dealers in Crimea, but claimed to have no control over them.[134] Nevertheless, the companies do not seem entirely comfortable with their own justification that implies that they are conducting their business as usual in Crimea and have also come up with other explanations—Volkswagen, for example, explained their presence in Crimea on the grounds that the company cares about their clients' needs.[135]

---

[131] "Ukraina nakonets uvidela v Krymu importnye mashiny," *Kommersant*, 27 December 2017, https://www.kommersant.ru/doc/3511778?query=крым%20санкции.

[132] Viktoriia Veselova, "V 'ob"ezd' sanktsii: kak inostrannye avtomobili popadaiut v Krym," *Krym.Realii*, 21 December 2017, https://ru.krymr.com/a/28931769.html.

[133] Andrey Gurkov, "Wie der Verkauf deutscher Pkw auf der Krim weitergeht," *Deutsche Welle*, 4 May 2017, https://www.dw.com/de/wie-der-verkauf-deutscher-pkw-auf-der-krim-weitergeht/a-38687520.

[134] "Ukraina nakonets uvidela v Krymu importnye mashiny," *Kommersant*, 27 December 2017, https://www.kommersant.ru/doc/3511778?query=крым%20санкции.

[135] Denis Trubetskoy, "Mit Krim oder ohne?" *Zeit Online*, 8 January 2016, https://www.zeit.de/wirtschaft/2016-01/ukraine-boykott-coca-cola-russland-karte-krim.

Legal assessment: the European export ban is not comprehensive and is restricted to the three key sectors of transport, telecommunications, and energy. Although the media reports labeled the case as a violation of EU sanctions, a closer look at the legal provisions nullifies this accusation. According to Annex II of the EU Council Decision 692/2014, the EU prohibited the delivery of vehicles that are suitable for ten or more people or special-needs vehicles such as wreckers or cranes.[136] The delivery of passenger automobiles is not included on the list and thus does not constitute an illegal activity. Juxtaposing companies' justification and the legal framework, it is interesting to observe that the companies do not openly acknowledge this loophole. Instead of directly referring to the Annex II in the EU legislation, the car manufacturers use other excuses such as client needs or the lack of control over gray dealers. This strongly underlines the fact that it is a high-risk activity for companies to conduct business as usual in Crimea. The companies evidently fear that by acknowledging their presence they will suffer reputational damage. In fact, after the Siemens scandal, Volkswagen sent a letter to its Russian car dealers, reminding them about the imperative to comply with the EU sanctions and specifying that the sale of trucks, commercial cars, and specialized vehicles is strictly prohibited.[137]

Under the current sanctions regime, this case represents an instance of sanctions avoidance. By exploiting the loophole in the sanctions regime and by bringing vehicles to Crimea from Russia without any Ukrainian authorization or Ukrainian customs registration, the Western companies *de facto* treat Crimea as part of Russia. This clearly contravenes the EU's non-recognition policy and breaches the spirit of the sanctions.

---

[136] Annex II, Council Regulation (EU) No 1351/2014 (18 December 2014) amending Regulation (EU) No 692/2014.

[137] Andrei Zagorskii, "Volkswagen razoslal pis'mo na pamiat'," *Kommersant*, 11 October 2017, https://www.kommersant.ru/doc/3435561.

Conclusion and Recommendations

Sanctions-busting behavior can be explained by companies' fundamental commercial interests. While the private sector bears the main costs of sanctions compliance, it has a strong economic motivation to avoid or evade sanctions in order to maintain its share of the Russian market. Although the Siemens case illustrated the importance of due diligence and the risks a foreign company faces when dealing with Russia directly or via local subsidiaries, the number of cases of sanctions circumvention has not decreased.

As this article has demonstrated, Western firms have employed various techniques to bypass the Crimea sanctions. The complex sanctions regime allowed them to exploit the loopholes within the sanctions framework and jurisdictions to lessen their exposure to compliance. First, Western companies used the get-out clause, by showing that they conducted due diligence. Ironically, due diligence was used as a convenient instrument for disclosing information while simultaneously suppressing information that could be harmful for companies. Stating that they had no reason to suspect that their activity would lead to a sanctions breach, companies claimed to be unaware of the true identity of the end user or the end destination, thus using the due diligence as proof of innocence. The second loophole was the re-registering of assets to Russian subsidiaries. As the latter is not covered by sanctions, Western firms created complex corporate structures or used intermediaries to distance themselves from their Russian entities. Despite the fact that those complex corporate structures have been revealed by investigative journalism, so far there are no legal consequences for the entities involved. Finally, the third loophole is the ability to operate on Russian territory. By claiming that they conducted activities in Russia and not in Crimea, companies argued that their activities are not subject to sanctions. Interestingly, none of the companies referred to the legal loopholes within the sanctions regime. Instead, companies used more complex justifications to distance themselves and to avoid the reputational risks.

The majority of the cases fall under the category of sanctions avoision, as the boundaries between law-abiding and law-breaking activities are blurred. Some cases constitute avoidance with elements of evasive practices (for example, the cases of the shipping and credit card companies), while other cases transgress into evasion in the process or are interspersed with such evasion (as in the cases of the bridge constructors). The absence of clear-cut sanctions evasion cases points to the amount of "creative compliance" that companies engage in so as to continue business as usual in Crimea. Many of them belong to global economic elites— they are large companies and corporations which employ professional services to exploit the letter of the law in order to stay within the legal brackets. They arrange their affairs so as to ensure compliance in form but not in substance. As a result, the spirit of the sanctions is breached, and their credibility and effectiveness is undermined.

The analysis of sanctions-busting points to ways in which the effectiveness of Western sanctions can be enhanced. First, staying agile and flexible will be the US' and EU's best response to countering sanctions-busting. Both actors should address the loopholes in their sanctions framework and prevent the emergence of new ones. Both should strengthen their leverage by anticipating how quickly and easily their sanctions might be evaded and avoided and include appropriate counter-measures at the design stage. In preventing sanctions-busting, systemic thinking is crucial. In contrast to targeting separate sectors and entities, whole systems and networks should be sanctioned. As suggested by Ukraine's Ministry of Foreign Affairs, to curtail the sanctions circumvention, the Crimea sanctions should be expanded to Russia's Southern Federal District where the majority of evasive practices takes place.

Second, the monitoring and enforcement mechanisms both in the West and in Ukraine should be significantly improved. The EU member states' and Ukrainian governments, in particular, clearly lack the political will to enforce sanctions effectively. For the EU, the costs of monitoring are high and time-consuming, while the value of illegal export-import is low. [138] For Ukraine, the implementation of full-scale sanctions would disrupt the business

---

[138] Lloyd's List, "Out of Sight, Out of Mind," 14.

structures of rent-seeking elites. So far, no US or EU companies implicated in sanctions breaches have been prosecuted, while the Criminal Code of Ukraine still lacks provisions on sanctions.[139] Borrowing experience from the North Korean case, a UN Panel of Experts would be helpful in early detection and effective countering of the sanctions-busting schemes. Prosecuting the sanctions evaders could repair the damage done to the credibility of Western sanctions and would deter companies from breaching them in the future.

Finally, better communication between the private and the public sectors is crucial, as is clear guidance from the authorities on implementation requirements. As suggested in the RUSI report, public-private partnerships will be quintessential for the enhancement of companies' compliance and thus sanctions' effectiveness. Moving from reactive and one-directional communication, an exchange between private businesses and government authorities at the early stages—during design and implementation—will be crucial for discussing the ways in which unintentional consequences can be avoided and alternative solutions forged. Although sanctions are first and foremost a foreign policy tool, business-government interaction can serve to enhance the understanding of the sanctions regime and its weak spots, and to enable the sharing of experience on best practice.[140]

---

[139] Oleksandr Humeniuk, Maksym Kytsiuk, Olena Loginova and Andrii Ianitskyi, "International Trade with Crimea Ongoing Despite Sanctions," *Organized Crime and Corruption Reporting Project*, 15 August 2015.

[140] Keatinge, Dall, Tabrizi and Lain, "Transatlantic (Mis)alignment," 13–14.

The Return to Patriotic Education in Post-Soviet Russia: How, When, and Why the Russian Military Engaged in Civilian Nation Building

Håvard Bækken

Abstract: *This article examines the military origins of the Russian State Program of Patriotic Education. It documents how the policy was incubated within the Ministry of Defense and had found much of its form and content before Vladimir Putin became Russia's president. To a degree often forgotten, patriotic education was shaped by circumstances of crisis and social destabilization. In response to failed nation building and rising concerns over youth behavior, military values and aesthetics were taken up as a means to cure social ills and moral vices and to counter the influx of western values. The military actors involved sought not only to increase the prestige of military service. Equally important was the fact that patriotic education served as a form of social outreach, based on a traditionalist worldview. Soviet and Russian soldiers were seen as important role models for the young, and the Armed Forces as a bearer of historical continuity and "Russianness." Thus, already before Putin's presidency, the regime invited the military into the heart of civilian affairs, presenting military traditionalism with a stronghold within the domain of official nation building. Under Putin, too, patriotic education policies continue to bear the strong imprint of their origins in crisis and failed nation building in the 1990s.*

Keywords: Russia, official patriotism, patriotic education, identity politics, militarization, militarism.

Introduction

Military-patriotic education[1] in contemporary Russia is frequently associated with a great power on the rise, with its international operations, and with President Vladimir Putin's personal engagement. There are good reasons to draw such connections. Following the ideological turn in official discourse in 2012, the Crimea annexation in 2014, and the subsequent war in Ukraine, traditional values and state patriotism have become increasingly central to Russia's nation building efforts. Moreover, Putin himself has done a great deal to reinforce his image as a patriot and a friend of the military. Yet, Russia's current president did not invent military patriotism, and his embrace of the policy largely followed up a trend started by his predecessor. Important, but often forgotten, is the fact that the State Program of Patriotic Education (henceforth State Program) that was launched in 2001 was in fact drafted in the mid- to late 1990s.[2] With both liberal and communist ideologies discredited, and in the midst of social turmoil and a collective identity crisis, the circumstances were ripe for a militarist comeback. Without the multifaceted crisis of post-communist Russia, patriotic education could arguably have had a considerably

---

[1] Even if "patriotic" and "military-patriotic" are often used interchangeably in Russian, the two terms have somewhat different connotations. In Russia, patriotic activities are sometimes separated into "civic-patriotic" *(grazhdanskoe-patrioticheskoe)* and "military-patriotic" *(voenno-patrioticheskoe)*, but "patriotic education" *(patrioticheskoe vospitanie)* when used alone is more strongly associated with the military than the civic aspects. In this article, "patriotic" (education) refers to the general project aimed at instilling patriotism, while "military-patriotic" (education) connotes the military aspects (objectives, agency, topics) of this practice. The term *vospitanie* may in turn be translated as both education and upbringing, relating to a dichotomy in Russian educational science, in which education is divided into academic *(obuchenie)* and moral-spiritual *(vospitanie)* counterparts. Education tends to be the most popular translation into English, but readers should be aware of these important nuances.

[2] While each of the five-year plans from 2001 were formally adopted as individual *programs*, I use the "State Program" as a collective name for all these plans and their related policy concepts, and "five-year plans" for what are officially called "programs." At least the first three five-year plans, while named "state programs," had unclear official status (Sanina 2017).

different character, or even be absent as a large-scale state program. As for the Putin administration, it did not change the core components of this policy much, and certainly not in Putin's first two terms as president. Misattributing the origins of patriotic education to the Putin government runs the risk of misinterpreting its ideological appeal and underestimating the massive effect that social crisis has had on post-Soviet Russian national consciousness and the political strategies of Russia's elites.

This article examines how, when, and why patriotic education was reintroduced to Russia after the demise of the Soviet Union. I claim that the policy was in large part a product of crisis and moral panics. Long before Putin declared patriotism "Russia's national idea" (*Moscow Times* 2016), traditionalist[3] circles within the Russian military[4] pondered how the army might serve as an example of Russianness in times of confusion and hardship. Importantly, the patriotic education discourse was staunchly inward-looking. More than a celebration of the contemporary state of affairs, or a preparation for grand military adventures, the State Program was a desperate attempt to address an army and a society in acute crisis, and to keep a disintegrating nation together. In a popular phrase at the time, patriotic education was a call to "love Russia in bad weather." Through the adoption of the State Program, I argue, political authorities invited the military into the heart of civilian affairs, presenting military traditionalism with a stronghold within the domain of Russian identity policy. This was the beginning of a phase of militarization of Russian society—a wave that has yet to break and ebb.

After a brief introduction to the salience and relevance of military patriotism today, the article proceeds to suggest a conceptual framework for assessing the character of military

---

[3] By traditionalism in the Russian context, I bear in mind an area-specific blend of social conservativism with characteristics such as a strong state identity, militarism, anti-Westernism, and defense-mindedness.

[4] This article treats the Ministry of Defense as a military institution. In the period in question, its leadership was completely dominated by military figures, as was its publication *Krasnaia zvezda*, which I use as an important source (see Betz 2002).

influence on nation-building, centered on the differentiation between militarization and militarism. Following this, I move on to consider how the Soviet experience created a template of militarism in identity policy that the traditionalists could resort to when other nation building attempts failed. The article then considers the reemergence of patriotic education in more detail. While the concept of patriotic education largely disappeared from state policies in the 1990s, the ideas survived within a sub-department of the Ministry of Defense, from where they would soon expand again. By persistently promoting the State Program as an anti-crisis measure to cope with social and moral disintegration, the advocates of patriotic education eventually managed to obtain Yeltsin's support and paved the way for the policy we know today. The remainder of the article examines how the moral indignation and military traditionalism carried over to the Putin era, in the form of actual policy documents as well as a generic entrenchment of military values in Russia's "patriotic infrastructure." When the Kremlin started to appeal more openly to traditional values after 2012, the military-patriotic complex was already developed and ready to serve.

Putinism and Resurgent Militarism in Russia

Under Putin's presidency, military patriotism has once again become a cornerstone of Russian identity policy. Under his auspices, the size of military parades escalated, official days of military glory were introduced (Laruelle 2009: 157–58), and military patriotism made headway way into schools, kindergartens, summer camps, cultural events, and state media (ICS 2018; Sanina 2017; Robertshaw 2015). The development was anchored in the State Program. Even if the actual resources allocated to the program remained quite modest,[5] its conceptual foundation was important for signaling the Kremlin's policy preferences to actors at lower levels. The program

---

5   The program's budget has increased sharply with every new five-year plan, also when adjusted for inflation. The budget of the current plan, about 1.7 billion roubles over five years, is certainly significant, but small in comparison to the total expenditure on military-patriotic policy.

has "inspired" the drafting of hundreds of other official programs regionally and within various state agencies (Sanina 2017). Other related large-scale projects from the past few years include the *Yunarmiia* (Young Army) youth organization, the multipurpose *Park Patriot* (Patriot Park), and a new official cemetery just outside Moscow—all created with the participation of military actors.

A chief goal of Russian official identity policy has been to increase and push to the fore the role of the *state* in every citizen's understanding of the self—to create Russian patriots and shape their individual characteristics, values, and loyalties into desired form. With this in mind, it has strived to tie the ideas of a strong state and an internationally great power to the current regime, to monopolize the concept of patriotism, and to discredit alterative visions of Russia as "unpatriotic" (see Bar-Tal 1997). Private businesses have long since jumped on the patriotic bandwagon (Norris 2011, 2012). In sum, the military patriotic theme has acquired a very significant presence in both official and everyday national culture.

To consolidate national identity based on symbols of war and the military may have particular relevance for foreign policy. Based on survey data, we know that armed conflict correlates with the Russian population's self-reported support for the political regime. The effect was hinted at by surveys following the August war against Georgia in 2008 and became much more clearly articulated following armed conflict in Ukraine from 2014 (Levada 2017). Seemingly, nothing unites the country like international confrontation and a war of limited impact on domestic affairs (see Kolesnikov 2016). While a rally-around-the-flag effect would probably be noticeable in any country, one could reasonably expect the positive effect of military confrontation to correlate with militaristic attitudes in the population. A society in which military penetration is especially high, may have greater tolerance for high military expenditures, as well as for the use of force in international and domestic conflicts (Danilova 2015: 214–16). At worst, the Crimea effect[6] suggests that Russia's rulers may resort to foreign policy aggression to shore up domestic support in times of falling legitimacy. Militaristic attitudes in the population at any rate contribute to the decision-making environment for the authorities and may thus influence decisions of huge consequence (Robertshaw 2015).[7]

To a certain degree, it makes good sense for Russian authorities to lean heavily on the military in nation building. Russian history is marked by revolutions and sharply diverging ideologies, but the military history and traditions work as a source of continuity that also transcends ethnic and religious borders. The importance of the Great Patriotic War in Russian national consciousness, the historical reliance on the military for education and indoctrination, and the securitization of traditional values—all these factors contributed to making the military a natural place to look when Boris Yeltsin's less traditional identity policy failed. The need for an epic and glorious past may be particularly salient in authoritarian states, where limited participation and economic redistribution make authorities dependent on other sources of legitimacy. In addition, the conflation of civilian and military values has proved useful to the regime in a more direct way. Traditional military values such as hierarchy, discipline, collectivism, and self-sacrifice go hand in glove with political loyalism.

At the same time, there are limits to how effective the current policy is for harnessing a common national identity or bolstering regime support. Research indicates considerable discrepancies between official and privately held conceptions of patriotism, and that state policy is often devalued among important target groups (Laruelle 2015; Goode 2016). The policy is vaguely formulated and

---

[6] The conflict and annexation of Crimea led to a surge in the self-reported support of Russians for their leadership and their Armed Forces. Also notable was an increased appreciation of everything else related to Russian state authority, such as its healthcare, education, and legal system (Levada 2017). The elevated levels of support were on most accounts maintained until 2018, when they dropped again in relation to the controversial pension reforms (the Levada Centre regularly post approval ratings on their webpage: https://www.levada.ru/en/ratings/).

sorely lacking in quality control, leading among other things to widespread instrumentalization of the patriotic infrastructure for a range of purposes (Goode 2016, Dauce et al. 2015, Sanina 2017). Even state actors involved in patriotic education in Russian schools frequently have little knowledge of official policy (Sanina 2017). Work in progress also suggests that military-patriotic ideology is more efficient for consolidating existing support groups than for bridging socio-economic, generational, demographic, and political cleavages among the Russian population. The same study, however, also suggests that the military is firmly anchored in Russian national identity, and that the typical Putin supporters overwhelmingly support military activity in the civilian sphere. Not only do they value the military's role in defending the country, in conducting international operations, and in increasing Russia's international prestige. They also cherish soldiers and military heroes as a source of pride and as positive role models for the young.[8]

Theorizing Military Impact on Nation Building

Traditionally, scholarship on nation building is structured around dichotomies like ethnic/civic, primordial/modern, and religious/secular. With regard to Russia, scholars have paid particular attention to the complexities arising from its imperial past and the ambiguous relationship between ethnic, religious, and civic understandings of the nation (e.g. Kolstø and Blakkisrud 2015). While these dimensions of national identity policy are very salient in Russia, this commonly employed approach tends to play down the significant military imprint on national identity. The rehabilitation of patriotic education in post-Soviet Russia is closely related to the Armed Forces, and the connection between traditional military values and "Russianness" is strong.

To deal with this phenomenon, I keep theoretically separate a "civilian" identity policy from a military "imprint" on this policy. Of course, no state's identity policy has ever been purely civilian in

---

[8] Bækken unpublished/forthcoming. The key evidence for these claims is a survey conducted in cooperation with ROMIR in 2018.

the sense that it has existed in complete isolation from the military realm. On the contrary, most nations have rallied around wars past and present, and conscription has been crucial to national socialization processes. The characteristics, purposes, and intensity of the military aspect in nation building, however, differ with circumstances. As concepts, militarization and militarism do not necessarily presuppose a binary approach and a before-after logic, as some critics suggest (e.g. Howell 2018). Instead, the terms can be useful for mapping out tendencies, developments, and processes. Militarization is not a state of affairs, but a direction of change.

Admittedly, military–society relations are not straightforward and cannot be reduced to simple claims about more or less military activity. Instead, the military imprint on civilian affairs can have diverse origins, purposes, and characteristics. A key tool for exploring the nature and ramifications of military influence on civil society is to distinguish between militarization and militarism. The two concepts are sometimes used interchangeably, but their theoretical separation is not new. In Stanislav Andreski's (1968: 185) definition, militarization connotes "the extensive control by the military over social life, coupled with the subservience of the whole society to the needs of the army." In another classic definition, Alfred Vagts (1959: 13) focuses on the latter element, seeing militarization (which he calls *the military way*) as a concentration of "men and materials on winning specific objectives of power." Understood as a direction or process, one could argue that Russia is remilitarizing, even if it will not return to Soviet levels anytime soon. Under Putin, Russia has refurbished its military-industrial complex, boosted its military expenditures, and engaged in costly operations abroad—presumably at the expense of its civilian economy. Though the drivers for this policy may be complex, Russia clearly shows a greater willingness to prioritize its Armed Forces than it did before 2010 (Hakvåg 2017).

The return of patriotic education in post-Soviet Russia, however, is arguably better captured in terms of militarism. Militarism (or, in Vagts' terms, the *militaristic way*), "covers every system of thinking and valuing and every complex of feelings which rank military institutions and ways above the ways of civilian life, carrying military mentality and modes of acting and decision into the civilian sphere" (Vagts 1959: 17). Militarism represents "an unquestioning embrace of military values, ethos, principles, [and] attitudes; as ranking military institutions and considerations above all others in the state; as finding the heroic predominantly in military service and action including war" (ibid.: 453). In Vagts' mind, the antonym of militarism is not pacifism, but *civilianism* (ibid.: 17). In some circumstances, the preoccupation of military institutions with militaristic rituals or practices may even harm their war-fighting capabilities. In Vagts' sense, militarism thus becomes not only separate from, but a conceptual opposite of militarization. It suggests an entirely different set of motivations and rationale behind the role of military actors, themes, and aesthetics in civilian affairs.

According to this terminology, making the military the centerpiece of a civilian identity program for social and moral purposes is a textbook example of militarism. In the patriotic discourse, soldiers are not simply glorified for their courage, sacrifice, and war-fighting capabilities—for defending Russian borders and national interests. They are also praised for their supposedly traditional "Russian" values: "The army embodies the nation" (Laruelle 2009: 188) and serves as a symbol of national continuity through political struggles. As will be made clear below, the engagement of military actors and themes in "civilian" identity policy is the continuation of a long tradition in Russia. In the Soviet Union, the Armed Forces were both an important agent of socialization and a showroom for Russianness and superior moral qualities.

The distinction between militarism and militarization therefore serves well to separate between the inward-looking and social-conservative militarism that developed in the 1990s, and the aggressive and outward-looking militarization that is sometimes attributed to today's Russia. Notably, the adaptation of militaristic policies in the 1990s did not put Russia on a war footing, since it was not followed up by extensive militarization. Today, the development of Russia has elements of both militarization and increased militarism. Part of the scholarly literature, however, has arguably neglected the latter element in Russian identity policy—the attempt to use the military for socializing Russia's youth into good citizens and human beings, unrelated to war-fighting capabilities or foreign policy goals.

The Russian Military and Soviet Identity Policy

While the first generation of Bolsheviks rejected military patriotism as reactionary (Rapoport 2012: 82), it soon became a prominent feature of Soviet ideology. Throughout history, the Russian military has been much more than a war machine. Various activities—such as public celebrations of military achievements of the past, the massive production of war-related fiction, the extensive practice of military patronage (*shefstvo*) in secondary education, and military exercises and indoctrination in the massive communist youth organizations—made military affairs an important and formative part of everyday life for Soviet youth. The Soviet military also took care of orphans and organized military sports camps and cadet schools (Sieca-Kozlowski 2010). By means of its multiple activities, significant ideological exposure, and not least its huge number of conscripts, the Red Army arguably became "the most important institution of social and ideological processing of the population" (Gudkov 2006: 41). It maintained a Marxist-Leninist façade, and even became a key symbol of the Soviet Union domestically and internationally. Yet, it was simultaneously an important carrier of tradition and historical continuity. Ironically, no modern world power at the time could compete with the Soviet army in terms of epaulettes and velvet lapels (Garthoff 1986: 250).

Under Brezhnev, the ideological role of the Red Army escalated and military-patriotic values soon became a "cornerstone of the official Soviet ethos" (Simes 1981: 141). The 1967 military service law replaced the first year of mandatory service with civilian-military preparation at secondary school, including rifle-handling, marching, and military tactics, as well as history and patriotic education (Odom 1976, Rakowska-Harmstone 1979). In the same period, membership of the Volunteer Society for Cooperation with the Army, Aviation, and Navy (DOSAAF), which conducted many of the same activities, mushroomed into seven- or even eight-digit numbers (Odom 1976: 44–45). Brezhnev officially declared the victory over Nazi Germany in 1945 to be the greatest achievement of Soviet socialism. When the military-patriotic infrastructure of the Soviet Union was eventually dismantled, the ideas and practices could easily be revived a few years later when the ideological transformation went astray. Both policy makers and local implementers in today's Russia typically belong to the generation shaped by this experience under Brezhnev, and today's practices in large part resemble those of the 1970s (Sanina 2017).

Multi-Faceted Crisis and the Collapse of the Military-Patriotic Complex

When the *glasnost'* policies expanded in the late 1980s, military patriotism was increasingly discredited. When the communist regime eventually collapsed, everything associated with the old ideology became tainted. In the first half of the 1990s, transitional politics of reform, demilitarization, democratization, and "westernization" drowned out traditionalist voices. In this period, the term "patriotism" once again dropped out of fashion and became associated with ageing communists and right-wing nationalists (Sperling 2009). The new constitution of 1993 banned state ideology, and the new leaders had no wish to engage in large scale nation building along the lines of promoting heroic historical narratives (Smith 2002). Departing from Soviet traditions, the attempts at active nation-building policies in the early 1990s were limited, ambiguous, contradictory, and ineffective for creating a sense of unity within the country (Shevel 2011). Besides the *ad hoc* projects of enthusiasts, patriotic education was largely confined to a special department at the Ministry of Defense, which organized patriotic education within the Armed Forces but hardly influenced civilian politics until years later.

As it turned out, Russia's ideological transition became just as confused as the economic or political. Failed attempts at nation building coincided with a wave of social problems that flooded the new Russian Federation and opened the way for a traditionalist counter-reform agenda. With liberalization came elections and new freedoms, but also an increase in prostitution, drugs, youth crime, corruption, and pornography. Attempts at propagating the good of the reforms and underpinning them ideologically were hopelessly inadequate to cushion their negative effects in the lives of the ordinary Russians. Instead, the extensive crisis came to instill negative and long-lasting associations with most ideas and concepts that were used to justify it. In the turmoil, Soviet nostalgia became widespread and produced a longing for safety and predictability. Even if they were sidelined in the early 1990s, the traditionalists were far from marginal in quantitative terms. Traditionalist forces contributed to numerous non-partisan organizations to save the country from new and "alien" values. More importantly, significant political parties like the KPRF, LDPR, and Our Home is Russia all rallied around a patriotic-traditionalist banner (Laruelle 2009).

At the margins of mainstream politics, military values were thus rehabilitated. The social and economic uncertainty contributed to this development in several ways. First, it produced a disenchantment with the "new" and "western" ideas, and thus caused a relapse to conservativism and nostalgia, which in the Russian case involves a stronger reliance on the military in both domestic and international affairs. Second, through its association with security, stability, and continuity, the military became a symbol of steadfastness in a wider sense than simply guarding the borders. It was a fortress of traditions and moral integrity, at least in its own eyes. A persistent securitization of national identity made this image particularly salient (Østbø 2016; Bækken 2017). Notably, the military institution managed to retain considerable popular support at an abstract level, even in times when few were willing to serve or send their sons to serve (Danilova 2015: 143).

The Armed Forces also suffered greatly under appalling economic and social conditions. Low education levels, discipline, and morale combined with high rates of corruption, theft, and *dedovshchina*, the infamous initiation rituals of new recruits (Herspring 1995). As the military's welfare and payment systems collapsed, the army faced mass retirements of junior and mid-level officers, and draft turnout declined dangerously. As of 1993, as many as half of the enlisted personnel positions were vacated, and dozens of soldiers deserted daily (Mendeloff 1994). The crisis, both within the armed forces and in society as a whole, spurred a patriotic counter-strike within military circles, not least among officials in military academies and in the Ministry of Defense. It was these initiatives that would eventually lead up to an official state program of patriotic education under Putin.

The Russian Military and the Rebirth of Patriotic Education

In late 1992, the Russian Ministry of Defense convened a roundtable on the social crises and lack of patriotism, chaired by then Deputy Minister Vasilii Mironov and with various specialists present. According to the Deputy Minister, the participants agreed with his conception that Russia needed "a scientific concept of education for future defenders of the motherland" (*Krasnaia zvezda* 1992). For this purpose, they laid plans for establishing an inter-agency commission *(ibid.)*. Mironov also compiled a report in which he focused on how to counter the growing "ideological disorder" (*ideinyi razbrod*) (Popov 1993). In the following years, Mironov promoted patriotic education through a series of interviews and articles in Russian media. In a two-part article in *Vestnik voennoi informatsii* named "We Should Raise Patriots" (1994a, 1994b), he formulated his opinion in clear terms. Not only did Mironov highlight the need for a more structured approach to patriotic education in the Armed Forces, but he also argued for the creation of a broader state program. "We need a deeply thoughtful and well-founded state policy in this field," he asserted, "the basis of which could be a corresponding federal program, prepared by the contribution of all branches of power, science, and civil society" (1994b). "Military-patriotic education," Mironov maintained, "is an issue for the whole state" *(ibid.)*. The same year, Mironov also presented a report on patriotic education to a special collegium within the ministry, which reportedly discussed the ongoing social processes in the country with great alarm (*Krasnaia zvezda* 1994).

Although there were at the time certain other initiatives which aimed at formalizing patriotic education at the federal level

(Tkachenko 2011), the military assumed leadership of these developments. For Pavel Grachev, Minister of Defense and General in the Russian Army, it was important to underscore that it was the Ministry of Defense that initiated the rebirth of patriotic education. In an interview, Grachev played up the military-patriotic link:

> More than anyone, the Army is aware of the danger of this degradation of spirits to us all, the neglect of patriotism and of ideas of serving the Fatherland. It is our duty to give a serious impulse on this important matter. It is a question of the spiritual health of society. It is a question of the Army's war-readiness and the security of the state (quoted in *Krasnaia zvezda 1994*).

At this point in time, the Ministry of Defense was surfing a wave of resurgent traditionalist patriotism in Russian politics and society. In the 1995 elections, the above-mentioned parties won a clear majority in the Duma.[9] For Yeltsin's camp, it became evident that his ideological platform had serious shortcomings in the eyes of a disillusioned electorate. In subsequent years, the Kremlin shifted towards a more centrist and consensus-seeking approach, not least with regard to national identity policy. In the process of recalibrating his political platform, Yeltsin made concessions to the Russian military and veterans by reintroducing military parades on Victory Day and supporting the further development of patriotic education inside and outside the Armed Forces (*Krasnaia zvezda* 1996).

An exact timeline of the various drafts and policymaking processes leading up to adoption of the State Program is not easy to draw. In an interview with *Na boevom postu* in 1998, the key policymaker Vladimir Lutovinov claimed that a first draft for an official "concept" (*kontseptsiia*) of patriotic education existed already in 1989, although "very far [from the 1998 version] in both form and content" (Ol'shevich 1998). According to the same source, a working group was set up in 1997 under Lieutenant-General

---

[9] Despite their differences, the three most successful parties were all buying into patriotic narratives. The Duma was thus dominated by the Communist Party (157 seats), Our Home is Russia (55 seats), and the so-called Liberal Democratic Party of Russia (51 seats). The more genuinely liberal democratic party, Yabloko, secured 45 seats.

Aleksandr Sinaiskii, leader of the University Department for Educational and Scientific Work at the Ministry of Defense, to formulate a draft "concept of patriotic education" *(ibid.)*. The Russian scholar V. Tkachenko (2011) mentions a *State Program for the Patriotic Education of Adolescents* that was developed in 1995/96, while another source from 1994 mentions a program bearing the same name, already under consideration by the government (Kovalev 1994). Lutovinov himself was also working on a draft state program on "patriotic education for youth," well before the Sinaiskii group was established (see Lutovinov 1998).[10] In this same general period, civilian and military authorities were developing regional programs of patriotic education (Sieca-Kozlowski 2010). By 1998, a significant number of Russian ministries and state agencies had engaged in projects of patriotic education, even if limited in scope and ambition (Lutovinov 1998: 227). To coordinate these and other initiatives and prepare the ground for a full-scale program, the state agency *Rosvoentsentr*[11] was set up in 1997 under the leadership of Yurii Kviatkovskii—a military professional with the rank of vice-admiral.

Whatever the exact drafts and procedures, the *Concept of Military-Patriotic Education for Adolescents* was completed and published in 1998 by a group of three authors working for a state body with a lengthy name: the Coordination Council under the President of the Russian Federation on Educational Work in the Armed Forces, Other Armed Units, Formations, and Organs. Vladimir Kulakov and the above-mentioned Lutovinov, then respectively head and deputy head of the Department for Patriotic

---

[10] Some or all of these authors may be referring to the subprogram *Development of Civic-Mindedness and Patriotism among Russian Youth* under the above-mentioned *Youths of Russia* program (see Tkachenko 2011). Others may have been alluding to unofficial or semi-official draft documents that did not appear online, such as the draft state program of 1996–2000 appearing as an appendix to Lutovinov's (1998) dissertation.

[11] The Russian State Military Historical-Cultural Center of the Government of the Russian Federation (Rosvoentsentr) was established on the foundations of a historical-cultural center for the Russian navy, headed by the same Kviatkovskii. Its webpage (http://www.rosvoencentr-rf.ru/o-rosvoentsentre/) became inactive a few years after they lost responsibility for coordinating the program.

Education at the Ministry of Defense, joined Sinaiskii to co-author the concept. This 1998 Concept has received little, if any, attention in English-language analysis. As its name suggests, it focused on adolescents, primarily with a view to boosting recruitment to the Armed Forces. At the same time, it had an explicit dual purpose of furthering the interests of the military and society alike (Kulakov, Lutovinov, and Sinaiskii 1998).

The same year as the concept of military-patriotic education was published, a Duma commission was set up to "unify and coordinate forces to activate the participation of society in the moral and military-patriotic upbringing of the young generation" (*Postanovlenie* 1998). Duma deputy Tarasov, who was in charge of the temporary commission to set up the state program in 1998, was a member of the Communist Party and an outspoken traditionalist.[12] Among his ambitions for the federal program was to facilitate "the spiritual-moral rebirth and consolidation of society" (*Suvorovskii Natisk* 1998). By November that year, a new concept had reportedly been through a considerable review process with federation subjects, ministries, and agencies, as well as a range of other organizations (*Suvorovskii Natisk* 1998). By all indicators, this same document was finally published as the *Concept of Patriotic Education for Russian Citizens* in 2003. The authors were a group headed by Kviatkovskii, the head of Rosvoentsentr. Lutovinov also participated, seemingly to decisive effect (see below). The 2003 concept had a much greater impact than its predecessor and became subject to academic analyses in international and peer-reviewed journals (e.g. Sperling 2003; Rapoport 2009).

When the 2001 five-year plan and the 2003 concept were released Putin had already been Russian president for some time. In many accounts of patriotic education, these documents mark the start of patriotic education in post-Soviet Russia. Yet while the 2003 concept stole all the limelight, in fact, it overlaps considerably with

---

[12] Tarasov served as deputy for the Communist Party fraction, and later became a member of the national-traditionalist organization Spiritual Heritage (*Dukhovnoe nasledie*) as well as the founder of the similarly minded organization Slavic Fortress (*Slavianskii posad*).

the previous concept. The documents are rather similar with regard to aims, content, and style. Moreover, a digital plagiarism tool reveals several identical phrases, and some whole paragraphs are very much alike. Lutovinov's participation in both author groups may explain the similarities. A review of patriotic policy documents from before and after the year 2000, shows no clear indication that the Russian presidents influenced them to any notable degree. Instead, the conceptual foundation for official patriotism seems heavily influenced by Lutovinov's personal perspectives (see Lutovinov 1998: 22-23). As we shall see below, both Lutovinov and others had broad visions for Russia's patriotic revival, extending far beyond military purposes.

The Military's Motivation for Promoting Patriotism

As mentioned above, military-patriotic education has traditionally been closely related to preparations for war. Rifle-handling and military games have gone hand in hand with ideological preparation in secondary education (Sanina 2017). Indeed, patriotic education is for a large part "a code phrase that implies military education, military training, and military preparation" (Rapoport 2012: 99). When the patriotic education was taking form in the 1990s and early 2000s, the Russian Armed Forces faced serious problems of an organizational and technical nature—not least highlighted by their poor performance in the First Chechen War (1994-96). The massive and conservative organization long proved resistant to reform, and problems were still evident in the short war against Georgia in 2008 (Renz 2012). Combat ineffectiveness correlated with widespread corruption, abuse, and poor material conditions, all contributing to defections and draft dodging. In the decade between 1982 and 1992, the percentage of conscripts that considered military service "an honorable duty" fell from 70 to 20 per cent (Danilova 2015: 142). As late as 2007, a survey indicated that only three per cent of Russian youth considered military service a "prestigious" profession, which was the lowest result in comparison with other occupations in the survey (*ibid.:* 181). It should not be surprising, then, that the State Program has been linked to the effort to recreate Russia as a military great power. By recruiting more and better soldiers, limiting corruption, and boosting morale within the Armed Forces, patriotic education could in theory boost military performance, which was indeed also one of its declared aims.

As Nataliya Danilova notes (2015: 180), studies of patriotic education in Russia have often emphasized the potential effect upon military preparedness. Marlène Laruelle (2009: 177), for instance, insists that the primary goal of patriotic education is "to reconcile draftees with their army." Similarly, Valerie Sperling (2009: 218) claims in one article that Putin's "reasons to rely on a militarized patriotism were straightforward. Russia's army ... hoped that such a campaign would enlist more soldiers into its ranks." Danilova (2015: 180–81) moderates this claim by pointing to the lack of policy success, and notes that the recruitment crisis did not end until almost a decade later. Yet, lack of efficiency does not equal a lack of ambition. In what follows, I therefore consider the arguments policymakers and other military actors used to promote the State Program when it was still under drafting. While the recruitment aspect indeed was one of the motivations behind it, the story behind post-Soviet patriotic education is certainly more complex. In particular, I will highlight how military actors have advocated the program as an instrument to promote their traditionalist worldview and social conservative agenda. My claim is not that moral and social concerns were the only considerations behind the program's promotion. My review of military periodicals from the time, however, suggests that these considerations were stressed to a degree at least equal to those of military security. The advocates of patriotic education repeatedly declared that civilian authorities had so far inadequately addressed the social and moral issues facing Russia; as one such advocate had it, "society is sick with non-spirituality [bezdukhovnost'], and the best remedy is patriotism" (Chupakhin 1994). In this regard, my findings support those of Elisabeth Sieca-Kozlowski (2010: 74), whose interviewees stressed patriotic education as a means to save children from "drugs, criminality and delinquency" and the influence of contemporary television.

Already in the late Soviet period, one could discern a trend of increasing attention paid in military periodicals to social issues as well as imperial history (Rumer 1994). Reportedly, "the organic unity of Russian military tradition and the spirit of the Russian state" was a popular theme at the time (*ibid.*: 10). The nationalist writer Aleksandr Prokhanov, for instance, argued that the military represented "the core of Russian society and state, a core that will carry the state's tradition throughout the upcoming crises and will serve as the basis of its restoration in the future" (*ibid.*). Many individuals within the military establishment were sharply critical of the liberalization agenda represented by Mikhail Gorbachev and later by Yeltsin. Even if the majority of the officer corps remained staunchly against political interference (Taylor 2003), this did not mean that all military actors shunned social engagement or masked their distinct ideological leanings.

Deputy Defense Minister Mironov's articles in *Vestnik voennoi informatsii* in 1994 represent an early call by a high-ranking Russian official for a broadly constituted patriotic education program. In these articles, Mironov worried about the poor state of recruits. The quality of the draftees, he lamented, was suffering under the rise of alcoholism, drug abuse, and youth crime in society, as well as under the recruits' low education and poor physical condition. From this point of departure, his argument quickly expanded: The whole of society would benefit from a patriotic education program, as it would serve as a remedy for the population's poor "spiritual health" (Mironov 1994a). In a manner typical to the national-patriotic discourse in Russia, the Deputy Minister proceeded to lash out against the cultural and moral decay of Russian society. The removal of military-patriotic content from education and culture, he contended, had led to the "depletion of primordial Russian spiritual values" and produced a moral vacuum that was now being filled with "low-grade propaganda of violence and sex" (Mironov 1994b).

In a number of articles, officials and policy makers within the military echoed Mironov's take on the desperate state of their motherland, and also shared his hopes that patriotic education might make things right. The liberal reforms had destroyed everything without building anything new, one argued.[13] His assessment of contemporary Russia was merciless: The behavior of Russian youth was but "an intuitive response to the spiritual and moral garbage in the midst of which they are living" (Kovalev 1994). Another officer agreed to the point of plagiarism,[14] upset by the moral policies of the liberal reformers, which had allegedly purged education plans for "everything that taught the young generation to love the Fatherland" (Bogdanov 1996). To strengthen Russian statehood, he maintained, the country was entirely dependent upon "military-patriotic ideas" *(ibid.)*. "The recent pacifistic euphoria has borne bitter fruits for Russia," a regional patriotic education leader stated in an interview in one year later (Pinchuk 1997). In his mind, the loss of "heroic-patriotic education" and preliminary military training had led to poor health, lack of spirit, and illiteracy among Russian youth *(ibid.)*. When patriotic education and Soviet-era wargames disappeared, another writer claimed, the youth started to make their living as racketeers and hitmen (Pasiakin 1997). For these writers, patriotic education seemed to symbolize everything they found good about the Brezhnev system, such as stability, law and order, a functioning education and welfare system—and certainly moral decency. Thus, their arguments can reasonably be seen as a nostalgic response to the contemporary developments.

In the late 1990s, when the first official policy documents were appearing, key policymakers legitimized patriotic education in a similar fashion. Even in the military press, where one would expect military matters to be given priority, they repeatedly stressed the issue of public morals. When a journalist pressed Lutovinov on why Russia wanted to return to a Soviet-style military-patriotic education, the Russian military academician legitimized it in the following fashion:

---

[13] Given the sparse information provided by *Krasnaia zvezda*, it is hard to verify the author's (military?) identity. It seems probable, however, that he is the same Aleksandr Kovalev that headed the education/upbringing department of the Red Army Automobile Construction College (KAKS-RANKHiGS).

[14] Several paragraphs of Bogdanov's text are unattributed reproductions from Kovalev's article two years earlier.

> [The youth environment] is swamped in drugs, prostitution, and crime. The family is less influential in the upbringing of youth. The 2.5 million homeless children in Russia bear testimony to this. Could we possibly leave them without attention and upbringing? ... And take contemporary pop-culture. It has in many ways a destructive influence on the mind, the youths' spirit—shaping [them into] faceless robots of consumer society. In aggressive television broadcasting [we can witness] the virtual zombification of Generation Pepsi,[15] as I call it (Ol'shevich 1998).

Lutovinov's academic works (1997; 1998) leave little doubt as to where his chief interests lie. Here, he underscored patriotic education's societal impact, and mentioned the potential benefit for the Armed Forces only in passing. In his dissertation (1998), Lutovinov warned against the influence of pro-western "pseudo values" (*ibid.*: 19) and a reorientation in society towards "individualism, thingism, snobbism, sexual dissoluteness, drug abuse, theft, prostitution, [and] homosexuality" (*ibid.*: 230). "The real power and attraction of patriotism as a value," he maintained, "lies within its spiritual-moral component" (*ibid.*: 256). Moreover, Lutovinov explicitly presented official patriotism as a counterforce to "anti-traditional and anti-Russian ... liberal-democratic ideology" which he saw as a threat to Russian collective values and national specificity (*ibid.*: 248–50). The poor state of Russian patriotism threatened to lead "not only to the loss of state authority, but also to irreversible processes of societal degeneration, the self-destruction and possible death of the Russian Federation as an independent state" (Lutovinov 1999). General-Lieutenant Kulakov (1999), one of Lutovinov's co-authors of the 1998 Concept, has expressed similar concerns for the moral degradation of Russian youth.

To summarize, when discussing patriotic education policy, the authors printed in the Russian military press typically focused on the ongoing crisis in Russian society, and often specified which moral vices they saw as especially troubling. The authors presented

---

[15] The term *Generation Pepsi* was made famous by Viktor Pelevin in the opening sequence of the book *Generation P* from 1999, but was evidently used before this date to signify the generation that chose the path of consumerism and foreign brands.

these vices as evils in themselves, and also as the foundation for the social ills with which Russia was plagued. Many also blamed liberal policies under Yeltsin in explicit terms, and called for a return to "Russianness" in a traditional sense. For problems big and small, patriotic education was presented as the universal remedy. In some articles, the authors connected moral issues to the quality of recruits to the Armed Forces, suggesting that patriotic education could help forge a social identity that would be useful in the conduct of war. Just as often, however, they stressed the benefits for society *per se*. The framing, language, and rhetoric of their arguments give a strong indication of a passionate traditionalist worldview and a resolute will to roll back harmful Western influences on Russian minds. More than anything, the call for patriotism was dominated by fathers disappointed and alarmed by the decadence of their sons.

Moral Security and Traditionalism in Patriotic Education Policy

The above review of the origins of patriotic education reveals how important military traditionalism and a notion of crisis was in shaping the arguments in favor of reintroducing large-scale patriotic education policies to post-communist Russia. One also needs to ask what real effect this had in the form of actual policies. Arguably, the debates of the 1990s entrenched patriotic education as a militarist bastion and carved out a place for it within the civilian realm. Even today, the field remains completely dominated by militaristic ideology, using the heroic imagery of the military for all that it is worth. Even if state policy gradually focuses less on the notion of an ongoing crisis, the alarmism and a sense of ideological threat is persistent. The most direct and tangible legacy of the debates and arguments discussed above, however, is the policy documents that have provided the conceptual core for patriotic education policy for the entire Putin era to date.

The first, and relatively unknown, 1998 Concept of Military-Patriotic Education took a broad approach to patriotism and set the standard for the years to come. This Concept linked patriotism to the "education of key spiritual-moral and cultural-historical values, reflecting the specific formation and development of our society and state, national self-consciousness, ways of life, the worldview and fate of Russians." The authors repeatedly linked these broad reflections to the making of an ideal soldier, yet also underscored how "the improvement of qualitative characteristics of contemporary youth can positively affect society as a whole" and to "an enormous degree," contribute to the "rebirth of Russia." The 1998 Concept aimed explicitly at overcoming the "period of crisis" in Russia's "historical development" (Kulakov, Lutovinov, and Sinaiskii 1998).

When the full-fledged State Program appeared under President Putin, it was no less replete with references to the spiritual revival of Russia and to purposes otherwise unrelated to war. The 2003 Concept took a broad approach and framed patriotism as having the potential to provide a boost to Russia's "spiritual health" and promote a "unified civil society." The first five-year plan of 2001 was explicitly framed as anti-crisis policy, to counter widespread "indifference, egoism, individualism, cynicism, unmotivated aggression, and disrespectful attitudes to state and social institutions" (Gospatriotprogramma 2001). The second plan (2006–2010) sought to establish patriotism as the "core spiritual component" of the country. Its three main goals concerned spiritual and cultural development, economic consolidation, and increasing Russia's international authority. Here, the relative lack of stated military aims is striking (Gospatriotprogramma 2006). In the third five-year plan (2011–2015), however, the military goals returned. A sense of crisis was still visible in the aims to *restore* Russian spirituality and *secure* and *stabilize* the country (Gospatriotprogramma 2010).

In 2014, Putin called for patriotic education to encompass new "really interesting, dynamic and relevant initiatives" for adults and youth alike (in Danilova 2015: 183). Perhaps as a response to this message, the publication of the fourth and current five-year plan in 2015 marked a shift in the style and framing of patriotic education policy in Russia. The lack of clear information at the time, however, caused confusion among observers. Rosvoentsentr seemingly interpreted Putin's advice as a call for a totalitarian turn, and produced a new and updated version for the next five years.[16] This document was also published on a semi-official webpage.[17]

Rosvoentsentr's version was eventually turned down, however, and it was a different version (but bearing the same name) that was actually adopted by governmental decree in December 2015 (Gospatriotprogramma 2015a). This version was developed by Rosmolodezh—a governmental agency for youth politics.[18] Rospatriottsentr, a subdepartment of Rosmolodezh, is officially the "operator" (*operator*) of the plan. Rosvoentsentr, the old coordinator, now plays a negligible role. Compared with previous plans, there is a lack of lofty references to morals, spirits, and similar terms. Furthermore, the sense of urgency and social crisis has been downplayed. For anyone intimate with the image of Rosvoentsentr, the shift in style should be obvious. In large part, Rospatriottsentr's personnel consists of relatively young civilians; their leader, Kseniia Razuvaeva, is a woman in her thirties. The web designs of the two agencies also suggest completely different orientations. Whereas the Rosvoentsentr webpage (rosvoencentr-rf.ru) is largely a bureaucratic database of reports, legal acts, and documents, Rospatriottsentr (rospatriotcentr.ru) offers a professionally designed webpage full of pictures, videos, and stories for its readers to explore. The online media content of Rospatriottsentr (as of 2018) downplays the military

---

[16] If Russia had indeed adopted the Rosvoentsentr draft, it would have given patriotic education policy a significant slant in an authoritarian or even totalitarian direction. The draft Concept calls upon Russians to sacrifice life and health for the undefined "interests" of the Fatherland, and seeks to mobilize all state and society actors in the service of bolstering patriotism and fighting unpatriotic expressions. Traditionalist militarist arguments emerge in the fight against "individual norms alien to the Russian," and for the protection of Russian culture and traditions. The document also stresses more strongly than preceding plans the ambition to increase military capabilities by means of patriotic education (Gospatriotprogramma 2015b).

[17] The document was published at http://gospatriotprogramma.ru, a website which was finally liquidated in late 2017.

[18] The full names of Rosmolodezh and Rospatriottsentr are the Federal Agency of Youth Affairs (FADM) and the Russian Center for Civic and Patriotic Education of Children and Youth, respectively. In 2018 the agency was moved from the Ministry of Education and Science and put under the direct supervision of the Russian government.

aspect more than the State Program would suggest. Rospatriottsentr's short summaries, presumably representing the center's distillate of the plan intended for a broader audience, do the same. In the official five-year plan and in the list of supported activities, however, the military imprint is both persistent and pervasive (see below). Despite its new wrapping, with less authoritarian language and a more modern style, the new operator is essentially marketing the same package as its predecessor. The new wrapping may therefore be the most important signal for the future development of patriotic education in Russia. Considering the skepticism of Russian youth about toward the bureaucratic outlook of patriotic education (see Daucé et al. 2015, Goode 2016), the shift seemingly signals renewed efforts to modernize its image and make it more appealing to the youth of today.

Military Objectives, Themes, and Agency in Patriotic Education

Figure 1. Percentage of all articles in Russian periodicals in 1997–2018 containing the phrase "patriotic education," categorized as "military" or "civilian" periodicals.

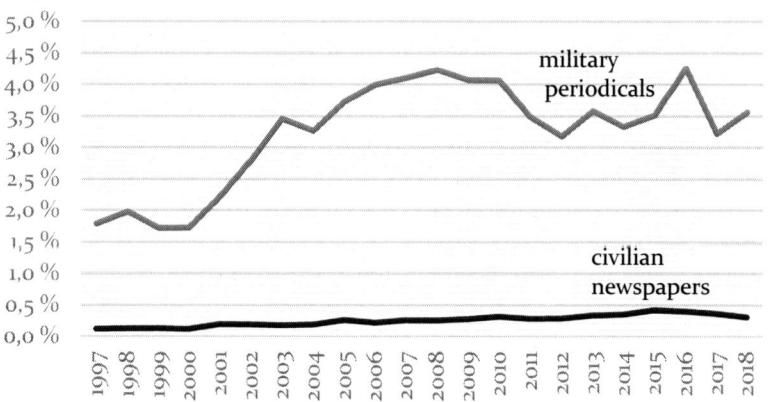

Source: Based on data from the Eastview databases.[19]

---

[19] Based on Eastview's categorization of "military and security periodicals" and "central newspapers." The timeframe is delimited by the available material in

Even though it was adopted partly for civilian purposes, and even if the State Program has recently acquired a more civilian-looking "operator," patriotic education remains a predominantly military term (see Figure 1). As a Russian officer put it, the notions of "army and patriotism are linked to each other like [Siamese] twins and cannot exist without each other" (Semenikhina 1999). Though the lion's share of funding from the State Program goes to the Ministries of Culture and Education, military actors are directly involved in the Program's implementation. The Ministry of Defense remains one of the most important partners of the Program, and military actors have also been directly involved in large-scale military patriotic projects such as the *Yunarmiia* (Young Army) youth organization, the new Federal Military Memorial Cemetary (Gabowitsch 2016), and the spectacles at the recently opened *Park Patriot*. They are also involved in everyday patriotic education at the local level. Recently, there has been an increased focus on military patronage (*shefstvo*) in secondary education, set to give the military institutions additional influence in the school system (Gospatriotprogramma 2015a). Veterans are often invited into schools (Sanina 2017), and frequently lead or participate in extra-curricular arrangements like military patriotic clubs (Laruelle 2015). They also act as organizers of activities under the State Program (Sieca-Kozlowski 2015). Moreover, when civil authorities plan and arrange patriotic activities, the responsible state officials often have military background even if they are not in uniform. Kathy Rousselet's (2015) article on, amongst other subjects, patriotic education and veteran priests in the Russian Orthodox Church, may serve as an illustration of how integrated military figures are in everyday practices.

In the two early concepts of patriotic education, the military purpose of patriotic education was highlighted, but hardly drowned out the other objectives and perspectives. Perhaps more striking, then, is the distinctly military *content* of patriotic education plans. Importantly, this is also the case with the most recent Rosmolodezh

---

this database, containing 5.1 million articles in 156 periodicals from this period. Exact numbers may vary over time, since Eastview's access to journals is not permanent.

edition. In the current five-year plan, words derived from "military," "war," and "martial" (*voenn*/voin**) occur 43 times on the 14 pages of large-font policy text. This comes in addition to the events financed under the program, which include war commemoration and repatriation groups, military exhibitions, war games and re-enactments, Victory celebrations, meetings with veterans, and a range of military-patriotic club activities. The most recent event list devotes a designated subsection to "Cossack activities" (*kazachestvo*) and eight out of ten media projects are clearly military in focus. Of the anniversaries supported, a majority concerns military figures like Zhukov or Kalashnikov (Gospatriotprogramma 2015a). The state-driven commemoration of the Great Patriotic War dominates both the five-year plans, and military patriotic policies in general. In Danilova's (2015: 182) words, the war has been transformed into a "master narrative of the Russian identity."

Insofar as the political leadership continues to embrace patriotism, it also embraces the importance of military values to civilian life and a reliance on the military for nation building. Russian authorities envisage Russia's military traditions as a primary driver of national pride, and soldiers as the chief example for today's patriots to emulate. Their fighting capabilities aside, the Armed Forces are seen as a valuable reservoir of people of superior moral qualities, and veterans are expected to "inspire heroic acts in the younger generation" (Sieca-Kozlowski 2010: 79). As frontliners of a Russian identity under siege, the burden put on their shoulders reminds us of soldiers under Brezhnev, who in his time as Soviet leader called upon the war veterans to suppress "signs of individualistic, consumerist orientation" among the youth (in Kucherenko 2011). Within this militaristic frame of mind, the perfect soldier is also the perfect citizen. Thus, the military is not only a beneficiary of the program, but is also used as a means to greater ends. Military aims and military means should not be conflated, even if the policy does contain both.

Military Patriotism and Traditionalism in Putin's Russia

Figure 2. Percentage of articles in Russian newspapers and periodicals that contain the phrase "patriotic education" (left y-axis), and "patriot*" (wildcard) (right y-axis) in the years 1998-2001.

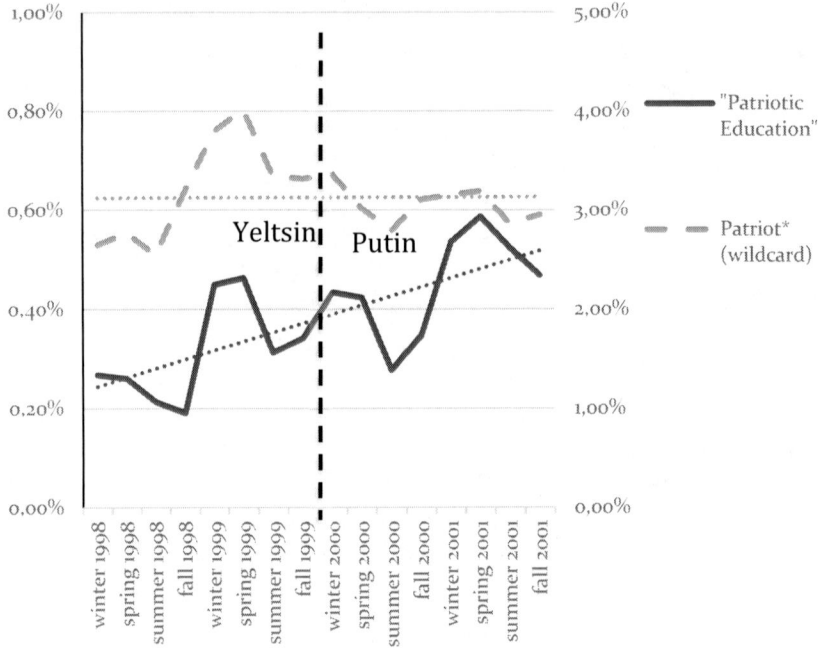

Source: Based on data from the Eastview databases.

In his first two terms as president, Putin consistently advocated a strong and sovereign state and marked a clear distance from his predecessor. By persistent efforts, the Putin administration eventually succeeded in wresting control of the "patriotic brand," previously an important ideological tool of Kremlin's traditionalist and nationalistic opposition (Laruelle 2009). As part of its co-optation of nationalist forces, military traditionalists were tolerated and even allowed to influence official policy. Part of his plan for Russia's revival was a more positive relationship with its past. Putin reinvigorated old state symbols, and championed Russia's cultural and ideological sovereignty. He also took a personal lead in elevating the memory of the Great Patriotic War to its former glory (Wood 2011). In this reorientation toward the past, the military and patriotic education were to play key roles. This does *not* however mean that the Putin regime invented patriotic education.

In Sperling's (2009: 218) account of patriotic education, "Putin's reign brought about a concerted effort to renew patriotic sentiment," and his regime "chose" to anchor these efforts in the Armed Forces and in the 1941–45 war against Nazi Germany. Douglas W. Blum (2006: 1–2) suggests that the new President "quickly moved" to establish the State Program, and Anna Sanina (2018) that the project was developed "in a hurry." Ekatarina Khodzhaeva (2017) explicitly claims that the first State Program was developed during Putin's presidency, and Francoise Daucé and colleagues (2015) leave the same impression. Indeed, explicit or implicit suggestions that the State Program was developed on Putin's initiative seem to be entirely commonplace. [20] As documented above, however, the development of a State Program was underway well before Putin emerged as a political force. Perhaps also in contrast with conventional wisdom, Putin's coming to power did not result in a sudden eruption of patriotic awareness in public debates. In fact, the numbers compiled in Figure 2 suggest that the press discussed patriotism more often in the Russian press in 1999 than in the year 2000. One could speculate whether the numbers for 1999 were inflated by the beginning of Russian military operations in Chechnya, perhaps leading to a patriotic surge. Searches on the Eastview databases, however, indicate that the war in fact carried greater impact on the figures for the year 2000.[21] As indicated by Figure 2, the term "patriotic education" appeared more frequently in 2001, but this growth was largely limited to military

---

[20] This is not to suggest that Sperling, Sanina, or others reject the emergence of patriotic initiatives in the late 1990s. They do, however, credit Putin's regime for the emergence of an official state program.

[21] The percentage of articles containing "patriot*" (*=wildcard) that also contained the phrase "Chechnya" was greatest for the year 2000 (18%), and about equal for the years 1999 (13%) and 2001 (12%),

periodicals and presumably related to the launching of the first five-year plan this year.

Instead of rushing to embrace patriotic education, Putin's adaptation of patriotic ideas was gradual and largely a continuation of late Yeltsin policy. Despite his considerable adjustment of Yeltsin's liberal position and his embrace of patriotism as a foundation for Russian identity, Putin's approach to politics long remained pragmatic and managerial, rather than ideological. It was not until the "morality turn" in Putin's third term from 2012 that traditionalism became a central legitimizing discourse for the regime (Laruelle 2014; Sharafutdinova 2014). In just a few years, social conservativism rose on the official agenda, becoming more visible and politicized than ever before in post-Soviet Russia. As part of this development, and certainly since the Crimea annexation in 2014, patriotism was elevated as close to a state ideology as it could get within constitutional limits. By 2018, the policy of patriotic education, which initially seemed to be a concession to the military traditionalist camp, seems a more or less natural part of Russian officialdom. In a sense, official patriotism seems headed into a new phase. Whereas the attention paid to both patriotic education and patriotism in general has actually been falling in Russian mass media recently (Figure 1), patriotism has conquered the legal realm where its inclusion in legal documents is on a sharp rise (Khodzhaeva 2017).

The crisis of the post-communist transition still haunts Russian national consciousness and influences political choice and rhetoric. Putin's political project has largely been legitimized precisely by virtue of its representing a counter position to both the commonly disliked Yeltsin regime and Russia's Western rivals, weaving several popular themes into a larger, pro-regime story of Russia and the world. In traditionalist-patriotic discourse, references to the West serve at least two purposes. First, the decadent and hypocritical West is cited to illustrate values purportedly alien to Russia—and to serve as an example of what Russia is *not* and should not become (Sharafutdinova 2017). Second, Russian traditionalism and military patriotism are associated with the belief that liberal influence in Russia can be traced back to anti-

Russian forces and even foreign intelligence. Liberals or critics may thus be framed as unpatriotic or even as foreign agents involved in ideological warfare. The hegemonic discourse in Russia today treats "spiritual-moral values" as "self-evident, eternal, absolute, and unchangeable—but also something that is under attack and must be protected" (Østbø 2016: 2). Both patriotic education and the more recent "morality turn" in official discourse thus serve to legitimate the regime not only as the moral champion of traditions and social conservativism at home and abroad but also as a bulwark against existential threats to Russian national identity. Given this securitized understanding of national identity, a reliance on security actors is only to be expected.

Conclusions

In post-Soviet Russia, like in the Soviet Union about 70 years earlier, state patriotism was initially discredited, then gradually reintroduced by means of militarist traditionalism. The process of officially rehabilitating patriotic education was relatively quick— from Mironov's first roundtable at the Ministry of Defense to the appointment of Tarasov's commission, it only took six years. In this period, the political leadership in practice moved to introduce a military identity concept for nation building. While recruitment of more and better soldiers to serve in the Armed Forces was, and still is, part of the programmatic aims, and while the policy may also serve to back up popular support for military spending and operations, this merely constitutes part of a much more complex story, in which the values-based argument plays an equally important role.

At least in part, Russia embraced militarism because the military represented a traditionalist stronghold in a time of uncertainty when civilian efforts proved inadequate. Confronted with economic crisis and disillusioned with liberal ideas, many Russians resorted to nostalgia and conservativism. While Soviet socialism could not be resurrected, its military-patriotic dimension proved appealing to many. It was thus the social crisis that opened the door for military expansion into the civilian domain. Even if the

Russian military is staunchly non-interventionist, its ideological leanings may very well have been decisive in its initiative to embrace patriotic education in the post-communist context. The Ministry of Defense identified a niche in "moral security," and took steps to appropriate this niche for itself. As a military journalist put it, "It's not the role of the army to education children. But in these difficult moments for the country, the military have taken it on, and society dares not criticize them" (quoted in Sieca-Kozlowski 2010: 74).

In general, despite recent elements of triumphalism, patriotism in post-Soviet Russia has not so much been a celebration of what Russia is, as it has reflected a sense of nostalgia for what it once was and a hope for what it may become in the future. Indeed, as we see from the above examples, many self-declared patriots within the traditionalist camp are furious in their criticism of contemporary Russia. They deemed patriotic sentiments necessary for Russia not despite the crisis, but precisely because of it. As Major General Nikolai Stoliarov (1992) put it: "Today, when it is hard, when freedom of choice mates with incredible hardships and losses, patriotism rallies us, helps people to stand on their feet, and Russia to find its new face."

For some reason, international scholarly analysis has largely bypassed the value-based arguments underlying patriotic education policy and misattributed its initiation to Vladimir Putin. Despite his declared break with the Yeltsin era, Putin never changed the configuration of patriotic education policy much. If we credit Putin for the patriotic revival, we are also buying his highly simplified narrative. By neglecting its institutional history and origins, moreover, scholars and policymakers alike run the risk of misjudging the role and appeal of militarism in Russia. In the last decade, and especially since 2014, the character of patriotic celebrations has evolved into new forms, and Rosmolodezh has given the State Program a more modern face. Today, we see signs that the social crisis of the 1990s is fading into the background of policymaking. Yet for two decades, it has had a profound impact upon the patriotic discourse in Russia, and traditionalism still holds a hegemonic position in arenas where the content and meaning of official patriotism are negotiated.

REFERENCES

Andreski, S. (1968) *Military Organization and Society*. Berkeley, CA: University of California Press.
Bar-Tal, D. (1997) "The Monopolization of Patriotism," in D. Bar-Tal and E. Staub (eds.) *Patriotism in the Lives of Individuals and Nations*. Chicago, IL: Nelson-Hall, 246-70.
Betz, D. J. (2002) "No Place for a Civilian? Russian Defense Management from Yeltsin to Putin. *Armed Forces & Society* 28(3): 481-504.
Blum, D. W. (2006) "Official Patriotism in Russia. Its Essence and Implications," *PONARS Policy Memo 420*.
Bogdanov, E. (1996) "Voenno-patrioticheskoe vospitanie poluchaet prezidentskuiu podderzhku," *Krasnaia zvezda*, 22 May.
Bækken, H. (2017) "Better Misled than Dead. Russian History Policy and the Securitization of National Identity." Working paper presented at the ASN World Convention, New York, 4 May.
Chupakhin, V. (1994) "Obshchestvo bol'no bezdukhovnost'iu, luchshee sredstvo ot etogo—patriotizm," *Krasnaia zvezda*, 22 April.
Danilova, N. (2015) *The Politics of War Commemoration in the UK and Russia*. Houndmills: Palgrave Macmillan.
Daucé, F., Laruelle, M., Le Huérou, A. and Rousselet, K. (2015) "Introduction. What Does it Mean to be a Patriot?," *Europe-Asia Studies* 67(1): 1-7.
Gabowitsch, M. (2016) "Russia's Arlington? The Federal Military Cemetery near Moscow," *Journal of Soviet and Post-Soviet Politics and Society* 2(2): 89-143.
Garthoff, R. L. (1968) "The Military in Russia, 1861-1965," in J. van Doorn (ed.) *Armed Forces and Society*. The Hague: Mouton.
Goode, J. P. (2016) "Love for the Motherland (or Why Cheese is More Patriotic than Crimea)," *Russian Politics* 1(4): 418-49.
Gospatriotprogramma (2001) "Gosudarstvennaia programma 'Patrioticheskoe vospitanie grazhdan Rossiiskoi Federatsii na 2001-2005 gody.'"
——— (2006) "Gosudarstvennaia programma 'Patrioticheskoe vospitanie grazhdan Rossiiskoi Federatsii na 2006-2010 gody.'"
——— (2010) "Gosudarstvennaia programma 'Patrioticheskoe vospitanie grazhdan Rossiiskoi Federatsii na 2011-2015 gody.'"
——— (2015a) "Gosudarstvennaia programma 'Patrioticheskoe vospitanie grazhdan Rossiiskoi Federatsii na 2016-2020 gody' [Rosmolodezh version]." Retrieved from: http://static.government.ru/media/files/8qqYUwwzHUxzVkH1jsKAErrx2dE4qows.pdf (accessed 4 August 2016).
——— (2015b) "Gosudarstvennaia programma 'Patrioticheskoe vospitanie grazhdan Rossiiskoi Federatsii na 2016-2020 gody' [Rosvoentsentr version]."
Goure, L. (1973) *The Military Indoctrination of Soviet Youth*. New York: National Strategy Information Center.

Gudkov, L. (2006) "The Army as an Institutional Model," in S. L. Webber and J. G. Mathers (eds.) *Military and Society in Post-Soviet Russia.* Manchester: Manchester University Press, 39–60.

Hakvåg, U. (2017) "Russian Defense Spending after 2010. The interplay of Personal, Domestic, and Foreign Policy Interests," *Post-Soviet Affairs* 33(6): 496–510.

Herspring, D. R. (1995) "The Russian Military. Three Years On," *Communist and Post-Communist Studies* 28(2): 163–82.

Holloway, D. (1980) "War, Militarism and the Soviet State," *Alternatives* 6(1): 59–92.

Howell, A. (2018) "Forget 'Militarization'. Race, Disability, and the 'Martial Politics' of the Police and of the University," *International Feminist Journal of Politics* 2(1): 117–36.

IGC (International Crisis Group). (2018) *Patriotic Mobilisation in Russia.* International Crisis Group, Brussels, https://www.crisisgroup.org/europe-central-asia/caucasus/russianorth-caucasus/251-patriotic-mobilisation-russia (accessed 9 November 2018).

Khodzhaeva, E. (2017) "Mobilizing Patriotism in Russia. Federal Programs of Patriotic Education," *Russian Analytical Digest,* 26 September.

Kolesnikov, A. (2016) *Do Russians Want War?* Carnegie Moscow Center, https://carnegieendowment.org/files/Article_Kolesnikov_2016_Eng-2.pdf (accessed 9 November 2018).

Kolstø, P. and Blakkisrud, H. (eds.) (2016) *The New Russian Nationalism. Imperialism, Ethnicity and Authoritarianism 2000–2015.* Edinburgh: Edinburgh University Press.

Kovalev, A. (1994) "Vospitanie patriota, voina, grazhdanina—segodnia eto glavnaia zadana din [sic] shkoly," *Krasnaia zvezda,* 20 October.

Krasnaia zvezda (1992) "Ot nashego informbiuro. Kto otvechaet segodnia za voenno-patrioticheskoe vospitanie!," *Krasnaia zvezda,* 23 December.

——— (1994) "Minoborony vystupaet initsiatorom vozrozhdenia patrioticheskogo vospitania," *Krasnaia zvezda,* 9 April.

——— (1996) "Ukaz Prezidenta Rossiiskoi Federatsii 'O merakh gosudarstvennoi podderzhki obshchestvennykh ob"edinenii, veduchshikh rabotu po voenno-patrioticheskomu vospitaniu molodezhi'," *Krasnaia zvezda,* 22 May.

Kucherenko, O. (2011) "That'll Teach'em to Love Their Motherland! Russian Youth Revisit the Battles of World War II," *Journal of Power Institutions in Post-Soviet Societies* 12, http://journals.openedition.org/pipss/3866 (accessed 15 February 2018).

Kulakov, V. F. (1999) "Moral'no-psikhologicheskoe obespechenie. Problemy i puti ikh reshenia," *Voennaia mysl',* 1 November.

Kulakov, V. F., Lutovinov, V. I. and Sinaiskii, A. S. (1998) "Kontseptsiia voenno-patrioticheskogo vospitaniia molodezhi," *Boevaia vakhta,* 16 September.

Laruelle, M. (2009) *In the Name of the Nation. Nationalism and Politics in Contemporary Russia.* Houndmills: Palgrave Macmillan.

———(2014) "Beyond Anti-Westernism," *PONARS Eurasia Policy Memo* 326.
———(2015) "Patriotic Youth Clubs in Russia. Professional Niches, Cultural Capital and Narratives of Social Engagement," *Europe-Asia Studies* 67(1): 29–48.
Lutovinov, V. (1998) *Patriotizm i problemy ego formirovaniia u rossiiskoi molodezhi v sovremennykh usloviiakh (sotsial'no-filosofskii analiz)* Doctoral dissertation in Philosophy, Moscow Military University. Copy retrieved at the Russian State Library, Moscow.
———(1999) "Patriotizm i ego formirovanie v obshchestve i Voorushennykh Silakh," *Voennaia mysl'*, 1 July.
Lutovinov, V., and Radionov E. (1997) "O Patrioticheskom Vospitaniimolodezhi [sic]," *Obozrevatel'* 3–4: 18–23.
Mendeloff, D. (1994) "Explaining Russian Military Quiescence. The 'Paradox of Disintegration' and the Myth of a Military Coup," *Communist and Post-Communist Studies* 27(3): 225–46.
Mironov, V. (1994a) "My dolzhny rastit' patriotov [1/2]," *Vestnik voennoi informatsii*, 1 April.
——— (1994b) "My dolzhny rastit' patriotiov [2/2]," *Vestnik voennoi informatsii*, 1 May.
Moscow Times (2016) "Putin Declares Patriotism Russia's Only National Idea," *Moscow Times*, 4 February.
Norris, S. (2011) "Memory for Sale: Victory Day 2010 and Russian Remembrance," *The Soviet and Post-Soviet Review* 38(2): 201–29.
———(2012) *Blockbuster History in the New Russia: Movies, Memory, and Patriotism*. Bloomington, IN: Indiana University Press.
Odom, W. E. (1976) "The 'Militarization' of Soviet Society," *Problems of Communism* 25(5): 34–51.
Ol'shevich, F. (1998) "Vospitanie patriotov, zadacha gosudarstvennaia," *Na boevom postu*, 6 June.
Pasiakin, V. (1997) "Rastit' patriotov. Est' post, kotoryi nikogda ne sdaiut," *Krasnaia zvezda*, 28 June.
Pinchuk, A. (1997) "Skol'ko stoit slovo vospitatelia. Voennaia reforma. Chelovecheskii faktor," *Krasnaia zvezda*, 2 October.
Popov, S. (1993) "Vospitatel'noi rabote nuzhny novye idei i novye liudi," *Krasnaia zvezda*, 20 July.
Postanovlenie (1998) *Postanovlenie Gosudarstvennoi dumy federal'nogo sobraniia Rossiiskoi Federatsii ot 20.03.1998 No. 2320-ii gd*, http://zakon.7 law.info/base46/part4/d46ru4979.htm (accessed 18 January 2019).
Putin, V. (2012) *Address to the Federal Assembly*, 20 December, http://en.kremlin.ru/events/president/news/17118 (accessed 15 February 2018).
Rakowska-Harmstone, T. (1979) "The Soviet Armed Forces as the Instrument of National Integration," in J. Erickson and E. J. Feuchtwanger (eds.) *Soviet Military Power and Performance*. London: Palgrave Macmillan, 129–54.
Rapoport, A. (2009) "Patriotic Education in Russia. Stylistic Move or a Sign of Substantive Counter-Reform?" *The Educational Forum* 73(2): 141–52.

———(2012) "Educating New Citizens. The Role of Patriotic Education in the Post-Soviet Countries," *Educational Practice and Theory* 24(2): 81–105.
Renz, B. and Thornton, R. (2012) "Russian Military Modernization. Cause, Course, and Consequences," *Problems of Post-Communism* 59(1): 44–54.
Robertshaw, S. (2015) "Voluntary Organizations and Society-Military Relations in Contemporary Russia," *European Security* 24(2): 304–18.
Rousselet, K. (2015) "The Church in Service of the Fatherland," *Europe-Asia Studies* 67(1): 29–48.
Rumer, E. B. (1994) *The Ideological Crisis in the Russian Military*. RAND Corporation, National Defense Research Institute.
Sanina, A. (2017) *Patriotic Education in Contemporary Russia. Sociological Studies in the Making of the Post-Soviet Citizen*. Stuttgart: ibidem.
Semenikhina, I. (1999) "Rastim patriotov. Liubite Rossiiu i v nepogodu," *Na boevom postu*, 19 March.
Sharafutdinova, G. (2014) "The Pussy Riot Affair and Putin's Démarche from Sovereign Democracy to Sovereign Morality," *Nationalities Papers* 42(4): 615–21.
———(2017) "Managing National Ressentiment," in A. Makarychev and A. Yatsyk (eds.) *Vocabularies of International Relations after the Crisis in Ukraine*. London: Routledge, 130–51.
Sieca-Kozlowski, E. (2010) "Russian Military Patriotic Education. A Control Tool against the Arbitrariness of Veterans," *Nationalities Papers* 38(1): 73–85.
Simes, D. K. (1981) "The Military and Militarism in Soviet Society," *International Security* 6 (3): 123–43.
Smith, K. E. (2002) *Mythmaking in the New Russia. Politics and Memory During the Yeltsin Era*. Ithaca, NY: Cornell University Press.
Sperling, V. (2003) "The Last Refuge of a Scoundrel. Patriotism, Militarism and the Russian National Idea," *Nations and Nationalism* 9(2): 235–53.
———(2009) "Making the Public Patriotic. Militarism and Anti-Militarism in Russia," in M. Laruelle (ed.) *Russian Nationalism and the National Reassertion of Russia*. London: Routledge, 218–71.
Stoliarov, N. (1992) "Patrioticheskaia Ideia. Vchera i segodnia," *Krasnaia zvezda*, 7 August.
Suvorovskii Natisk (1998) "Programma patrioticheskogo vospitania grazhdan," *Suvorovskii Natisk*, 17 November.
Taylor, B. D. (2003) *Politics and the Russian Army: Civil-Military Relations 1689-2000*. Cambridge: Cambridge University Press.
Tkachenko, V.V. (2011) "Patrioticheskoe vospitanie molodezhi," *Vestnik Brianskogo gosudarstvennogo universiteta* 4(2): 133–40.
Vagts, A. (1959) *A History of Militarism*, rev. ed. New York: Meridian Books.
Wood, E. A. (2011) "Performing Memory. Vladimir Putin and the Celebration of World War II in Russia," *The Soviet and Post-Soviet Review* 38: 172–200.
Østbø, J. (2017) "Securitizing 'Spiritual-Moral Values' in Russia," *Post-Soviet Affairs* 33(3): 200–16

Political Parties and the Institution of Membership in Ukraine, 1991–2014

Melanie G. Mierzejewski-Voznyak

Abstract: Between 1991 and 2014, the majority of political parties in Ukraine largely failed to develop the institution of membership. Minimal legislative input on party organization combined with an unwillingness on the part of the party leadership to reform party operational structures, resulted in parties that lacked internal democracy, demonstrated low levels of representativeness, and were tied to oligarchic groups and business elites. The weak relationship between Ukrainian political parties and society due to a strong party-state linkage based on rent-seeking behavior, has led to non-accountability and a disinterest among parties to function as membership organizations. Consequently, apathetic attitudes towards partisanship developed in Ukrainian society.

Introduction

Scholarship on post-communist political parties has found a clear set of features that tend to characterize political parties in Eastern Europe. In particular, the majority of parties in post-communist Europe display weak institutional structures and have failed to develop strong linkages with society (Spirova 2005). They have become professional in nature, have forged closer links with the state, and have generally eschewed the mass membership model (Golosov 1998; Toole 2003; van Biezen 2003; van Biezen and Poguntke 2014). The focus of many political parties in Eastern Europe has shifted from an organizational one (focused on building a party membership base) to an electoral one (focused on "catch-all" slogans aimed at any and every voter at the polls). Ukraine is no exception. Following the 2014 Euromaidan Revolution and the ousting of President Viktor Yanukovych, which subsequently led to government collapse and snap presidential and parliamentary elections, the Ukrainian political party landscape underwent some major changes. These changes raised questions about the overall functioning of party politics in Ukraine, particularly as concerns party system stability and the problem of weak partisan attachment.

The party system structures patterns of competition and affects public acceptance of democracy. Institutional rules and stability are crucial for a well-functioning party system and thus democracy. Rules provide parameters and shape the behaviour of actors (i.e. political parties). Stability—in electoral results, rules, and inter-party competition—creates continuity and provides for a well-functioning party system (Lindberg 2007; Przeworski 1975; Mainwaring and Scully 1995; Mair 2001).

Since independence, a major challenge for Ukraine has been overcoming the Soviet institutional legacy and lack of democratic political culture. The 1990s transition from the Soviet system saw Ukraine begin its transformation into a democratic state; however, a lack of structural reform and bureaucratic overhaul left in place many ineffective, poorly enforced rules not well suited for the development of a multiparty system. Parties themselves were rudimentary as were the patterns of competition between them, which led to decades of electoral volatility. The use of parties for personal political ambitions, a lack of liberal democratic ideological foundations, and the decisive influence of business interests on party activity—all these factors had an impact on Ukrainian parties' abilities to institutionalize and act as intermediaries between state and society over the past twenty years. The result, however, is not necessarily politically weak parties, but parties that failed to develop the institution of membership. The specific puzzle this research tackles, is why political parties have developed as non-membership organizations in Ukraine and to what extent this is impacted by parties' failure to develop meaningful relationships with society as a consequence of their increasingly pronounced linkage with the state.

The Meaning of Membership

It is important to understand not just how modern European political parties function within government and the laws that govern them, but what traditionally gives these organizations their vitality: party members (Widfeldt 1995: 135). Political parties long depended on a strong, mass membership base. Van Biezen, Mair and Poguntke (2012) posit that political parties continue to play key roles in the elections and institutions of modern European democracies, however, since roughly the end of the twentieth century they have failed to be the mass organizations connected to wider society they once were.

There is a well-documented, ongoing decline of party activism and party membership in Europe since the late twentieth century (Dalton and Weldon 2005; Mair 1994; Mair and van Biezen 2001; van Biezen and Poguntke 2014; Whiteley and Seyd 1998). Changes in political parties have resulted from changes in society as a whole. The post-war period has seen a reduction in the size of the working class and an increase in resources available to parties thanks to technology and public funding, both of which have reduced the need for a mass-member base (van Biezen and Poguntke 2014). Parties once were organizations with well cultivated political identities representing specific segments of the population. Political parties are now taking a more top-down approach favoring the political elite over the masses and failing to engage with citizens as they once did. Political party leaders now prefer to have internal meetings without the presence of party members and often communicate with the masses via press releases rather than town hall meetings.

Despite the changing nature of political parties, some researchers have argued that party members are still crucial to the functioning of the party organization, be it through campaigning efforts, funding, or simply voter loyalty (Seyd and Whiteley 1992; Scarrow 1999; Scarrow 2000; Spirova 2005; Whiteley and Seyd 2002; Ionascu and Soare 2011; Gherghina 2014). While some parties—particularly ideologically based ones—may still consider large membership bases important for building electoral support, enhancing legitimacy, and creating party stability, many have now eschewed the institution of membership altogether. Why is that? While members remain critical to mobilization, they are not mandatory. Social media and an internet-based society have in large part replaced the need for parties to have many members with whom they are in close contact. In other words, members are necessary but not sufficient for a party to be politically viable and successful in the 21st century.

Much of Eastern Europe has followed the trend seen in Western Europe, with political parties failing to develop into mass-membership organizations. Under Soviet rule, the Communist party was ideologically based and membership was exclusive. Following independence in post-Soviet countries, political parties showed disinterest in ideology, party programs, and even rank-and-file members.[1] As opposed to maintaining a traditional focus inwards on the concerns of party members, there has been a shift outwards toward concerns of the general voter (Farrell 2006: 122). It is widely accepted that parties are predominantly concerned with winning office and influencing policy. In many Eastern European countries, this is increasingly becoming possible without reliance on a mass base of party members. As numerous studies on parties in Eastern Europe have noted, political parties in former communist Europe are parliament-focused, lacking local branches, top-down in structure led by "professional" politicians, and disconnected from any grassroots social movements (Golosov 1998; Olson 1998; Szczerbiak 1999; Szczerbiak 2001; van Biezen and Poguntke 2014; van Biezen et al. 2012). As Yuriy Yakymenko with the Razumkov Centre in Ukraine posits, "political trade, the spread of regionalism and more leadership projects are the main trends of Ukrainian party construction" (2017). Across Eastern Europe, many political parties have developed as personal projects controlled by a group of elites, which view elections and fighting for power as their raison d'être.

---

[1] Based on statements made by Ihor Kohut, Chairman of the Board, Laboratory for Legislative Initiatives in Ukraine, made during an expert discussion of Ukrainian Political Parties hosted by Razumkov Centre, 27 May 2010, Kyiv.

So, what is the state of party membership in Ukraine? In the last twenty years, academics have vigorously worked to understand the declining role of party membership (Poguntke *et al.* 2016). Still there remains a lack of empirical analysis documenting how institutional constraints provide a framework that gives meaning to party membership. Political parties are institutions; thus, the meaning of party membership is shaped in part by institutional determinants (Ionascu and Soare 2011), specifically, *legislative inputs in the form of party laws* that define who can and cannot be a member and *political party statutes* that outline the role and attributes of members.

In democratic states, legislation governing parties is not meant to control party performance, but rather to provide guidelines—common standards—aimed at promoting good practices and internal procedures among parties as well as guarding against conflicts of interest and political biases. Party statutes should ensure member participation and non-discriminatory procedures, as well as provide mechanisms that promote internal democracy at all levels of the party organization. It is important that party laws include such measures because Ukrainian legislation on political parties *does not* protect the rights of regional party organizations, the rights of rank-and-file members, or the rights of internal party opposition (Pavlenko 2007). The inclusion of such criterion in party statutes will direct parties to foster a sense of membership that is instilled with meaning and avoid simply attracting volatile voter support that is election dependent.

When taken together, these two forms of legislative input shape the contemporary meaning of party membership. Both national legislation and political parties themselves restrict who can be a member of a political party, define what it means to be a party member, and assign the rights and duties associated with membership. A thorough explanation for the state of party membership in Ukraine must consider how the meaning attached to membership is a result of continuity or a disconnect between these institutional determinants.

Political Parties, Society, and the State

The development of parties as membership organizations has been shaped by the relationships between political parties and society as well as the linkages between parties and the state. Parties are political actors in the public sphere taking part in the exercise of power, but they are also private associations of citizens that are charged with defending the interests of specific societal groups. Parties have traditionally been defined in terms of their relationships with civil society. However, as the mass-based party model has declined, so has the party–societal linkage.

Parties are no longer outgrowths of society, willing and able to function as representative organizations (Kopecký 2006). The deterioration in the bonds between parties and society is illustrated by a decline in ideologically based parties, an increase in candidate relevancy for electoral choice, and an increase in electoral volatility (Dalton and Weldon 2005; Kreuzer and Pettai 2003; Poguntke and Scarrow 1996; Thomassen 2005; Schmitt 2003). However, as Mair noted, just because the mass party model has been in decline that does not mean that parties generally are in decline (Katz and Mair 1994: 2). The "catch-all" party as described by Kirtchheimer (1966) and the "electoral-professional party" as defined by Panebianco (1988), illustrate the organizational change parties have undergone.

As the linkage between parties and civil society has grown weak, that between parties and the state has strengthened. In these cases, the state has become an alternative source of resources necessary for party survival (Katz and Mair 1994: 7). Contemporary parties increasingly rely upon state funding as opposed to member financing, public media outlets, and access to state resources to sustain their organizations (Kopecký 2006; van Biezen 2003; Roper 2002). However, with this intensifying bond between party and state comes increasing state regulation of party affairs, which has fundamentally altered the way parties organize (Katz 2002). Parties are dependent on the state, managed by the state, and engage in rent-seeking behavior within state apparatuses.

In the post-Soviet region, weak ties between civil society and political parties have been countered by a pronounced linkage between parties and the state. As Kopecký (2006: 254) posits, in post-communist Europe, parties tend to be founded by elite groups within government rather than social movements based outside the state. As the post-Soviet state is fragile, lacking legitimate and strong institutions, parties have had a comparative advantage over their western European counterparts. They have been able to leverage their position in power to set the rules of the game (such as manipulating political party and/or electoral law) and use public office to their own advantage instead of the general good (via patronage and clientelism) (Kopecký 2006; van Biezen and Kopecký 2007; Kopecký and Scherlis 2008). This study confronts the paradox of political party development as membership organizations in Ukraine by 1) documenting a weak institution of membership among political parties as a result of discontinuity in institutional determinants; and 2) explaining this weak state of party membership by analyzing the linkages between political parties and a) society versus b) the state.

Methodology

This article first presents an empirical analysis of the weak state of party membership in Ukraine by examining the institutional constraints that have shaped political party development. I analyze external regulations on political parties and party membership as outlined in Ukrainian legislation in addition to examining internal regulations as described in party charters. Through these dual approaches, I am able to identify how party membership in Ukraine is conceptualized, the ways in which it exerts an impact on the value attached to membership, and the overall institution of membership. Second, I explain the empirical results of the weak institution of membership in Ukraine by analyzing the evolution of party development as concerns the linkages between political parties and a) society, as well as b) the state. Specifically, this study addresses how leader-based political parties and Soviet legacy have adversely affected the development of parties and their ability/desire to function as membership organizations. The weak linkage between parties and civil society is documented in addition to the increasingly close relationship between parties and the state in post-communist Ukraine, from 1991 to 2014.

Party membership is often measured through either political party reports or public opinion surveys. Both of these methods present problems for analysis. Political parties may overestimate their membership levels and often lack accurate recordkeeping concerning levels of membership as they rely on local branches to submit annual reports. Furthermore, party membership records may be grossly inaccurate because of issues such as multiple memberships and cases of non-membership (where candidates and elected officials may represent a party without actually being a registered member of a party). As van Biezen and Mair (2001: 7) note, parties tend also to grow concerned with the appearance of declining partisanship and thus may claim a larger number of active members than is actually the case.

Survey data also presents problems of measurement as mass survey data is infrequently available and there are problems with both survey collection and the reliability of respondents (van Biezen 2001: 6). First, regular survey collection that employs identical or at least similar phrasing that would lend itself to comparative analysis is not always available, as wording varies between years and among different polling organizations. Second, respondents may have different understandings of "party membership" and what it entails (i.e. belonging to a party, being an active member of a party, or just routinely voting for a party).

While party data for many Central European countries is readily accessible, this is not the case when it comes to Ukraine. Repeated outreach to Ukrainian political parties to ascertain their membership levels was met with no response.[2] Likewise, my communication with various Ukrainian think tanks revealed that concrete data about political party membership in the Ukrainian context may not be available. As one senior Ukrainian researcher at the Institute of Sociology at the Ukrainian National Academy of

---

[2] The author contacted the five main political parties whose party charters are analyzed in this article four times each between September 2014 and March 2015 via email.

Sciences (ISNANU) put it in a professional correspondence on this project: survey data about the number of Ukrainians in any party has not ever been collected, and furthermore reliable data about party membership would be difficult to obtain since parties in Ukraine are often custom tailored for each election.[3]

Nevertheless, we can in part get around this paucity of data. My analysis uses public opinion polls conducted regularly in Ukraine by the International Foundation for Electoral Systems (IFES), between 1997 and 2012, and the Razumkov Centre, between 2000 and 2015. While this data is incomplete, it nevertheless offers crucial insight about party membership in Ukraine. Where there is discrepancy in the wording of questions over time, I note the variation. Additionally, I draw from a variety of public opinion surveys about the perception of political parties in Ukraine conducted as recent as 2017. Further information about membership numbers is drawn from journalistic reports, which provide some specific figures for individual parties over the last decade.

My analysis of party laws relies largely upon primary sources—the Constitution of Ukraine and subsequent amendments, as well as other laws that specifically refer to political parties, in original Ukrainian as well as English translations. The political party statutes/charters analyzed here are those that were made available by the party or publically accessible online as of October 2014, in Ukrainian.

A dominant trend observed by scholars of party politics in Eastern Europe is the weak link between parties and civil society. I identify such patterns of party development in Ukraine by combining documented weak levels of party membership and party identification with declining voter turnout and high levels of electoral volatility. Information about party membership and voter interests are drawn from various public opinion polls from the aforementioned institutions. Societal appreciation (i.e. trust and acceptance) of political parties, and the party system as a whole, can also be measured by public participation in elections (Dalton and

---

[3] I. V. Burov, Deputy Director at ISNANU in a professional correspondence with the author in October 2014. Author's translation to English from Russian.

Weldon 2005; Grönlund and Setälä 2007). I therefore rely upon voter turnout to help assess the relationship between society and political parties. If parties are strongly rooted in society, considered legitimate representatives of the people's interests and institutionalized, then traditionally voter turnout should increase over time or remain at high levels.[4] I additionally analyze electoral volatility scores reported by the "WHO Governs in Europe and Beyond" database.[5] Electoral volatility demonstrates the durability of voter affiliations. The higher the volatility score the more vote switching is occurring, which signifies weak partisanship attachment and thus an erosion of bonds between parties and society.

In this study, I assess the ongoing development of the party–state linkage through an examination of the dependence of political parties on state financing and free media, the management of parties by the state as concerns regulations/laws pertaining to political parties (both laws concerning the internal activities of political parties as well as electoral law that structures how parties compete), and rent-seeking behavior by political parties. Particular attention is paid to the elevated role that governing parties play in shaping this state–party relationship. Additionally, I account for recent changes in party law in Ukraine and how this might affect the future state–party relationship. These indicators, when considered together, highlight the weak societal roots of political parties that have been replaced by a close party–state bond, and present a more nuanced explanation for why the institution of membership is underdeveloped in Ukraine.

Case Selection

Party membership has been studied in detail in Central Europe but neglected when it comes to Eastern European states. This analysis

---

[4] This is starting to change, as seen by increasing electoral volatility levels in Western Europe (Lane 2015).
[5] Casal Bértoa (2016) Database on WHO GOVERNS in Europe and beyond, Party Systems and Government Observatory, http://whogoverns.eu.

presents an in-depth case study of party membership in Ukraine. After twenty-five years of independence punctuated by political revolutions in 2004 and 2014, Ukraine is a developing democracy and political parties are continuing to evolve with each election cycle. The value of studying Ukraine, a country of 45 million, is not only to gain insight about local political phenomena, but because it will have comparative utility for future studies on political parties and the institution of membership in other Eastern European and Transcaucasian countries. While this study focuses on a single country, it is comparative in nature as it analyzes multiple parties within Ukraine's party system.

Political parties routinely emerge and fade into obscurity in Ukraine, thus a comprehensive analysis of all major parties since independence is not feasible. As of 2018, the number of political parties in Ukraine exceeded 350, and therefore only certain political parties could be selected for comparison. I draw on the cases of five political parties in particular, selecting my case studies for the purpose of analyzing parties that were the most influential in Ukrainian politics and which taken together constituted the dominant political actors in the party system from independence until 2014. The parties examined in detail are *Narodnyi Rukh Ukrainy* (People's Movement of Ukraine) (henceforth *Rukh*), the former *Komunistychna Partiia Ukrainy* (Communist Party of Ukraine), *Sotsialistychna Partiia Ukrainy* (Socialist Party of Ukraine), *Vseukrains'ke obiednannia "Bat'kivshchyna"* (All Ukrainian Union "Fatherland") (henceforth *Bat'kivshchyna*), and *Partiia Rehioniv* (Party of Regions).

These five cases were selected according to the following criteria:

1) parties must have competed in *and* won seats in at least four of the seven parliamentary elections—1994, 1998, 2002, 2006, 2007, 2012, and 2014; and

2) parties must have obtained at least two of the four parliamentary wins as individual, independent parties (not only as part of a larger electoral bloc).

The basis for these criteria is not only to limit analysis to the parties that were most relevant in politics, but also to limit the case studies to parties which achieved electoral success as an independent party and not solely as a result of carefully constructed political alliances (i.e., electoral blocs). It is important to note that with the exception of the Communist Party, all of these parties have competed in elections *and* won seats in parliament at one point or another as part of an electoral bloc. Table 1 presents an overview of the case selection. While this case selection encompasses the most pertinent parties in Ukraine's contemporary political history prior to the Euromaidan Revolution, the current status of these parties varies.

Bat'kivshchyna is the only party that remains truly politically active at the national level as of 2018. The Socialist Party of Ukraine, while still active, has been in deep decline since 2007. In May 2013, *Rukh* made a decision to merge with the Ukrainian People's Party (*Ukrains'ka Narodna Partiia*), but to retain *Rukh's* party statute and assume simply the name "*RUKH.*" Soon after, in June 2013, the former head of the People's Movement of Ukraine, *Rukh*—Borys Tarasyuk—as well as some other members of the newly formed *RUKH*, joined *Bat'kivshchyna*. The post-merger *RUKH* is still active at the local level and is registered to participate in the December 2018 elections for the newly established *obiednani terytorial'ni hromady* (united territorial communities—UTC), but is largely non-existent in national politics. The Party of Regions, while technically still in existence, became politically inactive after the deposing of the Yanukovych government in February 2014. This resulted in many former members of the Party of Regions running as candidates in the 2014 parliamentary elections on the election lists of the newly formed Opposition Bloc party. The Communist Party of Ukraine was officially banned on 15 May 2015 as a result of the new decommunization laws enacted by President Poroshenko. Law No. 2558, "On the Condemnation of the Communist and National Socialist (Nazi) Regimes, and Prohibition of Propaganda of their Symbols," in effect stripped the party of its legality and banned its registration.

Table 1. Case Selection

	Ideological positioning	Year Founded	Parliamentary wins
People's Movement of Ukraine (*Rukh*)	**Rightist liberal**	1990	1994, 1998, 2002, 2006, 2007
Socialist Party of Ukraine	**Leftist conservative**	1991	1994, 1998, 2002, 2006
Communist Party of Ukraine	**Strongly leftist with conservative tendencies**	1993	1994, 1998, 2002, 2006, 2007, 2012
Party of Regions	**Centrist liberal**	1997*	1998, 2002, 2006, 2007, 2012
All Ukrainian Union Fatherland (*Bat'kivshchyna*)	**Centrist conservative**	1999	2002, 2006, 2007, 2012, 2014

*Founded as Party of Regional Revival of Ukraine

Party Law and Party Membership[6]

The existence of Ukraine's multi-party system was first provided for legally in the 24 October 1990 amendment to the 1978 Constitution of the Ukrainian Soviet Socialist Republic and subsequently with the 1992 law "On Association of Citizens," which provided the legal basis for the formation of political parties and their activities. In 1996, Ukraine finally adopted its first constitution since independence, which further redefined the status of parties, imposing limitations on their formation and activities (Articles 36 & 37).[7] Citizens of

---

[6] Party law in this chapter refers to all laws that make reference to political parties in the title or text, including but not limited to the Constitution, laws on civic associations, and specific laws on political parties.

[7] An English translation of the 1996 Ukrainian Constitution can be found at "Ukraine's Constitution of 1996 with Amendments through 2004,"

Ukraine were declared to have the right to freedom of association within political parties to realize and satisfy their freedoms and political, economic, social, and cultural interests. Parties were, however, *forbidden* to promote the liquidation of independent Ukraine, to promote violence or war, and/or to encroach on human rights and freedoms. The substantial Constitutional amendments of 2004, following the Orange Revolution, elevated the status of parties in Ukrainian politics, with parties now having the right to form the government and influence the executive via the proposal and approval of the Prime Minister in parliament.[8] However, some inconsistencies in the 2004 amendments led to years of constitutional power struggles in Ukraine.

In 2010, under pressure from President Yanukovych, parliament reversed the 2004 Constitutional amendments, reverting back to the 1996 Constitution that greatly reduced the powers of political parties. Following the Euromaidan Revolution of 2014, there was a re-enactment of the Constitution as amended in 2004, with parties again playing a leading role in the formation of legislative and executive power (Razumkov 2015a). Political parties now play a vital role in Ukrainian politics, but there has been an overproduction of parties within the party system. In 2014, 37 political parties were registered, in 2015, 79 parties, and in 2016, 43 parties (CVU 2018). However, these numbers are rather misleading—as are all figures about political parties in Ukraine. This is because a large portion of registered political parties no longer exist, have been in the process of termination for years, or never actually functioned in the first place (Karmazina 2018). Also problematic is the fact that despite the influx of new parties, as of 2018, there remains still no more than a handful of ideologically based/grassroots organizations that have been established from the bottom-up, with genuine membership bases (e.g. *Pravyi Sektor, Svoboda, Samopomich*) (Razumkov 2015a).

---

      constituteproject.org, https://www.constituteproject.org/constitution/Ukraine_2004.pdf.

[8]   An English translation of the 2004 amendments can be found at *ibid*.

While legislative engineering of electoral law has been common in Ukraine, which will be discussed further in the section on party–state linkage, there have been few legal changes to laws governing political parties themselves. Still, Ukrainian legislation specifies certain provisions on the nature of political party development and party membership. The 2001 law "On Political Parties in Ukraine," stipulates the right of Ukrainian citizens to freely and voluntarily associate in political parties (Article 1).[9] Parties are defined as legally registered voluntary associations of citizens that must operate in Ukraine with nation-wide status (Articles 2 & 3). This stipulates, therefore, that not only is party membership limited to Ukrainian citizens, but that parties must be able to secure nation-wide support—encouraging all-inclusive representativeness over a regional or ethnic orientation. Despite a number of parties previously or currently being reliant upon strong regional networks of support (Party of Regions, *Svoboda, Samopomich*) (D'Anieri *et al.* 1999; Vistak & Myrosh 2017; Mierzejewski-Voznyak 2018)—Article 8 of the aforementioned law requires that the formation of a party be supported by the collection of at least ten thousand voter signatures obtained in at least *two-thirds of the districts in at least two-thirds of the 24 Ukrainian oblasts* and in the cities of Kyiv and Sevastopol as well as the Autonomous Republic of Crimea. Additionally, parties have six months from the date of registration to establish regional offices *in the majority of oblasts* in Ukraine.

Ukraine is home to an "ethno-cultural" geographical cleavage, particularly between the Center-West and South-East, which is based on ethnicity and language and a result of larger historical divides (Mierzejewski Voznyak 2018). Independent Ukraine is divided between Ukrainian-speaking Ukrainians in the West, that identify with more of an ethnic Ukrainian nationalism, and Russian-speaking Ukrainians and ethnic Russians in the South and East, who have historically allied more with a pro-Russian/Soviet nationalism (Shekhovtsov 2011; Umland 2013; Kuzio 2015). Historically, this

---

[9] An English translation of the law can be found at http://www.legislationline.org/documents/action/popup/id/7110.

divide has hindered the development of a single, unified Ukrainian national identity as it creates competing interests and geopolitical orientations. Therefore, to develop a truly nation-wide party as called for by Ukrainian law is in practice problematic. Parties' organizational structure begins with the voters. While parties need to project a certain amount of all-inclusiveness in order to meet registration requirements, the political reality is that parties in Ukraine still rely upon specific segments of the population to build up their membership and win votes.

Legal restrictions on party membership, as set out in Article 6 "On Political Parties in Ukraine," predominantly concern eligibility and ethical propriety. All Ukrainian citizens over 18 years of age, who are not of reduced mental capacity and not currently imprisoned, who wish to obtain membership must submit a statement expressing a desire to join a particular party. Citizens can only belong to one political party at a time and those holding certain public positions are not eligible for party membership. These include judges, officials of the public prosecutor's office, officials of the bodies of the interior, officials of the Security Service of Ukraine (SBU), and military service members. Amendments to the law in 2005 further prohibited officials of the State Tax Authority (formerly DPS, now the Fiscal State Service—FDS) from being members of political parties and the "Law on Amendments to and on Abrogation of Certain Legislative acts of Ukraine Pertaining to Operation of the State Penal Services of Ukraine" (April 2009) prohibited employees of the state penal service from holding membership (Kovryzhenko 2010: 40). While legal provisions are meant to safeguard against the appearance of impropriety, how membership is handled is at the discretion of the parties themselves.

All political parties in Ukraine are required to draft formal party charters that include procedure for admission, suspension, and termination of membership as well as the specific rights and obligations of members (Article 8, Law on Political Parties in Ukraine). While this allows parties a fair amount of discretion in how internal party politics are handled, Ukrainian law does attempt to curtail discrimination among political parties as concerns membership. Articles 6 and 7 of the Law on Civic Associations prevent party charters from containing any specific restrictions on the basis of sex or nationality and calls for an equality of all members.

National legislation on political parties predominantly pertains to the registration process when establishing a new party and general guidelines that aim at the creation of a well-functioning, more democratically minded party. In a democratic state, however, the government is not in a position to heavily regulate internal party procedures. For instance, there is no set requirement for the minimum number of party members. Additionally, while parties are required to form statutory bodies and conduct party congresses, there are no legal requirements as to the character of parties. Political parties, therefore, can choose to operate with or without internal democracy, and the role of individual members can vary greatly.

Legislation may have granted a privileged role to parties in Ukraine, but in the past couple of decades those parties have been operating more like well-designed machines, not organic associations of citizens who share a similar social and political outlook. This has diminished the role of the party member and the importance attached to such membership. For instance, it is common among the majority of parties that decisions such as name changes, amendments to party constitutions, or the elections of party leaders occur at party congresses that are attended by only 25 party members.[10] While this is an easy requirement to meet, it raises concerns about the involvement and value of party members to the larger political organization.

Arguably, the most substantive change to party law came in 2015 with the amendments to the Law "On Political Parties in Ukraine." These amendments 1) outlawed parties' use of Nazi and/or communist symbols as well as similar propaganda; and 2) provided for state financing of political parties.[11] This set of laws not only

---

[10] According to Olena Semiorkina, Director, Department of Legalization of Association of Citizens, the Ministry of Justice of Ukraine, expert discussion of Ukrainian Party System hosted by Razumkov Centre, 27 May 2010, Kyiv.

[11] The Laws of Ukraine "On Condemnation of Communist and National-Socialist (Nazi) Totalitarian Regimes in Ukraine and Ban on Propaganda of their

altered who could participate in elections but took a major first step in regulating the financial operations of parties. The results, de facto, banned the Communist Party and also introduced a new system of party financing and financial transparency (these latter changes will be discussed at greater length in the section on party–state linkage).

Legislative input concerning party registration and organization has been minimal in Ukraine, placing the responsibility for internal democratic development on the party itself. Parties have been allowed to define themselves and their activities, which include matters of party membership. Provisions have largely been limited to rules on the compatibility of party membership and employment in elected offices, ministries, or certain government sectors for the purpose of providing guidelines that will help parties avoid conflicts of interest and personal bias. Understanding party membership in Ukraine, thus requires additional analysis of the parties themselves to determine what trends can be observed among parties as concerns the value of membership.

Parties as Membership Organizations

Ukrainian law allows for an open interpretation of party membership; it is the party therefore, not the state, that attaches meaning to membership. To understand the significance of party membership and whether it carries the same value among different parties within the party system requires referencing individual party charters. Under Ukrainian law (Article 8, Law on Political Parties in Ukraine), all party charters must include the following:
- procedures for admitting new members;
- reasons and protocol for membership suspension;
- grounds on which membership can be terminated; and
- rights and obligations of active members.

Symbols" and "On Amendments to Some Legislative Acts of Ukraine on Preventing and Combating Political Corruption."

Party charters are important as they outline who can be a member and what a member's role will be in the party. A party's constitutional rules are thus valuable, as these provisions create an institution that individuals either do or do not choose to join. Analysis of the party charters across the five selected cases in Ukraine (Communist Party of Ukraine, Socialist Party of Ukraine, *Rukh, Bat'kivshchyna*, Party of Regions), finds that they all contain a similar structure, with the same wording and general terminology.[12]

The concept of membership can be understood as nearly identical across all the cases. All of the parties require an application or written statement requesting membership, refer to the same eligibility requirements as pertains to citizenship, age, and voter eligibility as outlined by Ukrainian law, and require that an individual belong to no other party.[13] In almost all cases, membership is approved by majority vote at the local level. All parties address membership termination, and in all cases this can result from voluntary withdrawal, loss of right to vote, or the decision of the party to exclude a specific individual as a member.[14] A common basis of exclusion across parties is the violation of party discipline or failure to adhere to the party charter that results in damage to a party's reputation.[15] While parties vary in whether there are warnings or reprimands that precede membership termination, all include

---

[12] This research references political party charters as published on the parties' websites as of October 2014, in the original Ukrainian. All translations are the author's own.

[13] *Statut Komunistychnoi Partii Ukrainy*, sections 2.1 & 2.4; *Statut Sotsialistychnoi Partii Ukrainy*, section 2.1; *Statut Narodnoho Rukhu Ukrainy*, sections 10-11; *Statut Partii Rehioniv*, sections 3.1–3.2; *Statut Vseukrains'koho obiednannia "Bat'kivshchyna,"* sections 3.1–3.2, 3.5.

[14] *Statut Komunistychnoi Partii Ukrainy*, section 2.5; *Statut Sotsialistychnoi Partii Ukrainy*, section 2.3; *Statut Narodnoho Rukhu Ukrainy*, section 20; *Statut Partii Rehioniv*, sections 3.6–3.9; *Statut Vseukrains'koho obiednannia "Bat'kivshchyna,"* section 3.6.

[15] *Statut Komunistychnoi Partii Ukrainy*, sections 2.5.3–2.5.4; *Statut Sotsialistychnoi Partii Ukrainy*, sections 2.5–2.6; *Statut Narodnoho Rukhu Ukrainy*, sections 21–22; *Statut Partii Rehioniv*, section 3.6; *Statut Vseukrains'koho obiednannia "Bat'kivshchyna,"* section 3.10.

provisions outlining a window for appeal of a termination decision (ranging from 30–60 days).

Despite the overall similarities between how political parties define and provide for membership (see Table 2), there are a few notable differences in membership provisions. In particular, the Communist Party highlighted the importance of the party's ideological underpinnings on membership by including a provision which states that members may only join other civil society organizations whose activities *are not* contrary to the goals of the party as outlined in the party program.[16] As the Communist Party of Ukraine was one of the only parties founded according to ideological beliefs, the internalization of such beliefs was expected of its members. *Rukh* as well as the Communist Party had additional requirements for membership, that required applicants to obtain the recommendations of two current party members who have held membership for at least a year. Parties also differ on their rules for obtaining membership if an individual previously belonged to another political party. The Communist Party required a one-year probationary period for those who have previously held membership in a different political organization and the Socialist Party requires a three-month probationary period *if* three years have not passed since membership in another party was terminated. Both parties also stipulated a one-year probationary period for those wishing to reapply to the party, while *Bat'kivshchyna* mandates that two years pass before reapplication is possible.

---

[16] *Statut Komunistychnoi Partii Ukrainy*, section 2.3.

Table 2. Membership Provisions Compared

	Bat'kivshchyna	Communist Party of Ukraine	Party of Regions	Rukh	Socialist Party of Ukraine
Eligibility	x	x	x	x	x
Application	x	x	x	x	x
Recommendation		x		x	
Exclusivity	x	x	x	x	x
Probation		x			x
Rights	x	x	x	x	x
Duties	x	x	x	x	x
Termination	x	x	x	x	x
Suspension	x	x	x	x	x
Exclusion	x	x	x	x	x
Regain Membership	x	x	x	x	x
Rewards	x	x			x

x- denotes that specific provisions are outlined in the party charter

Party membership in Ukraine is best conceptualized by the rights and obligations that parties attach to such affiliation. The difference between what members are entitled to versus what is expected of them denotes both their value and place within the institution (see Table 3). All parties require that members promote the party, campaign for its candidates, and adhere to party regulations.[17] These

---

[17] *Statut Komunistychnoi Partii Ukrainy*, section 2.2; *Statut Sotsialistychnoi Partii Ukrainy*, section 2.8; *Statut Narodnoho Rukhu Ukrainy*, section 17; *Statut Partii Rehioniv*, section 4.1; *Statut Vseukrainskoho obiednannia "Bat'kivshchyna,"* section 3.7. While *Rukh* does not specifically state that members must help

obligations are intended for the purpose of bolstering the party and its goals—be they ideologically based or primarily election oriented. Membership fees are also demanded of all members, although the amounts are unspecified. Interestingly, only *Rukh* does not specify the recruitment of new members as part of membership duties. This may in part be due to the party's longevity which has afforded it both legitimacy and name recognition. Regardless of the specific value parties attach to membership, Ukrainian political parties are aware of the need to build a visible membership base. This visibility is strategic, and three parties—*Bat'kivshchyna*, the Communist Party, and the Party of Regions—required their members to participate in party activities, political rallies, and promote the party publically. Interestingly though, while party members are necessary for public display of a party's strength, their contribution to internal party operations appears less valued.

---

recruit new members, it does oblige members to *strengthen Rukh's* influence and authority.

Table 3. Membership Rights versus Duties

	Bat'kivshchyna	Communist Party of Ukraine	Party of Regions	Rukh	Socialist Party of Ukraine
Rights:					
Elect or be elected to governing bodies	x	x	x	x	x
Participate in meetings	x	x			x
Propose policy initiatives/ party activities	x	x	x	x	x
Be nominated as candidate for election to government			x		x
Criticize party during private party meetings	x	x	x		x
Duties:					
Adhere to party regulations	x	x	x	x	x
Campaign	x	x	x		x
Demonstrate/ Participate in party activities	x	x		x	
Promote Party	x	x	x	x	x
Attract new Members	x	x	x		x
Pay membership Dues	x	x	x	x	x

x- denotes specific reference to that duty or right in the party charter

All parties have an open approach to member involvement, stating in their charters that members have the right to submit proposals for party activities or amendments to party programs as well as attend party meetings.[18] However, participation in the internal workings of the party is not required. The Communist Party only necessitated registration and work within a local party organization for the purpose of attracting new members, and *Rukh* as well as Party of Regions require that members be registered with a local party branch, but do not demand active participation within that body. Additionally, participation in the election of candidates to the governing or statutory bodies of a party is also a membership privilege, though it is not a task of membership. Furthermore, only two parties—the Party of Regions and the Socialist Party of Ukraine—state that members are entitled to be nominated as candidates for government office.

The emphasis placed on external involvement with party activities over internal involvement highlights the changing role of party membership in newer democracies. Visible party supporters help establish a party's legitimacy, demonstrating its representativeness (Scarrow 2000). This is increasingly important in Ukraine, as there is growing demand for parties that represent societal interests and not just those of a party leader or business group. The average party in Ukraine is leader-focused (Razumkov 2015). This has resulted in membership that is passive in nature as opposed to the classic conception of membership where participation in local associations is routine practice.

Why is the role of "party member" marginalized and the meaning of "membership" trivialized in Ukraine? The majority of Ukrainian parties have followed a top-down model, where ultimate power rests in the hands of the leadership. The notion that a political party is little more than a vehicle for obtaining power, is a byproduct of the Soviet institutions once in place in Ukraine. Party organizational development has largely been driven by individuals whose knowledge of parties was derived from personal experiences

---

[18] *Statut Komunistychnoi Partii Ukrainy*, section 2.3; *Statut Sotsialistychnoi Partii Ukrainy*, section 2.9; *Statut Narodnoho Rukhu Ukrainy*, section 18; *Statut Partii Rehioniv*, section 4.2; *Statut Vseukrains'koho obiednannia "Bat'kivshchyna,"* section 3.8.

with the Communist Party of the Soviet Union and the All-Leninist Communist Youth Union (Romaniuk 2018). What has resulted in Ukraine is a party system that consists predominantly of centralized parties; where the subordination and dependence of all party structures and members on central management is expected and levels of internal party democracy remain low (Romaniuk 2018: 360).

Parties do not require meeting attendance or voting in internal elections to executive bodies, as internal practices favor centralized decision making. Members are not an active, valued component of the party organization, they are literally more for "show." This is in large part a result of the reluctance of party leaders to engage ordinary members in agenda setting. Party leaders have an interest in strengthening their position in the party and limiting the control of party activities by party members (Romaniuk 2018). The average party member holds little influence on the decision-making process of both leadership and policy agenda. Survey results from 2010 find that a plurality of Ukrainians (42.9%) believe that it is just such a lack of internal party democracy that prevents young and promising party members from taking executive positions in a party or on party councils (Razumkov 2010a: 30). The top-down model of parties and the organizations' increasing linkages with financial groups and the state places unlimited power in the hands of the party elite. Thus, in many instances, party membership lacks value for the young and politically ambitious.

Bat'kivshchyna is one of the prime examples of a leader-based party where a lack of internal democracy is largely responsible for the declining value of rank-and-file members. Party leaders dominate over the party's governing bodies, which meet periodically based primarily on the needs of leaders (Romaniuk 2018). Additionally, party issues are typically addressed by a group *solely* compromised of party leaders and deputies—not exceeding 7 people and exclusive of ordinary party members. The use of closed electoral lists in Ukraine further empowers the leadership of all parties (Haggard and Webb 2004). Party leaders nominate candidates for parliament as well as fixing the order of candidates, determining the likelihood a specific candidate will be elected to office. Prior to 2014, primaries were largely non-existent and even the function of party representative bodies (i.e. congresses) were reduced to simple approval of the lists drafted by leadership (Razumkov 2010a).[19] Such practices diminish the notion that party membership holds a functional value in the majority of parties and that party members play a contributing role in internal party politics.

An additional problem concerning the organization of political parties is a general disconnect between the party and their supporters both in terms of activity and communication (Razumkov 2015e). Prior to the newly enacted decentralization reforms that saw the establishment of UTCs beginning in 2015, parties did not devote genuine efforts to developing local offices. According to opinion polls, half of citizens have never heard of local party organization activities in their regions (Razumkov Centre, 2010b: 64). Some exceptions do exist. For instance, the political party UDAR focused on strengthening its party at the local level since the early stages of party development back in 2010. In 2013, half of the heads of UDAR's regional organizations in each oblast' were MPs, which the party claimed were committed to maintaining their visibility at city council meetings and during local elections to build much needed public trust.[20]

A further issue regarding the value of party membership is that it is not a prerequisite for a political career in Ukraine. There are no legal requirements that make membership in a party mandatory in order to run in national elections on party lists. Taking for example the 2014 parliamentary election, the number of independent candidates included on a political party's list varied

---

[19] There are a few exceptions of parties that have made modest attempts to decentralize internal candidate selection. *Samopomich* held public primary elections for the position of Lviv mayor in 2015 (which will be discussed further in the section on post-Euromaidan trends). In the case of UDAR, the regional party branch in Ternopil oblast held a congress to elect the party's regional head, deputy, and executive council ("Na mistsevi..." 2014). Additionally, the UDAR party branch in Lviv oblast tasked its local party offices to elect candidates for the municipal elections in fall 2015 ("L'vivs'kyi UDAR..." 2015). In both cases, it is important to note that candidate selection took place at the regional and local levels and was not controlled by party head Klitschko or UDAR's central party leadership in Kyiv.

[20] These statements were made to the author during personal interviews with party representatives in Kyiv during June 2013.

among parties. The newly created Opposition Bloc (rebranded Party of Regions) had a high of 98% independent candidates on its party list; in other words, only 2% of the candidates held membership in the Opposition Bloc. In contrast, *Svoboda* had zero independent candidates and the Communist Party of Ukraine had only 1% (Kononchuk 2014: 5-6) (see Table 4). Even in the case of the President's namesake party, Bloc of Petro Poroshenko, only one of its top 10 candidates was a registered party member. Individuals can achieve political office and high-ranking government positions without committing to a party. This not only makes party membership unnecessary but potentially undesirable, as an elected independent member of parliament can strategically change his or her affiliation with parties to gain political advantage.

The issue of non-membership is not a new one in Ukraine, as parties have long included individuals who were not party members on their electoral lists. For example, all of the parties that crossed the five-percent electoral threshold in the 2012 parliamentary elections placed non-members on their electoral lists. Over 55% of the candidates on *Bat'kivshchyna's* list were non-party members, 13% of UDAR's candidates were not members, 8% of PR candidates were not members, and around 2% of CPU's and *Svoboda's* candidates were not party members.[21] There are various reasons a party would include non-members on their party lists. First, if the party list is a result of an electoral bloc and multiple parties are running as a coalition (such as the Ukrainian Democratic Alliance for Reform (UDAR) did with BPP in 2014), then there will be members of multiple parties running on a single list. For instance, the leader of UDAR—Vitali Klitschko—was actually the first candidate listed on the BPP electoral list as a non-party member, according to the Central Election Commission of Ukraine's website. Second, parties will typically include party sponsors—businessmen—who have financed the electoral campaign (Meleshevych 2016: 11). Third, a party may want to include well-

---

[21] Based on author's own calculations using data and candidate bios as found on the Central Election Commission (CVK) website about the 2012 parliamentary elections, available at: http://www.cvk.gov.ua/pls/vnd2012/wp001.

known public figures that will attract attention and win votes, regardless of whether the person is a party member.[22] This was highly relevant in the 2014 parliamentary elections, as all the major parties were interested in including either.

Table 4. Number of Party Members and Independent Candidates on Party Lists, 2014 Parliamentary Elections.

Party Name, year of registration	Number of party members to number of candidates on the party list, ratio as percentage	Number of party members among top ten candidates	Party Name, year of registration	Number of party members to number of candidates on the party list, ratio as percentage	Number of party members among top ten candidates
Bat'kivshchyna, 1999	94.3%	6	National Democratic Party, 2014	100%	10
Bloc of Left Forces, 2014	33%	4	Opposition Bloc, 2010	2%	0
Bloc of Petro Poroshenko, 2014	34.1%	1	Party of Greens of Ukraine, 1991	71.1%	10
Revival, 2004	75.2%	7	*Pravyi Sektor*, 2014	74.1%	8
Civil Position, 2010	88.3%	6	Radical Party of Oleh Liashko, 2010	63%	4

---

[22] In 2012, Taisiya Povaliy—a famous Ukrainian singer—was included on the Party of Regions electoral list, though she was not a party member. Mariya Matios—a Ukrainian poet and novelist—was listed second on UDAR's list, though she was not a party member (information available on the Central Election Commission website: http://www.cvk.gov.ua/pls/vnd2012/wp001.) In 2014, it was common practice for parties to include members of civil society who became famous during the Euromaidan protests and individuals who gained recognition for fighting the war in Eastern Ukraine (Meleshevych 2016) (see further the section on post-Euromaidan trends below).

Party Name, year of registration	Number of party members to number of candidates on the party list, ratio as percentage	Number of party members among top ten candidates	Party Name, year of registration (	Number of party members to number of candidates on the party list, ratio as percentage	Number of party members among top ten candidates
United Country, 2008	29.6%	2	Svoboda, 2004	100%	10
Zastup Party, 2014	46.9%	10	Strength and Dignity, 2009	59.7%	8
Green Planet, 2005	9.7%	3	Power of People, 2014	78.3%	6
Internet Party, 2011	47%	6	Mighty Ukraine, 2014	71.1%	6
Communist Party of Ukraine, 1993	99%	9	Solidarity of Women of Ukraine, 1999	49.1%	2
Liberal Party of Ukraine, 1991	75.3%	7	Ukraine – United Country, 2014	4.3%	3
People's Front, 2014	79.6%	6	Ukraine of the Future, 2008	88.2%	6
New Policy, 2011	91.6%	8	5.10, 2014	96.5%	9

Source: Kononchuk (2014).

Between 1991 and 2014, the majority of political parties in Ukraine did not develop the institution of membership. Members were not necessary to optimize electoral needs, which became satisfied by mass advertising campaigns during election time, nor were they financially necessary, as oligarchs and financial investment groups provided the majority of party funding. While the importance of a mass member base remained visually important for rallies and/or protests, it largely became an empty affiliation. Even party charters themselves were more about meeting legislative requirements than truly developing intra-party democracy that elevated the decision-making power of members and imparted meaning to the concept of party membership.

Party Membership and Organizational Linkages in Ukraine

According to the 13 surveys carried out by IFES between 1997 and 2012, an average of 2.33 percent of the Ukrainian electorate reported holding membership in a political party.[23] While membership was only at a reported one percent in the 1990s, this number hit a high of five percent in 2005, following the Orange Revolution. In the late 2000s, it continued to fluctuate but fell to an average of 2.86 percent. Razumkov Centre records slightly higher membership levels, with an average of 4.87% between 2001 and 2015, though it finds a similar pattern in membership levels, with a high of 6.7% in October 2005 and a low of 3.5% in November 2014 (2015d: 109).

To provide a baseline for comparison, an average of 7% of ethnic Ukrainians were members of the Communist Party of the Soviet Union as of 1 January 1989 (Tishkov 1991).[24] This is well over any reported average of party membership levels in independent Ukraine. To further contextualize this, Ukrainians accounted for just over 16% of all members of the Communist Party of the Soviet Union, second only to Russians who made up 58.64% of the party. Party membership levels in independent Ukraine are also lower than the 27-country European average of 4.7% reported for the late 2000s (van Biezen *et al.* 2012). However, Ukraine's average is similar to the average observed in the post-communist European Union (EU) member states; their average calculated to approximately 3%.[25]

---

23 IFES annual Ukrainian public opinion polls, available at: http://www.ifes.org/countries/Ukraine.aspx.
24 It should be noted that this figure refers to the number of ethnic Ukrainians in the whole of the Soviet Union and not the number of residents of the Ukrainian Soviet Socialist Republic.
25 The post-communist democracies included here are Bulgaria, the Czech Republic, Estonia, Hungary, Latvia, Lithuania, Poland, Romania, Slovakia, and Slovenia (van Biezen *et al.* 2012).

According to polls conducted by the Razumkov Centre in 2005 and 2009, the overwhelming answer as to why people do not belong to parties is a lack of need—56.8 and 64.1 percent respectively (Razumkov 2010b). This lack of need to belong to a party is likely tied to citizen expectations about party representativeness and opinions about whose interest parties serve. Between 2001 and 2015, a plurality of citizens believed that political parties primarily served the interests of financial and business circles, while an average of less than nine percent of citizens felt that parties served the interests of voters. A decline in party representativeness is also illustrated by the increased relevance of the party leader over party ideology. While only around a quarter of Ukrainians prefer an ideologically-based party (with a consistent party program), a majority of Ukrainians (42%) prefer a party with strong, popular leadership, that does not change over time (Razumkov 2015b).

Societal-Party Linkage

Since the establishment of a multi-party system in Ukraine, there has been an absence of stable connections between parties and specific social groups. Parties generally appeal to the "whole" of Ukraine as opposed to a specific social section. Attempts by a majority of parties to secure a wide electoral base has led to difficulties with the recruitment and retention of members, but as found by the Razumkov Centre (2010a), little if any analytical data is published by parties about their members. The diminished value of party membership as viewed by Ukrainian citizens mirrors the decreased value parties place in their members. As previously discussed, member participation is not essential to the internal workings of the party, and is a potential hindrance to how the party elite chooses to run the organization.

One way to assess the link between society and political parties over time is by voter turnout. Stable or increased voter turnout illustrates strong linkages between people and the political parties that are tasked to represent them; it means that parties are continually able to mobilize voters and keep them engaged in formal politics. To place these findings in a meaningful context, I compare voter turnout for parliamentary elections in Ukraine between 1994 and 2014 to the average of that found in Central and Eastern Europe (CEE) between 1990 and 2014. Average voter turnout in Ukraine since independence mirrors that of the CEE region—65% and 64% respectively. However, voter turnout in Ukraine has steadily decreased over time, on average 3.5% with each election.

While there are various explanations for decreasing voter turnout, one main reason is lack of trust in political parties. Less than seven percent of Ukrainians surveyed between 1996 and 2013 had any trust in political parties.[26] Additionally, an average of only 20.5 percent of respondents found that political parties had clear and distinct proposals to address the issues facing the country.[27] In a 2017 poll by Razumkov Centre, which asked whether there were any existing political parties (in or out of government) or movements that could be trusted to govern the state, a relative majority of 48.9% answered "no" with another 18% reporting it was "hard to say" (Razumkov 2017). Parties are the primary political actors in a democracy and if the public lacks confidence in them and their abilities, then this signals weakness in the organizational development of parties.

An additional measure of the bond between society and parties is electoral volatility. Electoral volatility in Ukraine between 1994 and 2014 reached almost 35%, one of the highest of any European country (Casal Bértoa 2016).[28] Net electoral volatility is considered high if it exceeds 10%. Ukraine's level of volatility fell during the mid-2000s, as few parties routinely passed the electoral

---

[26] Instytut sotsilohii NAN Ukrainy (2013) "Ukrains'ke suspil'stvo 1992-2013, stan ta dynamika zmin sotsiolohichnyi monitorynh," http://i-soc.com.ua/institute/soc-mon-2013.pdf (accessed 21 February 2017).

[27] IFES annual Ukrainian public opinion polls, available at http://www.ifes.org/countries/Ukraine.aspx. From 1997 to 2001, the specific wording of the question was, "Do you find there are clear differences between the various political parties and blocs in how they plan to solve problems facing Ukraine?" Between 2002 and 2012, the wording was, "In your opinion, do the major political parties in Ukraine have clear proposals to address the issues facing the country?"

[28] Ukraine's level of electoral volatility is exceeded only by Albania, Lithuania, and Turkey.

threshold—*Bat'kivshchyna*, Party of Regions, and the Communist Party of Ukraine. However, following the Euromaidan Revolution of 2014, the political landscape underwent significant changes. The ever-present Communist party of Ukraine was forced out of parliament in 2014 as a result of the new laws on decommunization. The Party of Regions collapsed and did not participate in the elections. The inclusion of a new nationalist party—*Pravyi Sektor*—meant that the radical-right vote was split and thus the surprise victor in the 2012 elections, *Svoboda*, failed to pass the electoral threshold in 2014. Additionally, the 2014 elections were won by a political newcomer: the Petro Poroshenko Bloc. Electoral volatility nearly doubled between the period of 2007–2012 and that of 2012–2014 due to a high level of instability of party representation (Razumkov 2015a: 13). The lack of a stable base of parties prevents high levels of predictability, and thus undermines the overall effectiveness of political parties as a link between state and society and the legitimacy of parties as membership organizations in general.

Low membership levels, decreasing voter turnout, lack of trust among parties, and high electoral volatility all indicate weakened linkages between parties and society. Generally speaking, political parties are not developing according to the mass-based model, as a professionalization of party politics has shifted emphasis to obtaining and maintaining power (Hooghe and Kern 2015). Parties are organizing in accordance with a top-down model, where the recognizability of party leaders is proving increasingly important at the polls and parties are operating with little input from rank-and-file members. As parties move away from civil society, their relationship with the state is intensifying and parties are becoming more reliant upon the monopolization of state resources for survival.

Party-State Linkage

Ukraine's constitution legally recognizes political parties and, like most post-communist countries, elevates them to a privileged position, defining competition and political participation almost solely in terms of the party (Kopecký 2006). As Kopecký (2006: 253) posits, political parties in Eastern Europe are in a "strong position to define the rules of the game so as to suit their private ends." Hence, these parties have had comparably more influence in determining their political environment than their Western European counterparts. In Ukraine, there has been substantial management of parties by the state as exercised through manipulation of electoral law. Whenever there are changes to laws there can be both intended and unintended consequences, thus electoral law directly affects the party system (Bille 1994).

A distinctive feature of Ukrainian elections is that they are often governed by a new set of laws. Four times between 1991 and 2014 the electoral law governing parliamentary elections has been changed. In 1990 and 1994 the elections were held under the majoritarian electoral system, the 1998 and 2002 elections were held under a mixed (proportional-majoritarian) system, the 2006 and 2007 elections were held under a proportional system, and the 2012 and 2014 elections reverted back to a mixed system (Razumkov Centre 2015a). Such frequent changes undermine the stability of the party system as the electoral system structures competition. This is particularly true in the case of Ukraine where changes were made during times of tough political struggle, in the run-up to an election.

New election laws have been used to manipulate competition, as they often have clear political intentions to suppress the opposition and/or create an advantage for the ruling party (Taagepera and Schugart 1989; Tan 2013; Way 2004). Changes to the electoral threshold were also intended to affect the composition of parliament. While the decrease from a four-percent to a three-percent threshold following the Orange Revolution was meant to increase representation of smaller parties, the increase to five percent in 2010 intended to favor the ruling majority and exclude smaller ideological parties. Another major change to electoral law that had implications for the interactions between parties was the banning of electoral blocs prior to the 2012 parliamentary election. The ruling Party of Regions attempted to limit collaboration among opposition parties by preventing them from allying at the polls. It was a clear attempt by the ruling authorities to secure a majority of seats for themselves by restricting interparty competition via a complete ban on blocs.

In the Ukrainian party system, reciprocity between parties and members does not exist. The parties do not work on behalf of their members and the party members in turn do not offer reliable allegiance and financial support. This points to a main problem with party organization in Ukraine: party financing. Ukrainian party law has not required the disclosure of what percentage of a party's budget is derived from membership dues, and therefore parties do not make exact figures available. However, most parties state that between 6 and 10 percent of their budget is derived from membership dues—not enough to finance party activities (Kovryzhenko 2010).

A problem with accounting for what part of party's budget is derived from membership fees is that this sum is often lumped together with members' voluntary donations—here the role of oligarchs should be noted. Journalistic reporting has produced some specific figures on membership dues *and* member donations in party financing over time, but it is the latter that provide the bulk of financial assistance ("Sered..." 2012; "Skil'ky koshtuie.." 2002). For instance, the minimum quarterly membership fee for the Party of Regions as of 2012, was five hryvnia. Although the fee is small, the party reported over 1.5 million members at the time which would amount to 30 million hryvnyas a year. The Communist Party earned over 112 million hryvnias in 2012, almost all of which came from voluntary donations. However, according to Petro Symonenko— party leader at the time—deputies of Parliament were subject to a deduction of twenty percent of their monthly salary, which went back to the party. In 2002, the Socialist Party of Ukraine required one percent of a member's monthly salary be donated to the party (less for retirees and students). The situation of *Bat'kivshchyna* is a bit more complicated due to a matter of semantics. In 2002, the party required a minimum of one hryvnia a year in voluntary donations. In 2012, the minimum membership fee was reported to be only one hryvnia a month, although leading party members reportedly paid more. For the year, membership fees *and* financial donations (no distinction between the two being made) amounted to over 114 million hryvnias. In 2013, *Bat'kivshchyna* reported having no fixed membership fees ("*Bat'kivshchyna, Svoboda...*" 2013). In 2016, *Bat'kivshchyna* reported *receiving* no membership fees for the second quarter of 2016, though it recorded 2,239,083 hryvnias in contributions (Kalmykov 2016).

In many European countries, parties have turned to the state for financial support, as private contributions are no longer sufficient to sustain party organizations and operations. In many Southern and Central European countries, the relationship between parties and the state has grown increasingly strong as state financing has become crucial for the maintenance and survival of parties—both in and out of government (van Biezen and Kopecký 2014). For most of independence, political parties in Ukraine only received indirect public funding. Some parliamentary elections have included reimbursement of election expenditures which were actually reimbursed (the 2006 election), while others have included similar reimbursement requirements that were never paid out as State Budget Laws did not provide the funds (the 2007 election) (Kovryzhenko 2010: 93). Thus, the most important funding sources for political parties in Ukraine remain oligarchs and their corporations.

Ukrainian parties have become clients of oligarchic clans, representing their interests in politics, and thus granting immense political influence and authority to big business (Matuszak 2012: 13). This situation results in parties that are led by or partner with prominent businessmen—notably President Petro Poroshenko, Ihor Kolomoisky, and Rinat Akhmetov—or business groups, such as the Lyovochkin–Firtash group. For most of its independence, Ukraine lacked a national broadcast system such as that found in most of Western Europe.[29] Thus parties turn to oligarchs not just for funding but for their mass communication needs, as the commercial

---

[29] Legislation was introduced in early 2015 that would create a public broadcasting company out of the already established state-owned media outlets. It would be under state ownership and controlled by a supervisory board comprised of one member of each parliamentary faction/group and various NGOs (Halling and Stewart 2016). The national public broadcasting company of Ukraine (UA:PBC) was registered 19 January 2017.

media sector is predominantly controlled by the same business groups that finance the parties (Razumkov 2015c; Kuzio 2016). For example, the following television channels are indirectly owned by Ukrainian oligarchs: *1+1* by Kolomoisky and Ihor Surkis; *Inter* by Dmytro Firtash, Valeriy Khoroshkovsky, Serhiy Lyovochkin and Svitlana Pluzhnykova; *STB/ICTV/Novyi Kanal* by Viktor and Olena Pinchuk (former President Kuchma's daughter and son-in-law); *TRK* by Rinat Akhmetov; *Telekanal 24* by Kateryna Kit-Sadova (wife of Lviv mayor and party head of *Samopomich*, Andriy Sadovyi) and Roman and Oksana Andriyko ("Vladel'tsy..." 2016).[30]

An important means of support oligarchs provide to "loyal" political parties is discounted airtime for political advertisements (Meleshevych 2016: 9). The Ukrainian Center for Independent Political Research found that the majority of party communication with voters is via mass media during election campaigns (Razumkov Centre 2010a: 27). During the 2014 parliamentary election campaign, parties relied upon TV advertisements as the main means of conveying information to voters (2015e).

As financial industrial groups remain the main financiers of parties, parties continue to represent the interests of the capital that funds them. This has allowed parties to avoid public accountability as they do not rely upon mass membership bases nor state financing for their survival. As a result, parties in Ukraine have developed in a very particular manner, similar to that observed by van Biezen and Kopecký (2014) in the cases of many African states. In Ukraine, parties have not become *dependent* upon the state, and the majority of the benefits that parties amass from the state are obtained from patronage, clientelistic practices, as well as corruption and are thus enjoyed solely by the electoral victors who control the state (Kopecký and Mair 2003; van Biezen and Kopecký 2014). As Fisun (2016: 199) notes, in Ukraine, "political parties are formed by political investors not to protect the interests of the electorate but to promote the quota based distribution of the rent-seeking

---

[30] The majority of these channels are owned by offshore companies that are owned by Ukrainian oligarchs that represent both Ukrainian and Russian interests.

positions in the Cabinet of Ministers and the rent-seeking apparatuses." This has allowed the parties in power to control state resources, and as a result, become deeply intertwined with the state.

The close linkage between the state and ruling parties has at times created parties of power, such as the Party of Regions. The result is the under-development of opposition parties who rarely make it into parliament and/or never join the ruling coalition. Furthermore, it has elevated the clientelistic party model over the mass-based party in Ukraine. Referring back to the emphasis placed on party leader over party ideology, this is largely because a party that organizes itself around a strong leader who can assume the top executive office, is a party that will be able to amass wealth and secure public office as well as associated privileges for its rent-seeking entrepreneurs (Hellman 1998; Fisun 2016). Political leadership projects have long been part of Ukraine's party history, and in 2017 there were more than ten parties registered with the Ukrainian Ministry of Justice which bear the names of their leaders—such as Petro Poroshenko Bloc "Solidarity," Radical Party of Oleh Liashko, Ukrainian Sea Party of Serhii Kivalov, and Public Political Platform of Nadia Savchenko (Yakymenko 2017).

Patronage routinely occurs in Ukraine's civil service system, as documented in the cases of the Party of Regions both at the end of the 1990s/early 2000s and between 2010–2013, Our Ukraine and *Bat'kivshchyna* in the mid-2000s, and the Petro Poroshenko Bloc following its 2014 win (D'Anieri 2005; Kudelia and Kuzio 2015; Melnykovska 2016).[31] The system of patronage in Ukraine allows the ruling party to redistribute rents to maintain party operations and control key positions at all bureaucratic levels (Kudelia 2016). For instance, after the Party of Regions won the 2006 parliamentary

---

[31] Ukraine's political system is characterized by presidential patronage, where the power center is the president and parties act as the structural framework for the patron–client relationships. Examples of patronage–clientelist practices include collecting votes, buying places on party lists, nepotism over government appointments, the introduction of legislation to target specific oligarchs or business groups, and threats of prosecution to coerce business/political rivals. See Melnykovska (2015) for a detailed history of state–business relations in Ukraine.

elections, its oligarch backers—Rinat Akhmetov, Andrii Kluiev, and Dmytro Firtash—assumed important cabinet positions (Kudelia 2016: 71). Similar was the case following *Bat'kivshchyna's* 2007 win in the early parliamentary elections, with Serhiy Buryak, Vitaliy Haiduk, and Tariel Vasadze, receiving key government posts.[32] Big business has also benefited from clientelistic practices that sees them receive special benefits/privileges in return for their political support and financial backing. Such was the case with Dmytro Firtash and his RosUkrEnergo group's cooperation with Yushchenko, which allowed the group to be the sole intermediary agent in Russian gas imports to Ukraine between 2004–2009 (Melnykovska 2015). Parties also draw support from their patron–client networks in other ways, such as establishing local "charities" to mobilize voters, and selectively implementing policies at the regional level so as to maintain the support of economic and regional elites (Fisun 2016; Wilson 2005).

It should be noted that important elements of how Ukrainian parties organize may be changing, which will inevitably impact the relationship between parties and the state. In October 2015, the Ukrainian parliament adopted the law "On Amendments to Some Legislative Acts of Ukraine on Preventing and Combating Political Corruption" (No.2123a), which officially introduced state funding of political parties. Additionally, it requires greater financial transparency and accountability of political parties, as well as increasing liability for violations of the laws on party financing (Razumkov 2015a: 11). This law came into force 1 July 2016 and provided direct state funding of political parties and reimbursements of campaign costs for members of parliament beginning in January 2017. Ninety percent of the funding allocated for party financing is proportionally distributed, according to votes received, among parties that cross the five-percent threshold in parliamentary elections. The remaining 10% of funding is to be

---

[32] Serhiy Buryak was a former Ukrainian banker who was appointed Head of the Tax Administration of Ukraine; Vitaliy Haiduk was founder of the Industrial Union of Donbas who was appointed to serve as Yushchenko's head of the National Security and Defense Council (RNBO); Tariel Vasadze is chairman of UkrAvto automobile empire and received a position as an MP in *Bat'kivshchyna*.

distributed among parties entering parliament that see women make up at least one-third of the MPs. The law further stipulates that parties are now required to submit quarterly reports on their property, income, expenses, and financial obligations to the National Agency on Prevention of Corruption (NAZK). Based on the 2016 third-quarter results, most parties were fulfilling the financial disclosure requirements. While NAZK found more than 500 violations, they tended to be of one type, which is the failure of local party chapters to open bank accounts. *Bat'kivshchyna* was found to be the primary offender. However, by October 2017, 162 registered political parties had not submitted current financial statements, and while some parties were later convinced by NAZK to submit the required documents, 86 requests for financial disclosures were returned because the addresses listed in the official register were either incorrect or out-of-date (Yakymenko 2017).

Parties in Ukraine—particularly the electoral winners—have used their close linkage with the state to operate without transparency and are thought of more as part of the state than as representatives of civil society. Due to the immense power of oligarchs and business groups, parties have not traditionally been highly dependent upon the state in Ukraine. Furthermore, state resources are not universally enjoyed by parties but rather only the electoral winners, thus parties continue to develop unevenly, and the sustainability and growth of party organizations is in large part a result of clientelistic practices within state institutions. Whether the new legislative change on the state financing of parties will weaken ties between parties and oligarchs, as intended, remains to be seen. However, this new law raises many questions about the future of the party–state relationship. Will parties become increasingly dependent on the state as the sources of party financing change? Furthermore, what effects will the increased oversight of parties by the state have, as parties are now subject to greater financial regulation? Lastly, will the state look to become further involved in internal party affairs, broadening their oversight from financial matters to other aspects of party conduct?

Post-Euromaidan Trends in Party Organization

As of early 2015, party membership in Ukraine remains at nearly half of that seen in Western Europe, averaging just above two percent (Razumkov 2015a). Despite the 2004 Orange Revolution that placed political parties at the center of national political debate, partisanship did not see a drastic *and* stable increase. Parties remained leader-based projects where little value was attributed to the ordinary member. Following the 2014 Euromaidan Revolution, some new trends can be observed in party politics, which will likely have an impact on the future of the institution of membership in Ukraine. If parties continue to devote efforts to developing party organizations from the ground-up and engage with civil society, citizens will likely find parties more representative and association with them to be more fulfilling. This in turn could infuse the concept of party membership with some much-needed value.

The first major trend is the entry into the national political arena of grassroots based parties. While these parties are still associated with strong, prominent leaders, the party organizations were built from the bottom-up. Two prime examples are *Samopomich* (Self Reliance) and *Pravyi Sektor* (Right Sector).

Samopomich was one of the unexpected stars of the 2014 parliamentary elections, coming in third. The party ran in the early elections without a single former parliamentarian deputy on its electoral list, instead turning to medium-sized business owners, local entrepreneurs and civic volunteers for support (Sindelar 2014; Razumkov 2015e; Olszański 2016). Furthermore, a quarter of the party's electoral list consisted of female candidates (Goncharova 2014). *Samopomich* established a local presence and demonstrated how a political party should facilitate representativeness, additionally evidenced by its internal party procedures. The party held public discussion over mayoral candidate selection and chose to hold public primary elections between 15 June and 15 July 2015 (Makarov and Kaplan 2015). While questions did surround the level of transparency of these primary elections, the fact that they were held at all signifies a major first step in increasing the level of internal party democracy among Ukrainian parties.³³

Pravyi Sector began as a small, radically nationalist, extra-parliamentary umbrella-association in November 2013. It was a coalition of radical right-wing activists from organizations such as *"Tryzub"* ("Trident"), *"Patriot of Ukraine,"* UNA-UNSO, Social-National Assembly, C-14 (or Sich), and "White Hammer" (Shekhovtsov & Umland 2014). In March of 2014, *Pravyĭ Sektor* became a political party. The political party had developed from the ground up, as a paramilitary group during the Euromaidan Revolution who created a grassroots network of volunteers to protest Yanukovych's authoritarianism and fight the riot police in Kyiv. The organization then shifted its focus to Eastern Ukraine where it continued its paramilitary activities with the establishment of the "Donbas" battalion that took part in defending Ukraine against the Russian military and proxy forces occupying Donetsk and Luhansk regions.

Similar to *Svoboda*, the political arm of *Pravyi Sektor* was founded upon a strong right-wing, nationalist ideology. It was based not around a leader, but around political ideals.³⁴ *Pravyi Sektor* proved the development of a grassroots political organizations in Ukraine is possible, given the presence of a common set of core values and a vast network of human resources (Mierzejewski-Voznyak 2018). However, it also attested to the fact that there are few political prospects at the national level for ideological parties in Ukraine's current political system, as witnessed with the 2014 parliamentary results (Razumkov 2017). *Pravyi Sektor* received 1.8 percent of the vote in the early elections with fellow right-wing party *Svoboda* capturing only 4.71 percent and the CPU obtaining merely 3.88 percent.

---

33 See "HO 'Samopomich' provodytyt' [sic] pershi v Ukraini vidkryti 'Praimeriz'," *Visti Kalushchyny*, 26 May 2015, http://visti-kalush.com.ua/news/2015/05/26/12066/view; "'Samopomich' obmaniuie frankivtsiv?" *Versiyi.if.ua*, 8 July 2017, http://versii.if.ua/novunu/samopomich-obmanyuye-frankivtsiv/.

34 The party in fact experienced a change in leadership in 2016, with Dmytro Yarosh being replaced by Andriy Tarasenko. However, this did cost the party around 20 percent of its members (Melkozerova 2016).

A second trend is the inclusion of not just seasoned politicians and businessmen on party lists, but also civil society activists, journalists, battalion commanders, and Anti-Terrorist Operation (ATO) volunteer participants (Olszański 2014; Razumkov 2015e). This is important for party representativeness as there was societal demand for wide sweeping political change and greater inclusion of civil society representatives in the political process. A poll carried out by the Razumkov Centre prior to the 2014 parliamentary elections found that 68 percent of respondents had a positive view on political parties placing civil society activists on their electoral lists and over 60 percent responded favorably to the inclusion of volunteer battalion commanders, military servicemen, and ATO participants (Razumkov 2015e: 23–24).

Parties' motivation for including such individuals varies. In the case of *Samopomich*, the party itself began as an NGO and after registering as a political party it continued to work with civil society. It was logical for the party to include NGO leaders on its electoral list. The most notable party member was Hanna Hopko, who headed *Samopomich's* electoral list and as of December 2018 is Head of the Foreign Affairs Committee in the Ukrainian parliament.[35] Hopko has a long history of activism including working for the Ukraine Citizen Action Network, leading the campaign for tobacco control in Ukraine, and working as an advocacy expert for the National Democracy Institute (NDI). The party also placed on its list Iryna Suslova, a civil activist (although in 2016 she joined the leading faction of Petro Poroshenko Bloc after being kicked out of the *Samopomich* faction) (Zhuk 2016).

For other parties, such as Bloc Petro Poroshenko, *Bat'kivshchyna,* and People's Front, including members of civil society was strategic—those names (i.e. "new personalities") acted as a counter to the seasoned politicians and businessmen that made-up the bulk of the list.[36] For example, Bloc Petro Poroshenko

---

[35] Hopko was ousted from the party in 2015 due to her voting in parliament in support of draft amendments to the constitution for decentralization.
[36] While many oligarchs previously associated with Yanukovych disappeared from party lists, other representatives associated with the Firtash-Lyovochkin group

included journalists Serhiy Leshchenko, Mustafa Nayyem, and Olha Chervakova on its list; *Bat'kivshchyna* included on its list Alyona Ivanivna Shkrum, a human rights activist and lawyer, and Oleksiy Ryabchyn, an academic, freelance journalist, and development specialist; Tetiana Chornovol, a journalist and civic activist, was included on the People's Front's list. Additionally, three battalion commanders—Semen Semenchenko, Yuryi Bereza, and Andriy Teteruk—were elected to the parliament on the lists of *Samopomich* and People's Front (*Obiednannia Samopomich* 2015).[37]

Conclusion: The Underdeveloped Institution of Membership in Ukraine

Between 1991 and 2014, the institution of membership was underdeveloped in Ukraine. However, this has in large part been a deliberate choice. During the Soviet period, the Communist party held definitive power, was deeply intertwined with the state, and was not truly representative of the people. Political parties born out of this legacy have shown difficulty eschewing these tendencies. Independent Ukraine has seen a blurring of boundaries between political regime and state on more than one occasion. Contemporary political parties in Ukraine are more concerned with amassing power than a large membership base, as winning elections and controlling government does not require parties to actively recruit and retain party members.

A political party's struggle for power is generally a battle for control of resources rather than a fight for implementing a specific political agenda. This is because a party with privileged access to the *"administratyvnyi resurs"*—the ability to mobilize state institutions and resources to achieve political objectives—tends to be in a better

---

and oligarch Ihor Kolomoisky were heavily represented on the lists of Bloc Petro Poroshenko and People's Front.

[37] Semen Semenchenko is the commander and founder of the "Donbas" defense battalion located in Donetsk; Yuryi Bereza is the commander of the Dnipro 1 battalion; Andriy Teteruk is the commander of the Myrotvorets battalion. Semenchenko ran on *Samopomich's* list while Bereza and Teteruk ran on the list of People's Front.

position to fend off competitors and protect the status quo, especially if it is willing to break or bend the rule of law. To be sure, it is not just the political context that has impeded the development of the institution of membership among Ukrainian political parties. The internal organizational dynamics of parties themselves has been a hindrance. Parties are top-down machines that lack internal democracy, predominantly work for themselves and represent the interests of oligarchs or oligarchic groups, and have thus let societal interests fall by the wayside. If proper democratic mechanisms of decision-making are absent within the party structure, it affects the political culture, which is often expressed in societal distrust of parties and the party system (Tymchenko 2015).

National legislation has provided minimal guidelines as concerns the development of parties and the role of party members. In the case of Ukraine, the party system would likely benefit from further national oversight in the form of additional amendments to the 2001 Law "On Political Parties in Ukraine." First, the matter of non-party members should be addressed. Legislation should stipulate that top party positions should only be held by registered members of the party and more importantly, the number of non-party member candidates that run on a party's list should be limited. Not only should a quota be set, that requires a minimum of 70% of a party's electoral list be comprised of registered party members, but it should also be stipulated that the top 10% of candidates listed must also be registered party members. This would improve transparency in the electoral process, as voters would more clearly be able to ensure that when they vote for a candidate representing a party that politician will continue representing that party throughout the entire term. Furthermore, it would help curtail the increasingly problematic issue of "free agents" in parliament who switch factions at any given time.

Second, there should be enhanced criteria to establish and register a new political party. Specifically, there should be a change from requiring signatures in support of a new party to requiring applications for party membership in the proposed new party. Similar criteria ensuring representativeness should apply (applications must come from two-thirds of the districts in two-thirds of the oblasts). Both of these changes would place greater emphasis on partisanship, making it a goal for parties which in turn might result in greater value being placed on members themselves.

Parties have been responsible for defining the functions of party members and choosing to what extent value is attached to such membership, as outlined in their party charters. However, just as ideological programs have declined among parties in Ukraine, interest in rank-and-file members has also waned. Parties were not established as representative organizations, and party loyalty has shifted from members to financial backers. Furthermore, parties have found that electoral success can be guaranteed even without a wide member base as long as there is a prominent, popular party head. While national legislation protects against conflicts of interest and bias, as concerns party membership, parties themselves need to ensure the well-functioning of their own organizations by establishing internal regulations and procedures that will decentralize decision-making and engage party members in the agenda setting.

In Ukraine today, there is an overall disconnect between citizens and party elite. This may in part explain why new parties are able to rise to power overnight, since old parties have not established roots in the consciousness of the average voter. For most of Ukraine's independence, party membership has failed to have relevance or a function for the majority of Ukrainians. However, it is possible that if parties continue to actively engage with and incorporate members of civil society, apathetic attitudes towards partisanship will decrease in years to come.

References

Bat'kivshchyna. (2014) *Statut Vseukrains'ke obiednannia "Bat'kivshchyna,"* http://Bat'kivshchyna.com.ua/statute.html (accessed 30 October 2014; URL inactive as at 5 August 2019).

"Bat'kivshchyna, Svoboda i Udar rozpovily, khto ikh finansuie" (2013) *TSN*, 21 April, https://tsn.ua/politika/lideri-opoziciyi-rozpovili-za-chiy-rahunok-isnuyut-yihni-Partiï-291451.html.

Bille, L. (1994) "Denmark: The Decline of the Membership Party?" in R. Katz and P. Mair (eds.) *How Parties Organize: Change and Adaptation in Party Organizations in Western Democracies.* London: Sage, 134–57.
Burnell, P. and Ware, A. (eds.) (1998) *Funding Democratization.* Manchester: Manchester University Press.
Casal Bértoa, F. (2016) "Database on WHO Governs in Europe and Beyond," *Party Systems and Governments Observatory*, whogoverns.eu (accessed 21 February 2017).
CVU (2018) "V Ukraini zupynyvsia partiinyi bum," *Committee of Voters of Ukraine*, 30 January, http://www.cvu.org.ua/eng/nodes/view/type:news/slug:v-ukraini-zupynyvsia-partiinyi-bum (accessed 1 December 2018).
Dalton, R. and Wattenberg, M. (eds.) (2000) *Parties without Partisans.* Oxford: Oxford University Press.
Dalton, R. J. and Weldon, S. A. (2005) "Public Images of Political Parties: A Necessary Evil?" *West European Politics* 28(5): 931–51.
D'Anieri, P. (2005) "What Has Changed in Ukrainian Politics?: Assessing the Implications of the Orange Revolution," *Problems of Post-Communism* 52(5): 82–91.
D'Anieri, P. J. (1999) *Economic Interdependence in Ukrainian–Russian relations.* New York: SUNY Press.
Farrell, D. M. (2006) "Political Parties in a Changing Campaign Environment," in R. S. Katz and W. Crotty, W. (eds.) *Handbook of Party Politics.* London: Sage, 122–33.
Fisun, O. (2016) "Neopatrimonialism, Rent-seeking, and Regime Change," in H. Hale and R. W. Orttung (eds.) *Beyond the Euromaidan: Comparative Perspectives on Advancing Reform in Ukraine.* Stanford, CA: Stanford University Press, 105–23.
Gherghina, S. (2014) *Party Organization and Electoral Volatility in Central and Eastern Europe: Enhancing Voter Loyalty.* London: Routledge.
Golosov, G. V. (1998) "Who Survives? Party Origins, Organizational Development, and Electoral Performance in Post-communist Russia," *Political Studies* 46(3): 511–43.
Goncharova, O. (2016) "New Faces in Parliament Possible with Samopomich Party," *Kyiv Post*, 23 October, https://www.kyivpost.com/article/content/oct-26-parliamentary-election/new-faces-in-parliament-possible-with-samopomich-party-369116.html (accessed 1 December 2018).
Grönlund, K. and Setälä, M. (2007) "Political Trust, Satisfaction and Voter Turnout," *Comparative European Politics* 5: 400–22.
Haggard, S. and Webb, S. B. (2004) "Political Incentives and Intergovernmental Fiscal Relations: Argentina, Brazil and Mexico Compared," in A. P. Montero and D. J. Samuels (eds.) *Decentralization and Democracy in Latin America.* Notre Dame: University of Notre Dame, 235–70.
Hale, H. and Orttung, R.W. (eds.) (2016) *Beyond the Euromaidan: Comparative Perspectives on Advancing Reform in Ukraine.* Stanford, CA: Stanford University Press.

Halling, S. and Stewart, S. (2016) "Deoligarchisation in Ukraine: Promising Visions, Murky Realities," *Stiftung Wissenschaft und Politik*, Deutsches Institut für Internationale Politik und Sicherheit 51, http://nbn-resolving.de/urn:nbn:de:0168-ssoar-49684-6 (accessed 21 February 2017).

Hellman, J. S. (1998) "Winners Take All: The Politics of Partial Reform in Postcommunist Transitions," *World Politics* 50(2): 203–34.

Hooghe, M. and Kern, A. (2015) "Party Membership and Closeness and the Development of Trust in Political Institutions: An Analysis of the European Social Survey, 2002–2010," *Party Politics* 21(6): 944–56.

Ionascu, A. and Soare, S. C. (2011) "Cultivating Large Membership Rolls: The Romanian Case," in E. van Haute (ed.) *Party Membership in Europe: Exploration into the Anthills of Party Politics*. Brussels: Editions de l'Université de Bruxelles, 61–76.

Kalmykov, D. (2016) "Deshcho pro formu ta zmist shchokvartal'nykh zvitiv politychnykh partii, Tsentr polityko-pravovykh reform, 21 October, http://pravo.org.ua/ua/news/20871759-descho-pro-formu-ta-zmist-schokvartalnih-zvitiv-politichnih-partiy (accessed 2 December 2018).

Katz, R. S. (2002) "The Internal Life of Parties," in K. R. Luther and F. Müller-Rommel (eds.) *Political Challenges in the New Europe: Political and Analytical Challenges*. Oxford: Oxford University Press, 87–118.

Katz, R. S. and Crotty, W. (eds.) (2006) *Handbook of Party Politics*. London: Sage.

Karmazina, M. (2018) "'Liudyna, shcho hraiet'sia': politychni partii v Ukraini," *Mirror Weekly*, 31 March, https://dt.ua/internal/lyudina-scho-grayetsya-politichni-partiyi-v-ukrayini-273771_.html (accessed 13 December 2018).

Katz, R. S. and Mair, P. (eds.) (1994) *How Parties Organize: Change and Adaptation in Party Organizations in Western Democracies*. London: Sage.

Kirchheimer, O. (1966) "The Transformation of Western European Party Systems" in J. Lapalombra and M. Weiner (eds.) *Political Parties and Political Development*. Princeton, NJ: Princeton University Press, 177–200.

Kononchuk, S. (2014) "Perspectives on Political Responsibility of Ukrainian Parties," *Ukrainian Center for Independent Political Research*, 20(13/723), available at: http://www.ucipr.kiev.ua/publications/perspectives-on-political-responsibility-of-ukrainian-parties/lang/en (accessed 31 October 2014).

Kopecký, P. (2006) "Political Parties and the State in Post-communist Europe: The Nature of Symbiosis," *Journal of Communist Studies and Transition Politics* 22(3): 251–73.

Kopecký, P. and Mair, P. (2003) "Political Parties and Government," in M. A. Salih (ed.) *Political Parties in Africa*. London: Pluto, 275–92.

Kopecký, P. and Scherlis, G. (2008) "Party Patronage in Contemporary Europe," *European Review* 16(3): 355–71.

Kovryzhenko, D. (2010) "Regulation of Political Parties in Ukraine: Current State and Directions of Reforms," Kyiv, Agency for Legislative Initiatives and OSCE/ODIHR.

Kreuzer, M. and Pettai, V. (2003) "Patterns of Political Instability: Affiliation Patterns of Politicians and Voters in Post-communist Estonia, Latvia, and Lithuania," *Studies in Comparative International Development* 38(2): 76–98.

Kudelia, S. (2016) "Corruption in Ukraine: Perpetuum Mobile or the Endplay of Post-soviet Elites," in H. Hale and R. W. Orttung (eds.) *Beyond the Euromaidan: Comparative Perspectives on Advancing Reform in Ukraine.* Stanford, CA: Stanford University Press.

Kudelia, S. and Kuzio, T. (2015) "Nothing Personal: Explaining the Rise and Decline of Political Machines in Ukraine," *Post-Soviet Affairs* 31(3): 250–78.

Kuzio, T. (2015) "Competing Nationalisms, Euromaidan, and the Russian-Ukrainian Conflict," *Studies in Ethnicity and Nationalism* 15(1): 157–69.

Kuzio, T. (2016) "Oligarchs, the Partial Reform Equilibrium, and the Euromaidan Revolution," in H. Hale and R. W. Orttung (eds.) *Beyond the Euromaidan: Comparative Perspectives on Advancing Reform in Ukraine.* Stanford, CA: Stanford University Press.

Lane, J. (2015) "Volatility and Western European Party Systems: Two New Approaches," *Baltic Journal of Political Science* 4(1): 7–22.

Luther, K. R. and Müller-Rommel, F. (eds.) (2002) *Political Challenges in the New Europe: Political and Analytical Challenges.* Oxford: Oxford University Press.

"L'vivs'kyi UDAR vyznachyvsia z kandydatom na mery L'vova" (2015) *Varianty*, 10 July, https://varianty.lviv.ua/27694-lvivskyi-udar-vyznachyvsia-z-kandydatom-na-mery-lvova (accessed 13 December 2018).

Mair, P. (1994) "Party Organizations: From Civil Society to the State," in R. S. Katz and P. Mair (eds.) *How Parties Organize: Change and Adaptation in Party Organizations in Western Democracies.* London: Sage, 80–108.

Mair, P. and van Biezen, I. (2001) "Party Membership in Twenty European Democracies," *Party Politics* 7(1): 5–21.

Makarov, H. V. and Kaplan, Iu. B. (2015) "Mistsevi vybory 2015: problemy orhanizatsii, pidsumky, tendentsii," *National Institute of Strategic Relations*, Kyiv, http://www.niss.gov.ua/content/articles/files/vuboru-f2365.pdf (accessed 3 March 2017).

Matuszak, S. (2012) "The Oligarchic Democracy: The Influence of Business Groups on Ukrainian Politics," *Ośrodek Studiów Wschodnich Studies* 42(1): 13–22.

Meleshevich, A. (2016) "Cost of Parliamentary Politics in Ukraine," *Kyiv-Mohyla Law and Politics Journal*, 29 December, 2: 147–70.

Melkozerova, V. (2016) "Yarosh Launches a New Movement, Leaves Right Sector," *Kyiv Post*, 22 February, https://www.kyivpost.com/article/content/ukraine-politics/yarosh-launches-a-new-movement-leaves-right-sector-408646.html (accessed 1 March 2017).

Melnykovska, I. (2015) "Big Business and Politics in Ukraine: The Evolution of State–Business Relations," *Employment and Economy in Central and Eastern Europe* 1, available at http://www.emecon.eu/fileadmin/articles/1_2015/1%202015% 20MelnykovskaN.pdf (accessed 1 March 2017).

Mierzejewski-Voznyak, M. G. (2018) "The Radical Right in Post-Soviet Ukraine," in J. Rydgren (ed.) *The Oxford Handbook of the Radical Right*. New York: Oxford University Press, 608–29.

"Na mistsevi vybory partiia 'UDAR' ityme samostiino" (2014) *Za Zbruchem*, 15 December, https://zz.te.ua/na-mistsevi-vybory-partiya-udar-jtyme-samo stijno-2/ (accessed 13 December 2018).

Obiednannia Samopomich (2015) "Five Deputies Expelled from the 'Samopomich' Faction," *Obiednannia Samopomich*, 31 August, https://samopomich.ua/uk-5-deputativ-vyklyuchyly-z-fraktsiji-samopomich/ (accessed 1 March 2017).

Olson, D.M. (1998) "Party Formation and Party System Consolidation in the New Democracies of Central Europe," *Political Studies* 46(3): 5–21.

Olszański, T.A. (2014) "Before the Parliamentary Elections in Ukraine," *Ośrodek Studiów Wschodnich*, 16 October, https://www.osw.waw.pl/en/publikacje/osw-commentary/2014-10-16/parliamentary-elections-ukraine (accessed 2 February 2018).

Panebianco, A. (1988) *Political Parties: Organization and Power*. Cambridge: Cambridge University Press.

Partii Rehioniv. (2014) *Statut Partii Rehioniv*, http://pr.kharkov.ua/ru/article/static/id/18/ (accessed 30 October 2014).

Pavlenko, I. A. (2007) "Stratehiia vnutrishn'oi demokratyzatsii politychnykh partii v Ukraini," *Stratehichni priorytety* 2(3): 175–82.

Poguntke, T. and Scarrow, S. E. (1996) "The Politics of Anti-party Sentiment: Introduction," *European Journal of Political Research* 29(3): 257–62.

Razumkov Centre (2010a) "Present State of Political Parties and the Party System: Key Problems and Shortcomings," *National Security and Defense* 5: 21–30.

Razumkov Centre (2010b) "Ukraine's Political Parties and the Party System in the Public Eyes," *National Security and Defense* 5: 58–62.

Razumkov Centre (2015a) "Party Systems of Ukraine in 2010–2015: Stages and Special Aspects of Evolution," *National Security and Defense* 6–7: 3–17.

Razumkov Centre (2015b) "Development Prospects of Political Parties: Content of Public Demand," *National Security and Defense* 6–7: 34–46.

Razumkov Centre (2015c) "Political Parties in Ukraine: Expert Opinion," *National Security and Defense* 6–7: 74–92.

Razumkov Centre (2015d) "Political Party and Party System of Ukraine at Present: Public Opinion," *National Security and Defense* 6–7: 106–44.

Razumkov Centre (2015e) "Party System after Maidan: Implications and Factors," *National Security and Defense* 6–7: 18–33.

Razumkov Centre (2017) "Political Culture of Ukrainian Citizens: Special Aspects and Trends," *National Security and Defense* 3–4: 3–73.

Romaniuk, A. (2018) "Vnutrishn'opartiina demokratiia iak chynnyk rozvytku ta otsinky politychnykh partii Ukrainy," *Visnyk of the Lviv University. Series Philos.-Political Studies* 18: 354–62.

Roper, S. D. (2002) "The Influence of Romanian Campaign Finance Laws on Party System Development and Corruption," *Party Politics* 8(2): 175–92.
Scarrow, S. E. (1999) "Parties and the Expansion of Direct Democracy Who Benefits?" *Party Politics* 5(3): 341–62.
Scarrow, S. E. (2000) "Parties without Members? Party Organization in a Changing Electoral Environment," in R. Dalton and M. Wattenberg (eds.) *Parties without Partisans*. Oxford: Oxford University Press, 99–101.
Schmitt, H. (2003) "The Eurobarometers: Their Evolution, Obvious Merits, and Ways to Add Value to Them," *European Union Politics* 4(2): 243–51.
"Sered ukrains'kykh partii naibil'she zarobliaie PR, naimenshe – 'Svoboda'." (2013) *Finance.ua*, 25 May, https://news.finance.ua/ua/news/-/302383/sered-ukrayinskyh-partij-najbilshe-zaroblyaye-pr-najmenshe-svoboda (accessed 3 December 2018).
Seyd, P. and Whiteley, P. (1992) "Labour's Vote and Local Activism: The Impact of Local Constituency Campaigns," *Parliamentary Affairs* 45(4): 582–95.
Shekhovtsov, A. (2011) "The Creeping Resurgence of the Ukrainian Radical Right? The Case of the Freedom Party," *Europe-Asia Studies* 63(2): 203–28.
Shekhovtsov, A. and Umland, A. (2014) "Ukraine's Radical Right," *Journal of Democracy* 25(3): 58–63.
Sindelar, D. and Tereshchuk, H. (2014) "Can Lviv Mayor Change Ukrainian Politics Once and For All?" *Radio Free Europe Radio Liberty*, 31 October, https://www.rferl.org/a/ukraine-reforms-elections-self-reliance-party-sadoviy-profile/26668300.html (accessed 3 December 2018).
"Skil'ky koshtuie staty chlenom partii" (2002) *Ukrains'ka Pravda*, 29 May, https://www.pravda.com.ua/news/2002/04/29/2988529/ (accessed 3 December 2018).
Spirova, M. (2005) "Political Parties in Bulgaria: Organizational Trends in Comparative Perspective," *Party Politics* 11(5): 601–22.
Sotsialistychnoi Partii Ukrainy. (2014) *Statut Sotsialistychnoi Partii Ukrainy*, http://www.spu.in.ua/uk/about/statut_partii (accessed 30 October 2014).
Statut Komunistychnoi Partii Ukrainy. (2014), http://www.kpu.ua/ru/page/statute (accessed 30 October 2014).
Statut Narodnoho Rukhu Ukrainy (2014), http://www.nru.org.ua/pro-partiiu/statut-rukhu (accessed 30 October 2014).
Szczerbiak, A. (1999) "The Impact of the 1998 Local Elections on the Emerging Polish Party System," *Journal of Communist Studies and Transition Politics* 15(3): 80–100.
Szczerbiak, A. (2001) "Party Structure in Post-communist Poland," *Journal of Communist Studies and Transition Politics* 17(2): 94–130.
Taagepera, R. and Schugart, M. (1989) "Designing Electoral Systems," *Electoral Studies* 8(1): 49–58.
Tan, N. (2013) "Manipulating Electoral Laws in Singapore," *Electoral Studies* 32(4): 632–43.
Thomassen, J. (2005) *The European Voter: A Comparative Study of Modern Democracies*. Oxford: Oxford University Press on Demand.

Tishkov, B.A. (1991) "Natsional'nost'-Kommunist? (Etnopoliticheskii analiz KPSS)," *Polis. Politicheskie issledovaniia* 2(32): 32–43.
Toole, J. (2003) "Straddling the East–West Divide: Party Organization and Communist Legacies in East Central Europe," *Europe-Asia Studies* 55(1): 101–18.
Tymchenko, M. M. (2015) "Osnovni formy rozvytku vnutrishn'oi demokratyzatsii politychnykh partii v umovakh modernizatsii politychnoi systemy," *Hrani* 1 December (128): 25–30.
Umland, A. (2013) "A Typical Variety of European Right-Wing Radicalism?" *Russian Politics and Law* 51(5): 86–95.
van Biezen, I. (2003) *Political Parties in New Democracies: Party Organization in Southern and East-Central Europe*. Basingstoke: Palgrave.
van Biezen, I. and Kopecký, P. (2007) "The State and the Parties: Public Funding, Public Regulation and Rent-seeking in Contemporary Democracies," *Party Politics* 13(2): 235–54.
Biezen, I. V. and Kopecký, P. (2014) "The Cartel Party and the State: Party–State Linkages in European Democracies," *Party Politics* 20(2): 170–82.
van Biezen, I., Mair, P. and Poguntke, T. (2012) "Going, Going... Gone? The Decline of Party Membership in Contemporary Europe," *European Journal of Political Research* 51(1): 24–56.
van Biezen, I. and Poguntke, T. (2014) "The Decline of Membership-Based Politics," *Party Politics* 20(2): 205–16.
van Haute, E. (ed.) (2011) *Party Membership in Europe: Exploration into the Anthills of Party Politics*. Brussels: Editions de l'Université de Bruxelles.
Vistak, O. and Myrosh, M. (2017) "Electoral Activity of the Population of Western Ukraine Border Territory," *Journal of Geography, Politics and Society*" 7(2): 73–80.
Way, L. (2004) "The Sources and Dynamics of Competitive Authoritarianism in Ukraine," *Journal of Communist Studies and Transition Politics* 20(1): 143–61.
Whiteley, P. F. and Seyd, P. (1998) "The Dynamics of Party Activism in Britain: A Spiral of Demobilization?" *British Journal of Political Science* 2(1): 113–37.
Whiteley, P. F. and Seyd, P. (2002) *High-intensity Participation: The Dynamics of Party Activism in Britain*. Ann Arbor, MI: University of Michigan Press.
Widfeldt, A. (1995) "Party Membership and Party Representativeness," in H. Klingemann and D. Fuchs (eds.) *Citizens and the State*. Oxford: Oxford University Press, 134–82.
Wilson, A. (2005) *Ukraine's Orange Revolution*. New Haven, CT: Yale University Press.
Yakymenko, Y. (2017) "The Best Party: What Influences the Development of Ukrainian Political Parties," *Razumkov Centre*, 15 September, http://razumkov.org.ua/en/comments/the-best-party-what-influences-the-development-of-ukrainian-political-parties (accessed 3 December 2018).

Zhuk, A. 2016. "Iryna Suslova: Parliament Members Wants to Boost Status of Women in Politics, Military, Education," *Kyiv Post*, 1 December, https://www.kyivpost.com/special/iryna-suslova-parliament-member-wants-boost-status-women-politics-military-education.html (accessed 3 December 2018).

Reviews

Ognian Shentov, Ruslan Stefanov and Martin Vladimirov, *The Russian Economic Grip on Central and Eastern Europe*. New York: Routledge, 2019. 258 pp.

The Russian Economic Grip on Central and Eastern Europe contributes to our understanding of how Russia uses economic channels to shape the politics of the countries that used to be under Soviet influence but have embraced democracy for almost three decades. The authors expand on their pioneering 2016 analysis, *The Kremlin Playbook: Understanding Russian Influence in Central and Eastern Europe* policy report, which estimates the Russian economic footprint in five CEE countries and assesses the different amplifiers Russia has used to transform its economic influence into political leverage.[1]

The book does not shy away from tackling an empirical investigation of an inherently opaque set of mechanisms. The authors begin by developing a common theoretical framework that highlights the root causes of Russia's influence more broadly. This framework could be labeled "economic realism": a strategic shift away from military and ideological power to economic influence. This move, it seems, has worked well in an era when the superficial embrace of market capitalism has allowed Russia to subvert the levers of power and re-establish its impact on the political life of nine foreign countries: Bosnia and Herzegovina, Bulgaria, Hungary, Latvia, Lithuania, Macedonia, Montenegro, Serbia, and Slovakia.

The book could not be more timely: recent developments in the United States have turned "Russian meddling" into a popular catchphrase. This study reminds us that, in Eastern Europe, Putin's regime does not "meddle": it has established a firm grip. Contrary to "end of history" proclamations from the early 1990s that rejoiced in the Soviet regime's loss of political influence over the region, Russia has managed to gradually restore its political clout by embracing certain economic levers of power.

---

[1] Published by the Center for the Study of Democracy in Sofia, and available online: http://www.csd.bg/artShow.php?id=17805.

Russia's approach has been both systematic and multifaceted. As argued in a chapter on structural economic vulnerabilities, the CEE countries have relied heavily on energy imports. Russian energy giants have entered the countries' markets to meet this demand but have then developed offshore and foreign entities with convoluted ownership structures and have expanded to other sectors of the economy, such as construction, engineering, media, real estate, and transportation. This has turned energy dependence into a complex web of state capture due to the sheer size of the businesses and their astute involvement in tax schemes, winning of government procurement projects, and media control, among others. The unclear ownership and accountability structures of these economic conglomerates have made it difficult to track their activities and precise impact. Russia experts have long known about this feature of Soviet and now Russian rule, often referred to as the "sistema." It is characterized by informal networks and weak formal institutions, shadow structures of governance that operate in parallel to, and instead of, the official ones. Shentov *et al.*'s edited volume illuminates just how "sistema" works to serve Putin's foreign policy goals.

Unraveling at least parts of this complex web of influence is the edited volume's greatest strength, as exemplified by the case study chapters devoted to each of the nine countries. This features meticulous analysis of FDI data to estimate the true share of Russia's economic footprint in each respective country that combines official and offshore accounts and tracks revenue, assets, and employment figures to get a comprehensive sense of the sheer size of the Russian impact. In addition, the volume is unmistakably social scientific in nature. In explaining the extent to which Russia has managed to influence the political and economic climate, two main causes emerge. The first one is based on domestic vulnerabilities: corruption, lack of transparency, and poor regulatory quality and enforcement are among the key domestic preconditions for successful state capture by the Russian economic agents. The second is related to the extent to which international actors other than Russia have stayed economically engaged with the host countries: Russian investment is opportunist and readily fills the vacuum left by the West.

The theoretical clarity of the book enables it to draw some interesting policy recommendations. The West's over-reliance on economic sanctions towards Russia is insufficient when Putin's regime has become so good at diversifying the ownership and geographic structure or its otherwise hierarchical economic weaponry. The volume should be considered a powerful reminder that, while the West is countering Russia directly, Russia is waging a much less visible, but more nuanced and sophisticated, economic proxy war that has had profound impact deep into the supposedly unified and open European political and economic union.

While the policy recommendation for greater Western involvement is quite clear, the book leaves some doubts about the feasibility of this happening. As acknowledged by the authors of the chapter on state capture, European crises beget a stronger Russian grip. As Western actors deal with their own economic and political problems in an age of budget deficits, populism, and democratic malaise, one cannot help but think that Central and Eastern Europe is destined for dependence not only on Russia, but on other powerful illiberal regimes, such as China, Saudi Arabia, and Turkey. This logic is further supported by the fact that these countries face lower transaction costs of doing business due to the lower accountability and transparency standards that they abide by.

At the same time, the book would have benefited from a more open acknowledgment of the fact that even the illiberal foes of the Western powers are facing some immense challenges. As Vladimir Putin, Crown Prince Mohammed bin Salman, and Recep Tayyip Erdogan continue to bend formal and informal institutions in their favor, they have also faced crises escalating in severity and frequency. CEE countries, therefore, should be analyzed as small actors caught in the middle of an economic war of attrition. To be sure, their fate depends on the short-term levels of state capture by illiberal actors. However, it also depends on the ability of those actors to avoid abrupt and cataclysmic regime changes —something they tend to be especially prone to.

In conclusion, the book fills a key missing link in the analysis of the malign Russian influence in Europe. It does so by disentangling how Russian actors capitalize on the governance deficits in the different countries—an approach that could be applied to assessing the Russian economic footprint in Western Europe too.

KIRIL KOLEV
Department of Politics and International Relations
Hendrix College

Alexander Cooley and John Heathershaw, *Dictators Without Borders: Power and Money in Central Asia*. New Haven, CT: Yale University Press, 2017. 312 pp.

A landlocked region at the crossroads of the interests of a range of different international actors, Central Asia is most often portrayed as an autocratic region, lacking true agency, and generally closed off from globalization. In this book, Alexander Cooley and John Heathershaw set out to challenge this conventional view through an exploration of the impact of the global market on the economic development of the five republics and their leadership.

Political scientists focusing on political and economic developments in the former Soviet Union, Alexander Cooley and John Heathershaw take an unprecedented step here in presenting raw data about offshore dynamics in Central Asia. Building upon the publicly available data and on their experiences in the field, the authors aim to decipher the connections between state-owned companies, Central Asian presidents and their families, well-established Western banks, offshore accounts, and investments.

Published five years after Alexander Cooley's *Great Games, Local Rules: The New Great Power Contest in Central Asia* (Oxford University Press, 2012), *Dictators without Borders* describes the impact of the opening of Central Asia to the world, which has determined not only political and security dynamics in the region, but also the creation of transnational economic links, both onshore and offshore. The goal of the book, as stated in the introduction, is three-fold. First, it sets out to promote a better knowledge of the cross-border mechanisms used by the Central Asian leadership to launder money and exert political influence over dissidents. Second, the book indicates what changes in the regulatory and enforcement system are necessary in order to tackle transnational corruption. Finally, the authors try to shed light on how the domestic policy of Central Asia affects its foreign policy, especially concerning the regime's opponents, a topic that is the subject of John Heathershaw's ongoing research.

In the first chapter, "Inside-Outside, Onshore-Offshore: How Central Asia Went Global," the authors analyze the transition dynamics in Central Asia, both regionally and nationally. As a unitary region, Central Asia has some common characteristics, which contribute to the perpetuation of a series of longstanding myths, whose influence extends to regional political systems, public opinion, and academia (including Western academia). For example, the conventional image of Central Asia as a geographically isolated region, and thus ignorant of and immune to global dynamics, has fostered the widespread belief that the failure of economic liberalization and political evolution in Central Asia was determined mainly by the local and cultural conditions. The book debunks these myths through detailed case studies of the money laundering and political opposition practices in each of the five republics.

The case studies also focus on the national legal instruments put in place by the Central Asian authorities for handling political dissidents, while preserving the appearance of respect for international law and promoting a positive image for their governments. On one hand, the Central Asian republics were involved in multilateral processes of promoting democracy and human rights, while, on the other hand, their leadership consolidated their political position, including by targeting political defectors abroad through their national security services and portraying them as threats to national security.

Each of the following four chapters deals with a particular Central Asian country, exploring the national political set-up and the most prominent cases of embezzlement. The case of Mukhtar Ablyazov in Kazakhstan is discussed in the second chapter. This case study gives an account of the measures undertaken by the Astana leadership to seize the media outlets and the business shares of Ablyazov, a vocal member of the Kazakh political and economic elite. The case of Ablyazov is very interesting and controversial, showing the difficulties of understanding all the nuances of Central Asian politics. Despite his protestations, Ablyazov was not acting in good faith and for the benefit of a democratic society when he financially supported opposition media in Kazakhstan. He established himself as a banker and real-estate tycoon in Eurasia, attracting the envy of the Kazakh government and later triggering a highly publicized and costly hearing in London. The Kazakh authorities made lengthy efforts to bring Ablyazov to justice in his home country for embezzlement, fraud, and support of violent protests against the state, even by using his family as leverage. The use of Interpol's Red Notice system which allowed for the possible extradition of Ablyazov to Russia was later dismissed as politically motivated by numerous Western states where Ablyazov and his associates resided. In July 2017 Interpol canceled the Red Notices against the names of Ablyazov and several of his partners.

The next chapter focuses on Tajikistan and the state-owned Talco enterprise, an aluminium producer benefiting from state-subsidized electricity, and perhaps the greatest economic asset of the economically impoverished country. Talco followed a complicated pathway to secure offshore accounts and became subject to a London litigation between 2004 and 2008, with the aim of consolidating President Rahmon's control over it. The importance of the case resides in the silent approval of the Western partners, such as Norway's Hydro Aluminium, part of Norsk Hydro, whose majority shareholder is the Norwegian government, as well as the World Bank and the European Bank for Reconstruction and Development. Talco's history of changing owners reveals the continuity of corruption and lack of transparency, which took place at the expense of the Tajik citizen, with the naïve and even complicit participation of Western entities. The reinvestment of Talco's offshore profits was directed to the building of private properties, a hotel, and lobbying in the US Congress. Using the funds provided by Talco, Fabiani & Company lobbies for a favorable position in the building of Rogun Dam, a 42-year project for the tallest hydropower dam in the world, which was until recently opposed by Uzbekistan and the US for environmental reasons. In November 2018 however, President Rahmon inaugurated the dam's first turbine, built with an Italian-based company, while the second unit is scheduled to be launched in 2019.

Until the death of Islam Karimov, Uzbekistan was one of the most closed and repressive of the five Central Asian states. However, the connections of Gulnara Karimova, first daughter of the leader, with the global financial world, her diplomatic activity, and her allure as a Central Asian pop star dismantled the myth of the anti-Westernism of Central Asia, as the book's third case study shows. Illustrative for Uzbekistan's endemic corruption are the schemes through which Gulnara Karimova and her associates dealt with the licenses for access to the Uzbek telecommunication market for foreign companies. Despite her success and contribution to her father's authority, Karimova's growing dissension with the chief of the National Security Service, a close advisor of her father, led to her disgrace and house arrest. The President agreed to bring his daughter to justice in order to be absolved of any responsibility and knowledge of her schemes.

The final case study sheds light on Maxim Bakiyev's activities to centralize the control of Kyrgyzstan's assets in the hands of his family, during the five years of the Bakiyev regime (2005–2010). The local and international business aiming to gain access to "the Switzerland of the East" (as Kyrgyzstan came to be known during the 1990s) was not vetted by democratic institutions, but by the omnipresent and omnipotent hands of "Prince Maxim," as Bakiyev was nicknamed. The process was complete when powerful international banks became part of the scheme to launder money for Maxim, but it backfired when the Bakiyev regime was ousted. Nevertheless, Maxim currently enjoys political asylum in a luxurious London apartment.

In the sixth chapter, "The New Offshore Silk Roads," Cooley and Heathershaw summarize the story of an insufficiently regulated global financial world, in which corrupt Central Asian elites use the backdoors for their personal interests, with the help and blessing of

Western companies. Moreover, the authors point out that all these offshore transnational routes are commonly exploited by the US for military and strategic purposes and by the Chinese for their energy interests.

A chapter entitled "Political Exiles and Extraterritorial Repression," is dedicated to the categories of political exiles, including former regime insiders, secular activists, and banned clerics. The chapter also explores the threat that these dissidents face of being brought back to their countries, through the politically motivated misuse of legitimate international instruments. The chapter builds upon the work done by John Heathershaw's team in the Exeter Central Asian Studies Network, which has pulled together publicly available information into a database of Central Asian Political Exiles (CAPE).

One of the book's drawbacks is that it does not deal with the case of Turkmenistan, presently the most closed country of the five in the region. Although the book's initial argument focuses on the privileged position of Deutsche Bank and other German and French companies in the Turkmen economic system, these relations are not scrutinized in a thorough case study similar to the other four Central Asian states. Such analysis would have provided a context for the Turkmenistan's recent preoccupation with illegal economic activities, as shown by the October 2017 OSCE seminar focused on preventing money laundering through offshore zones and designed for Turkmen governmental experts and representatives of the business community. Additionally, according to the International Consortium of Investigative Journalists (ICIJ), there are Turkmen connections to offshore accounts belonging to various branches of Russian (Exxon, Kamaz) and American companies (Unocal, USA International).

The "pay-to-play" formula exposed in *Dictators without Borders*, whereby US government agencies bribe and compromise in order to maintain their military presence in the Central Asian countries, is not new and was discussed by Alexander Cooley in his previous work *Great Games, Local Rules*. However, the novelty of *Dictators without Borders* is that it provides detailed raw data for activities that cannot be justifiable, even under the motivation of the global war on terror or the interests of US national security.

The authors base their research on data that has been made public because of legal proceedings, government investigations, and leaked information. In doing so, they have synthesized and connected the dots of a huge volume of sources, with the aim of producing a largely empirical work that can serve as a basis for further research on the region. As the authors themselves note, there are currently insufficient instruments for validating the accuracy of data provided in courtrooms or even in politically motivated leaks. This may prove to be a challenge for parsimonious research, yet the data merely point to another dimension that confirms the characterization of the Central Asian states as patrimonial and autocratic regimes, with leaders interested above all else in their own survival.

Nevertheless, *Dictators without Borders* is mandatory reading for those wishing to understand the power dynamics in the region, without falling into the trap of erroneously viewing Central Asia as a region that is closed off from the rest of the world. *Dictators without Borders* represents a laudable attempt to present a clearer and more accurate image based on the most recent data, as a basis for future in-depth analysis regarding the role and place of Central Asian states in the world order.

ANA-MARIA ANGHELESCU
National University of Political Science and Public Administration
(SNSPA) Bucharest

Irene Kacandes and Yuliya Komska (eds.), *Eastern Europe Unmapped: Beyond Borders and Peripheries*. New York and Oxford: Berghahn Books, 2018. 300 pp.

Intrigued by the promise of an "unmapping" of Eastern Europe, I was excited to review this edited collection. The book begins with a substantial introduction by *Yuliya Komska*, discussing Eastern Europe under the notion of being "discontiguous." The introduction and the critique of "mapping" opens with an anecdote about the second Molotov-Ribbentrop Pact, or, to give its official title, the "German–Soviet Treaty of Friendship, Cooperation and Development," signed on 28 September 1939 and leading to what the author calls a "cartographic mandate," with wide-ranging geopolitical consequences. Komska critically assesses the histories of land-locked nationalism and border issues, often associated with cores, peripheries, and colonies in Eastern Europe. The book proposes to "unmap" Eastern Europe by bracketing these hegemonic notions related to the region and, consequently, decolonizing our thinking on the region.

The other contributions are divided into five parts. Part I, "Re-placed Religion," comprises two contributions: on Jewish cultural and ethnic plasticity (*Miriam Udel*); and on periodization and Muslim subjectivities in the Balkans (*Piro Rexhepi*). Part II, "Dislodged Dissent," provides a chapter on Belarusian intellectuals (*Tatsiana Astrouskaya*); and a critical rereading of the Polish émigré journal *Kultura* (Jessie Labov). Labov sees the journal as "suspended between the regional (Eastern Europe) and the global (Polish-language diaspora)," and working "at a scale that we do not yet know exactly how to name" (p. 104). Part III, "Fictional Cartographies and Temporalities," analyzes Central European literature (*Daniel Pratt*) and the transnational matrix of post-communist spaces (Ioana Luca), arguing for a comparative approach as an important tool to be added to traditional geographic tools such as maps and statistics. Luca's quest is to see the Eastern Europe through relationships; this chapter combines literary analysis with Doreen Massey's ideas on relational space and how certain stories of spaces become dominant. Part IV, "Appropriated Afterlives," analyzes instances of the appropriation of the past through the cases of the New Synagogue in Poznań and Olsztyn's Bet Tahara (*Sarah M. Schlachetzki*) and Bruno Schulz's Murals, *Oyneg Shabes* (*Adam Zachary Newton*). Part V, "*Elective Affinities*," presents chapters on Balkan travel (*Ann Cvetkovich*) and Polish childhood (*Irene Kacandes*). These two chapters use imaginative and reflective approaches, demonstrating *relation*ships to places through subjectivities and biographies. Finally, the book concludes with the chapter "Afterword/Afterward: Eastern Europe, Unmapped and Reborn," by *Vitaly Chernetsky*.

Clearly, the collection has an emancipatory aim of shedding light on overlooked histories, blind spots on the scientifically discursive and geopolitical "map" of social and cultural theory. I appreciate the effort to argue against framings whereby post-socialist Eastern Europe is superficially and unjustifiably portrayed as a consumer and a non-producer of theoretical and methodological innovations. I welcome the experimental, provocative, and creative style of writing that is on display here. However, the aftertaste of the book is eclectic and uneven. Perhaps the most important contribution of this book can be summarized in Ann Cvetkovich's words in the chapter "The Balkan Notebooks": "I try to see something else, to move between visible and invisible as icons and ruins both require, while also acknowledging my own ignorance and inability to see" (p. 245). Hegemonic notions of Eastern Europe are so strong and difficult to overcome. The collection tries to move beyond seeing the region as one of "misery," as a border region, or a region defined by all kinds of "posts-" (post-social, post-colonial, post-occupied, post-oppressed). The book sets out to understand the region's diverse histories and cultures from various viewpoints, spatially and temporally. This book asks questions, proposes critiques, acknowledges our own inability to breakthrough existing views, but does not really come up with coherent propositions. Some chapters engage with relational and contextual critique; others pursue very particular insights. In sum, the collection joins a growing dissatisfaction on how we see, interpret, and portray Eastern Europe, but suggests that the main work—coming up with new theories and understanding—is still to be done. Finally and positively, this collection is refreshingly rich in references to lesser known recent texts on Eastern Europe, many of which have been neglected in the Anglophone literature.

AIJA LULLE
Loughborough University

Chris Miller, *Putinomics: Power and Money in Resurgent Russia*. Chapel Hill, NC: University of North Carolina Press, 2018. 217 pp.

Since the onset of the war in Ukraine in 2014 and the subsequent deep crisis in Russian–Western relations, public debate and to a certain extent also research on contemporary Russia have been largely dominated by security- and foreign policy-related topics. Against this background, Chris Miller's new book provides a timely update on Russia's economic policy and its challenges.

Miller starts with a thought-provoking thesis. He states that while a great share of the literature focuses on missed opportunities and policy failures, Russia has actually fared surprisingly well in economic terms since the 1990s and even exceeded most expectations. To illustrate this observation, the author compares Russia with another country with similar characteristics, Venezuela. In 1999, both Venezuela and Russia were middle-income countries whose economies were heavily dependent on the export of natural resources and that were governed by increasingly authoritarian and security-oriented regimes. Almost 20 years later, however, Russia has experienced a period of impressive economic growth, rising living standards, and political stabilization, while today's Venezuela makes headlines with consumer good shortages, runaway inflation, and military-enforced food requisitions.

Although the title might at first glance suggest otherwise, *Putinomics* adds an important alternative perspective to a genre that is largely dominated by studies that focus on the shortcomings and weaknesses of the Russian economic and political system and that ascribe all problems to Putin and Putin alone. Miller outlines his main argument in the book's preface. He suggests that since the beginning of the Putin era, the Kremlin's decisions have been guided by a clear general strategy. According to Miller, "the three pillars of Putinomics" (p. xiii) are, in order of priority: strengthening and preserving the central (political) authority; preventing popular discontent by providing sufficient social security; and improving economic efficiency, if necessary by cooperating with private business. Thus, the regime's rationale throughout the 2000s was much more complex than simply stuffing the pockets of a kleptocratic elite. Sound economic policies and stable growth were oft-times considered just as important as they secured political stability in the medium to long term.

In the following chapters, the author illustrates how this overarching strategy influenced decision making in different areas of the Russian economy, such as the energy sector (Chapter 3), the financial sector (Chapter 4), and the industrial sector (Chapter 5). Chapter 6 covers the field of social policy and explains how rising living standards formed the basis for Putin's political rule (the so-called "social contract" between the regime and the Russian society).

The central factor that contributed to Russia's economic success was the prudent monetary and financial policy that was propagated by liberal economists such as finance minister Aleksei Kudrin, but also supported by Putin personally and defended against societal and political forces that called for more government spending. Thus, when historically high energy prices in the early 2000s brought the Russian government billions of dollars in taxes, this additional income was not (entirely, at least) embezzled or spent on populist social programs, but put in a Stabilization Fund. These savings later allowed Russia to go relatively unharmed through the severe economic crisis of 2008/2009.

It is only in the last chapter (Chapter 8) that Miller comes to more recent developments of the post-2014 period. The political controversy with the West and the resulting international sanctions as well as other factors such as the low global energy prices and rapid devaluation of the ruble caused a serious economic crisis in Russia. This time, however, the Russian government has far fewer resources to balance its economic and social effects. The author thus concludes that "tough choices" (p. 156) are ahead for the regime that could potentially endanger political stability.

Although many important points and observations are made in this chapter, it remains a somewhat cursory overview of complex and highly interesting processes that could determine much of Russia's political and economic future. In this sense, it would have been desirable to dedicate more space to the last five years. This impression is also amplified by the fact that some issues and empirical examples discussed for the 2000s are not entirely new but rather seem to belong to the standard repertoire of publications on the Russian political economy: be it the Yukos Affair to illustrate the turn to more state control or Putin's trip to the mono-industrial city of Pikalevo to stress the personal managerial style of Russia's political leaders.

Despite these minor shortcomings, *Putinomics* provides an extensive and well-written overview of major developments in Russia's economic and political system during the Putin era. Detailed empirical descriptions, clear and nuanced explanations of complicated processes as well as historical contextualization make the book accessible for a broad audience of scholars and non-scholars alike. Another strength of *Putinomics* is the comprehensive analysis of specific economic mechanisms, e.g. fiscal and monetary policy instruments. Such economic background is not always seen in studies on Russian politics.

The last chapter of the book asks whether *Putinomics* can survive. Miller argues that the Putin regime faces very different economic challenges today than it did in the early 2000s. Back then, an inefficient tax system, lack of access to credit, and legal instability were the primary obstacles for private business initiative and thus stable economic growth—problems that the Putin administration was largely able to solve. Today, however, the challenges are far more complex. For example, years of austerity have left healthcare and the education system underfinanced, but government spending is difficult today due to economic stagnation, low global energy prices, and external pressures (sanctions).

At the same time, the introduction of comprehensive reforms would contradict Putin's main goal of retaining his political rule. Thus, real change is not to be expected any time soon. According to Miller, *Putinomics* may survive, even if this means permanent stagnation and declining living standards. It remains to be seen, however, whether the Russian public will indeed be willing to endure this situation in the long term and what will happen to *Putinomics* without Putin, that is after the end of his fourth presidential term in 2024.

VERA ROGOVA
PhD Candidate
Peace Research Institute Frankfurt

Marci Shore, *The Ukrainian Night: An Intimate History of Revolution*. New Haven, CT & London: Yale University Press, 2017. 290 pp.

This book starts from the premise set by the Polish philosopher Stanislaw Brzozowski, when he wrote that "what is not biography—is nothing at all." Shore undertakes the important task of highlighting the individual stories, voices, and experiences of those who participated in the 2014 Ukrainian Maidan Revolution, otherwise known as the "Revolution of Dignity." The first half of *Ukrainian Night* deals with this mission exclusively, chronologically exploring the main events on the Maidan from the end of November 2013 up to the start of the war in the Donbas in March 2014. Shore utilizes the powerful stories of protestors and activists who were on the Maidan to reveal a new side to the crisis, one that was often overlooked in mainstream media coverage and subsequent political analysis. The second half of the book continues in this biographical style, but addresses the evolving war in the Donbas, as the author solicits further insights into the conflict that rapidly engulfed the Donetsk and Luhansk Oblasts in 2014. In this fascinating exploration into the emergence of the war, Shore engages not only with the subjects who featured prominently on the Maidan in Kyiv, who provided the bulk of the insight for the first half of the book, but she also tells the stories of Ukrainians in the restless cities of Odessa, Dnipro, and Kharkiv, enriched with occasional narratives of those from Donetsk and Luhansk.

The highly readable *Ukrainian Night* sets a quick tempo, employing short chapters often centred around particular questions from the author or a particularly illuminating response from an interviewee. This style creates an ascending crescendo of anticipation, as the reader is brought into the lived experiences of those who protested, fought, and died on the Maidan, always with the sense that a new crisis is just around the corner. The interview style of this book, threaded together masterfully by Shore, gives it this great strength of allowing the reader to relive both the depths of human tragedy and the heights of exuberant triumph experienced by those on the Maidan. However, *Ukrainian Night*'s biggest asset is also a methodological weakness. Throughout the entirety of the narrative focusing on the Maidan, there appears to be much greater time and space given to those of a similar cultural, class, and geographical background; namely, Ukrainians originating from the west of the country, with at least middle-class credentials, and a high level of education (a pertinent illustration is a lone critic of this aspect of the Maidan cited in the book, who describes the Maidan as "a bourgeois interest in the well-being of the upper classes"). This demographic is certainly not the sole focus of Shore's narrative, but it seems that the views and experiences of these individuals are given much greater attention and credence. Partly because of that, there is an intense romanticism in Shore's account of Ukraine's European integration, when it comes to her handling both of the political union itself and of the "idea" of Europe that Shore attributes to the Maidan protestors, as comprising "human rights, the rule of law, the dignity of being treated as a subject, not an object." Although European integration, in either a political or idealist form, is certainly supported by many Ukrainians, and was a major motivating factor in the Maidan, the monocular focus on this aspect of the Maidan also diminishes the voices of those who may have had different reasons to struggle. This stance further glorifies a process that has still not brought a lot of tangible benefits for many Ukrainians, and mystifies the pain that economic reforms and restructuring, demanded by the European Union, has inflicted on most Ukrainians. A richer exploration of the Maidan would have included a diverse range of voices from varying backgrounds, and further problematized the European integration from a more holistic perspective with the inclusion of dissenting standpoints.

The stories of heroism and civic resistance continue in the second part of the book, told through from the perspective of Ukrainians at the front line of tension and conflict in the country's east. Shore skilfully documents the immense role that the Ukrainian civil society played in defence of their homeland as pro-Russian separatists took control of government buildings and claimed to have founded people's republics in Donetsk and Luhansk. With the Ukrainian government in disarray, civilian volunteers and trained soldiers supplied the army with equipment and food, negotiated hostage exchanges, and provided medical care for the wounded. The narrative switches between a focus on the heroism of the Ukrainian people in government-controlled areas, and the horrors committed by separatists in the Donbass, which is a compelling read. However, this type of story-telling sets up a huge divide between the good and "glorious Ukraine" of the west, and the evil demagoguery of the east. There is quite a bit of brushing-off of alleged Ukrainian Army crimes against prisoners and civilians, which have been extensively documented by Amnesty International, the United Nations (UN) Subcommittee on Prevention of Torture, and the UN Human Rights Monitoring Mission. Although Shore also, very briefly, addresses some concerns over the activities of Ukrainian volunteer battalions, such as the Right Sector whom the author visits, there is a minimal critical exploration of these groups, who have, at best, been described in the academic literature as ultraconservative groups with a neo-Nazi fringe.

Ukrainian Night is an engrossing study of key perspectives on the Maidan protests from 2013 to 2014 and presents a lived experience of these tumultuous and uncertain days for Ukrainian society. The pace and style of the book thrusts the reader intimately inside this uncertainty, as the anticipation quickly builds to materialize in the crisis of Ukraine's east, as pro-Russian separatists take control of Donetsk and Luhansk, and war explodes in the Donbas. Shore's unique account of the events guarantees a stimulating read, though the apparent bias in the interview method does make *Ukrainian Night* a biography of, and for, a particular audience.

ELLIOT DOLAN-EVANS
PhD candidate
Monash Gender, Peace and Security Centre
Monash University

Lawrence Douglas, *The Right Wrong Man: John Demjanjuk and the Last Great Nazi War Crimes Trial*. Princeton, NJ and Oxford: Princeton University Press, 2016. 332 pp.

Lawrence Douglas offers a sliver of positive analysis to the traditionally critical assessment of postwar, transnational justice for crimes perpetrated during the Holocaust. *The Right Wrong Man: John Demjanjuk and the Last Great Nazi War Crimes Trial* tells the story of Ivan Demjanjuk's prosecution—a story that began in 1975 and only ended in 2011. The work carries its readers to three judicial sites of exploration: the United States, Israel, and Germany. Demjanjuk's story offers Douglas a vehicle of analysis to investigate the legal, historical, and geopolitical layers in the process of postwar transnational justice. Though he does not question the poor records of western states in effectively prosecuting individuals responsible for war crimes, he argues that courts and bureaucratic investigatory bodies have made some progress in instituting important adjustments in their proceedings.

He sets up his argument by situating the Demjanjuk case among the Nuremberg Trials, from 1945 to 1946, and the Eichmann case from 1961 to 1962. In doing so, Douglas argues for a particular trajectory of postwar transnational trials. On one hand, the Nuremberg Trials relied heavily on statistics and proceeded in a dry, documentary-like fashion. On the other hand, the Eichmann case was driven by victim testimony. The Demjanjuk trial, however, departs from the preceding cases in its use of history, and historians, to contextualize the crime and drive the prosecution forward. More importantly, the successful prosecution of Demjanjuk has set a positive precedent for future cases in Germany.

Douglas's cast of characters includes a colorful range of historians, lawyers, judges, bureaucrats, and survivors. The leading personality, Ivan Demjanjuk, was both ordinary and unique. Born in present-day Ukraine, Demjanjuk was drafted into the Red Army during the Second World War only to be captured by the Germans and become a prisoner of war, working in various camps. After the war, Demjanjuk settled in Cleveland and lived comfortably for thirty years. The crux of the narrative takes places between 1975 and 2011 when he was mistakenly identified as a camp guard in Treblinka, denaturalized as a US citizen, and tried in Jerusalem where he served time until the real identity of the Treblinka guard was found. After returning to the United States for eight years he was then, in 2001, correctly identified as a guard in Sobibor, denaturalized again, and this time sent to Germany where he endured trial, was convicted, and lived out the last few months of his life in a nursing home in Upper Bavaria until 2012.

The book follows a chronological structure and sets out much of the historical, bureaucratic, and legal context that drove Demjanjuk's prosecutions in Ohio, Jerusalem, and Munich. Douglas discusses the postwar and early Cold War period as a background to situate the ways in which the United States developed its Displaced Persons laws and the Office of Special Investigations. In his section on Israel, Douglas sheds light on the closeness of Demjanjuk's trial with society more broadly, as well as on the use and failure of witness testimony. Finally, in Munich, he gives a detailed background on German legal behavior prior to Demjanjuk, particularly when it came to identifying and properly prosecuting perpetrators. By outlining the legal limitations within which judges and experts were forced to work, he argues that the German Central Office's successful prosecution of Demjanjuk in 2011 demonstrates a positive progression rather than yet another failure.

There are a few points that allude to the importance of the Soviet Union's role in inhibiting a comprehensive investigation. Douglas also briefly mentions how the Soviet Union's collapse affected Demjanjuk's case. However, the work could have benefitted from more contextual information regarding the Soviet Union's role in postwar justice and East-West legal power struggles. These elements were particularly important as they affected why the West was reluctant to send back former Soviet citizens to the Soviet Union and why, in turn, the Soviet Union stalled in its full cooperation in investigations. This background would have further underscored the precariousness of Demjnajuk's situation and the legal tensions between the United States and the Soviet Union.

One of the most important contributions of this work is Douglas's transnational approach, which departs from existing scholarship.[1] In applying this perspective, he successfully demonstrates the necessity for multiple regional perspectives to understand one case and, at the same time, he makes use of Demjanjuk's case to unpack the legal, historical, and political challenges within each of the three countries. To solidify his argument, Douglas uses substantial court material from the trials in the United States, Israel, and Germany but it is his personal experience attending the Munich trial that adds to the rich insight he offers, particularly in the later portion of the book. Readers benefit from the experience of Douglas who not only attended the trial itself but personally comments on his interactions with lawyers and Holocaust survivors—most of which happened when proceedings were cancelled for those days. This personal element also enriches his writing, which reads smoothly and will appeal to legal experts, historians, and general audiences alike.

As each case developed over the years in different countries, the role of historians in providing necessary context on the nature of the camps was crucial. The role of historians also becomes increasingly more important as fewer and fewer survivors are able to testify. The other "heroes" of this story are legal experts who worked with historians to engage with existing legal parameters in order to offer some paths to the successful prosecution of

---

[1] While the existing scholarship is rich in its in-depth analysis of legal structures and treatment of former wartime collaborators in one country, Douglas's work departs in its inclusion of multiple regional sites for exploration. See for example: Richard Breitman and Norman J.W. Goda, *Hitler's Shadow: Nazi War Criminals, US Intelligence and the Cold War* (Washington, DC: National Archives and Records Administration, 2010); Roger Daniels, *Guarding the Golden Door: American Immigration Policy and Immigrants Since 1882* (New York: Hill and Wang, 2004); John Loftus and Mark Aarons, *The Secret War Against the Jews; How Western Espionage Betrayed the Jewish People* (New York: St. Martin's Press, 1994); and Kerstin von Lingen, *Allen Dulles, the OSS, and Nazi War Criminals; The Dynamics of Selective Prosecution*, trans. Dona Geyer (New York: Cambridge University Press, 2013).

perpetrators. Collectively, the greatest legacy of cooperation between historians and legal experts, seen in Demjanjuk's trial in Germany, is that they offer a nuanced view of legal understandings of the Holocaust. Rather than criticizing German courts for doing too little, Douglas acknowledges their efforts to adapt the law creatively with a view to improving the procedures for prosecuting different kinds of perpetrators.

Aleksandra Pomiecko
University of Toronto

ABOUT THE CONTRIBUTORS

GERGANA DIMOVA is currently an Associate Lecturer in Politics at the University of Winchester in the UK. She received her PhD from Harvard University and was a Jeremy Haworth fellow in politics at the University of Cambridge. She is the chair of the UK Political Science Association Anti-Politics group. Her forthcoming book is entitled *Democracy beyond Elections: Government Accountability in the Media Age* (Palgrave 2019).

ANDREAS UMLAND (Dr.Phil. FU Berlin, Ph.D. Cambridge) is Senior Research Fellow at the Institute for Euro-Atlantic Cooperation in Kyiv, and general editor of the book series *Soviet and Post-Soviet Politics and Society* (ibidem-Verlag, 2004–) distributed, since 2014, by Columbia University Press. His articles have appeared in, among other journals, *e-Foreign Affairs, e-Foreign Policy, Political Studies Review, Perspectives on Politics, European Political Science, Journal of Democracy, Europe-Asia Studies, European History Quarterly, Problems of Post-Communism, Communist and Post-Communist Studies, Russian Review, Nationalities Papers, East European Jewish Affairs, Journal of Slavic Military Studies, Demokratizatsiya, Internationale Politik, Österreichische Zeitschrift für Politikwissenschaft, Osteuropa, Jahrbuch für Ostrecht,* and *Voprosy filosofii.*

HÅVARD BÆKKEN is Senior Researcher at the Norwegian Institute for Defence Studies, Norwegian Defence University College. He obtained his PhD in Russian Area Studies from the University of Oslo (UiO) in 2014. He has worked as a research fellow at the Norwegian Institute of International Affairs (NUPI) and as guest researcher at the Norwegian University Centre in St. Petersburg and the EU–Russia Centre in Brussels. He has taught Russian politics and history at the Institute of Literature, Area Studies, and European Languages (ILOS) at UiO, and Russian language at Nansen Academy. He is the author of *Law and Power in Russia. Making Sense of Quasi-Legal Practices*

(2019). His current research examines resurgent military patriotism in Russia.

DASHA DUBINSKY (BA in Social Studies; Certificates in International Relations and Social, Cultural, and Critical Theory) is a Ukrainian-American graduate of Wesleyan University. As an undergraduate, she authored a thesis, *Lawyers or Liars: An International Law Perspective on the Role of Russia in the Annexation of Crimea*, earning High Honors and a Phi Beta Kappa selection. While at Wesleyan, she also competed in Tennis at the Varsity Level, earning an ITA Division III Scholar Athlete Selection. She will begin her Juris Doctor candidacy in Fall 2019 at Harvard Law School.

AGATA KLECZKOWSKA (Ph.D. in public international law) is Assistant Professor at the Institute of Law Studies of the Polish Academy of Sciences. She is currently leader or participant in a few research projects, concerning, *inter alia*, unrecognized subjects in international law; customary law on the use of force; and the responsibility of armed non-state actors. In 2018 she was a Fellow at the Max Planck Institute for Comparative Public Law and International Law. Her first monograph, *The Use of Armed Force by States in the Light of Customary International Law* (in Polish), was published in 2018. She is also an Oxford International Organizations (OXIO) Rapporteur.

MELANIE G. MIERZEJEWSKI-VOZNYAK received her Ph.D. from the University of Illinois, Chicago. She is an independent researcher who focuses on party politics and democratization in Ukraine and Georgia. She has worked for think tanks in Washington, DC and Europe and has lectured at universities in the US, Central Europe, and Central Asia. Her research has appeared in *East European Politics*, *New Eastern Europe*, and *The Oxford Handbook of the Radical Right* (Oxford University Press, 2018).

PETER RUTLAND is a Professor of Government at Wesleyan University in Middletown, CT and Associate Editor of *Russian Review*. Recent articles include "US Foreign Policy in Russia," in

Mick Cox and Doug Stokes (eds.), *US Foreign Policy* (Oxford University Press, 2018).

MARIA SHAGINA is a Japan Society for the Promotion of Science (JSPS) Postdoctoral Fellow at Ritsumeikan University, Japan. She was a visiting fellow at the Centre for Russian, European and Eurasian Studies, University of Birmingham and is currently affiliated with the Geneva International Sanctions Network. She holds a PhD in Political Science from the University of Lucerne, Switzerland. She is the author of *Joining a Prestigious Club: Cooperation with Europarties and Its Impact on Party Development in Georgia, Moldova, and Ukraine 2004–2015* (Soviet and Post-Soviet Politics and Society Series) *ibidem:* Stuttgart, 2017).

ibidem.eu